Queering the Church

Queering the Church

The Theological and Ecclesial Potential of Failure

Penelope Cowell Doe

scm press

© Penelope Cowell Doe 2024

Published in 2024 by SCM Press

Editorial office
3rd Floor, Invicta House,
110 Golden Lane,
London EC1Y 0TG, UK
www.scmpress.co.uk

SCM Press is an imprint of Hymns Ancient & Modern Ltd
(a registered charity)

Hymns Ancient & Modern® is a registered trademark of
Hymns Ancient & Modern Ltd
13A Hellesdon Park Road, Norwich,
Norfolk NR6 5DR, UK

All rights reserved. No part of this publication may be reproduced,
stored in a retrieval system, or transmitted,
in any form or by any means, electronic, mechanical,
photocopying or otherwise, without the prior permission of
the publisher, SCM Press.

Penelope Cowell Doe has asserted her right under the Copyright, Designs and
Patents Act 1988 to be identified as the Author of this Work

British Library Cataloguing in Publication data
A catalogue record for this book is available
from the British Library

ISBN 978-0-334-06562-3

Typeset by Regent Typesetting

Contents

Preface	vii
Acknowledgements	ix
Introduction	1
1 The Hermeneutic Lenses of Church Discourses	29
2 The Authorized Afterlife of the *Pilling Report*	57
3 The Unauthorized Afterlife of the *Pilling Report*	93
4 Queering Hermeneutics	117
5 Church Discourses and 'The Queer Art of Failure'	145
Bibliography	168
Index of Biblical References	191
Index of Names and Subjects	192

Preface

> If we think that conflicts within the church over gender and sexuality can be solved by listening exercises, reports or other forms of information gathering, we'll never be able to face up to the fact that's what's really going on is a struggle between incompatible visions of what is good for human beings.[1]

This observation from Marika Rose's latest book, on the failure of theology, encapsulates my own reflections on the failure of church reports on sexuality to deliver what they hope for and their incapacity for seeing failure as a tenuous telos to the wrestling with incompatible views and exhausting debates about the licitness of (homo)sexuality in the life of the Church of England. My focus here is on the *Pilling Report*[2] and its afterlife, using this report and the processes that it initiated to queer institutional bodies and practices and their constructions of power, privilege and authority. In one sense this is a snapshot of the Church at a moment of deliberation, yet *Pilling's* tentacles reach into past debates and future resolution of the 'problem' of (homo)sexuality for the Church. It is my hope that this methodology may be adopted to interrogate further institutional responses to this 'problem', such as the *Living in Love and Faith* resources and the ecclesial response to these.[3]

I read Marika's book while I was editing this – which is an updated version of my doctoral thesis for the University of Exeter – and found much in her theology which echoed my own work on the potentialities of failure to critique dominant, hegemonic epistemologies of progress and capitalist practices of growth and success to which the Church has succumbed in the latter half of the twentieth century and the beginning of the twenty-first.

In this book I que(e)ry those epistemic practices and the institution (the Church of England), which continues to deploy and produce them. The Church has concluded that consensus on 'issues' of human sexuality has not been reached, may be unattainable even, but it has not therefore understood that the search for harmony is problematic. In what follows I work with the 'queer art of failure' and the queer temporality of Holy

Saturday[4] as a space of abnegation and alterity to suggest alternative ways of being and doing in the pursuit of theological and ecclesial answers to questions on (homo)sexuality. The queer art of failure recognizes that failure is part of the human condition and for Christians an inherent part of our fallen nature. Failure may be faithfulness to an apophatic tradition, inhabiting the unknowingness of Holy Saturday and the queer temporality of living in the 'not yet'.

Notes

1 Marika Rose, *Theology for the End of the World* (London: SCM Press, 2023), 39.

2 The Archbishops' Council, *Report of the House of Bishops Working Group on Human Sexuality* (London: Church House Publishing, 2013).

3 *Living in Love and Faith: Christian Teaching and Learning About Identity, Sexuality, Relationships and Marriage*, https://www.churchofengland.org/resources/living-love-and-faith (accessed 14.2.24).

4 J. Halberstam, *The Queer Art of Failure* (Durham, NC: Duke University Press, 2011); Karen Bray, *Grave Attending: A Political Theology for the Unredeemed* (New York: Fordham University Press, 2020).

Acknowledgements

My thanks are due to David Shervington and all at SCM Press, whose faith in this project and invaluable help and advice have helped to usher this work into life as a book.

For supervising the original thesis on which this work is based I want to thank Professors Louise Lawrence and Susannah Cornwall, whose enthusiasm, wise counsel and unfailing support kept me buoyant when I was in danger of sinking below the pressures of the task and who helped me to think theologically and to find a voice.

Most of all, however, I would like to thank my husband, Bernard, whose belief in my abilities never wavers and who has, through over 30 years of marriage, encouraged my every endeavour. This work would not have been started or completed without his steadfast support (or constant nagging). He encouraged me to persist even when he was suffering from serious illnesses and undergoing life-changing treatment. When he could no longer proofread or suggest edits because he had lost his sight, Bernard remained absorbed by this project, even when he didn't entirely agree with the direction that it was taking! So, thank you to a great critic and cheerleader.

Introduction

Queer studies offer us one method for imagining, not some fantasy of an elsewhere, but existing alternatives to hegemonic systems.[1]

In this book I propose to que(e)ry official Church of England discourses on sexuality (which is invariably a cipher for homosexuality), and to interrogate the constructions of authority and power that generate these reflections and debates. My primary focus will be on *The Report from the House of Bishops Working Group on Human Sexuality*, hereafter the *Pilling Report* or *Pilling*,[2] and on its afterlife, both official and non-official, in continuing debates and discussions. The profuse resources provided by the Living in Love and Faith initiative – a substantial outcome of the *Pilling* process – will not be examined in any detail, but the ensuing discussions and debates at General Synod and elsewhere will be analysed as a continuation of the afterlife that *Pilling* initiated.[3] Time has allowed some perspective on *Pilling* and its immediate afterlife, enough to consider the report as an exemplar of the ways in which church discourses construe authority, power and privilege and what they judge to be normative and canonical despite their claims to provisionality.

The terms 'que(e)ry'/'que(e)rying' here denote the critical interrogation of the hermeneutics chosen by the writers of *Pilling*, the queering of the cisheteronormative (often white and male) epistemological assumptions that inform their writing, and the structures of power and privilege that underlie their publication and their influence in the Church (and, to a lesser extent, in secular society since the Church of England is a state church established by law). In particular, this work posits the queer art of failure as a response to the ways in which the institutional Church, particularly the Church of England, both reflects and reproduces a neoliberal culture that expects enterprise to solve issues and answer questions satisfactorily; that is, in a way that is amenable to the mechanisms that are doing the reflecting and enquiring.[4] Enterprise in this context is the working out of a discourse, or series of discourses, in which a particular model of debate and discussion is devised as the process by which consensus or solutions may be reached. The mechanisms that undertake such deliberations are themselves synthetic bodies, particular constructions of authority, power and privilege. In the Church of England these bodies are church reports, official working parties and synods, which initiate process and determine teaching and doctrine. They are predicated on a neoliberal model that sees success in terms of positive and measurable outcomes, or at least regards the processes by which such outcomes are sought as legitimate and progressive. An alternative is failure which, as a 'queer art', is a refusal

> to acquiesce to dominant logics of power and discipline and as a form of critique. As a practice, failure recognizes that alternatives are embedded already in the dominant and that power is never total or consistent; indeed failure can exploit the unpredictability of ideology and its indeterminate qualities.[5]

My intent is to que(e)ry the authority of these synthetic and dominant bodies and their constructions of power and privilege, which look innocent but are full of artifice, and to interrogate their propulsion towards conclusion and consensus by suggesting that failure to agree and to conclude may be a 'solution' to the intractability of competing Christian (and post-Christian) narratives. The motif of failure as a 'queer art' derives from J. Halberstam's *The Queer Art of Failure*, which posits failure as a kind of 'victory' for those who fall outside the cisheteronormative models enforced by neoliberal patterns of success and progress. Often using animated and 'trash' films, antisocial negativity, countercultural lifestyles and images of gay Nazis, Halberstam's work disrupts

> commonsense narratives about emergence and suppressions ... [where] redeeming the gay self from its pathologization have been replaced by emphases on the negative potential of the queer and the possibility of rethinking the meaning of the political through queerness precisely by embracing the incoherent, the lonely, the defeated and the melancholic formulation of selfhood that it sets in motion.[6]

It is my contention that by adopting the potential of failure as a means of que(e)rying the hegemonic assumptions of church reports and report writers, the Church of England might be able to embrace 'the incoherent, the lonely, the defeated and the melancholic'. The *Pilling Report* and its 'afterlife' showcase mostly those voices whose authority and whose meanings derive from their participation in the hegemonic norms of neoliberal ideas of progress and success, albeit norms that are represented as Christian – and often as traditional or orthodox Christianity.

INTRODUCTION

Epistemological enquiries, which appear 'commonsensical' to the authors and creators of church reports, and the debates that ensue, often exclude those who do not conform to the dominant narrative. Moreover, these prevailing ways of knowing disregard the possibilities suggested by the failure of progress, success, knowing, agreeing and predominating. The institutional life of church reports and debates, which is predicated on the belief in the unassailability of church polity, could, perhaps, seek for ways of knowing outside this dominant framework. Rather than 'success' and 'progress', failure's art embraces the queer hope of unbecoming, undoing, unknowing; the ways of negativity, passivity and immaturity. Halberstam focuses on what Foucault calls 'subjugated knowledge' – cultural understandings that have been regarded as childish and foolish notions of possibility.[7] It is, perhaps, ironic that a religion that enjoins its followers to be childlike has such a problem with the radical and anarchic potentialities of childishness. I will return to the trope of potentially redemptive failure and negativity throughout this book, engaging with its possibilities for the queering of ecclesial discourses in the final chapter. I also reflect upon the ways in which the academic or quasi-academic language of church reports and debates gatekeeps this discourse, making access difficult for those who do not 'speak' the scholarly or ecclesial vernacular. Halberstam's appeal to the silliness and childishness of some subcultures and popular culture reminds us that meaning is made outside 'proper' knowledge in failure, forgetfulness, wandering and improvization.[8] My suggestion is that one kind of redemptive failure could be learning to dwell in the 'queer temporality' of Holy Saturday,[9] in which the prospect of resolution is tenuous and uncertain.[10] Failure and the almost fugue state of Holy Saturday are the suggestive 'solutions' I offer to the peculiarly intractable 'issues' that sexuality, or rather homosexuality, pose for the Church.

In late 2013, the Church of England published the *Pilling Report*. I first read the report as an investigation of the sources that could inform the Church about the licitness of homosexual relationships, and that might provide answers to the problem that homosexual relationships – particularly monogamous ones – pose for the Church. My observation that it didn't do those things very well was a response to the report's success on its own terms. Through reflecting on these reactions and observations I realized that *Pilling* was a type of institutional construct that relies for its authority on unexamined assumptions about the unmarked power and privilege that it embodies. Que(e)rying these assumptions would thus entail not only interrogating the hermeneutical lenses that the report deploys, but also deconstructing the paradigm of reports themselves as neoliberal mechanisms for delivering success and progress. What is being queered here is not just the text of a church report but also the apparatus behind the text and the synthetic constructions of power and authority that the chosen text represents. This book aims to queer a church institution using *Pilling* as its chosen paradigm, suggesting that the queer art of failure may offer a paradoxical resolution that the decidedly unqueer art of success cannot.

Pilling followed a series of documents, over a period of 34 years, commissioned by the Church of England both to examine human sexuality and to offer teaching about Christian marriage as the proper place for 'sexual intercourse, as an expression of faithful intimacy'.[11] Five reports, published between 1979 and 2013, and discussions at General Synod[12] and elsewhere have focused more particularly on homosexuality and homosexual relationships and on whether there is any proper place for them in the life and teaching of the Church. All these reports – whether they have been construed as 'liberal' or 'conservative' – have addressed, principally, the status of homosexuality and of gay people in the life of the Church of England, with very little reflection on the theology of sexuality and marriage, beyond a concern about homosexual orientation and relationships. As the 1987 General Synod concluded, 'homosexual genital acts ... fall short of ... ideal and are to be met by a call to repentance and the exercise of compassion'.[13] Gay relationships, even those that are permanent and faithful, are judged here to fall short of the ideal of Christian marriage, a union between one man and one woman.

The begetters of the *Pilling Report* – like the authors of all Church of England reports – showed little sign that they were aware of treating a whole section of humanity as an issue for the Church, to be solved by analysis, discussion and theological reflection, some of it sympathetic and orientated towards inclusion, but all carried out with the overriding assumption that, although the Church may have erred historically in its treatment of gay people, the norms that made the authors insiders and the subjects liminal remained largely unchallenged. Thus *Pilling*, although more culturally sensitive in its treatment of gay people than some earlier reports, nevertheless 'others' gay people by seeing homosexuality as a problem to be tackled by those who hold canonical authority and who are willing to pathologize queer sexuality[14] simply because it is non-normative and, therefore, beyond the fences and the walls that the Church has built to safeguard orthodoxy and orthopraxy (and also, perhaps, to exclude the possibility of taint[15]). It is difficult, if one is cis[16] and straight, not to use the terms 'they' and 'it' when writing about gay and trans people and about homosexuality and gender transition, for one cannot write 'us' and thus colonize their lives and experience. But, in church reports, LGBTIQ+[17] people are always 'they' because the reports are invariably written from the perspective of the cisheterosexual[18] norm. No matter how sympathetic they are to the disadvantages, prejudices and abuses experienced by gay, trans, bi and non-binary people, the author(itie)s (the writers of *Pilling* and earlier reports) regard those with non-normative loves and experiences as 'them' – alien, different, other.

Queering an Institution

The idea of queering the *Pilling Report* arose from the realization that church reports – like decisions made by Synod and by the House of Bishops – rely upon the readers' assumption that, while those writing and debating are, structurally, the arbiters of canonicity and orthodoxy, they are more particularly the representatives and possessors of unquestioned, and even ordained, norms, whether the authors and participants themselves are aware of this or not. This book will que(e)ry the aims and methodology of church discourses, such as the *Pilling Report* itself more than its subject matter: purportedly 'human sexuality', but really a code for homosexuality; for nowhere in this report is the subject of heterosexuality discussed, beyond asserting that it is the divinely ordained norm for humankind, and never is this assertion queried in any of the report's reflections. For several decades there have been womanist and feminist, post-colonial and decolonial, liberation and queer theological responses about bodies that the churches have, at times, labelled aberrant.[19] This is, I think, the first time that an attempt has been made to queer institutional reports and debates, to que(e)ry their methodologies and their constructions of power and authority, their choices of who writes the reports and on who speaks, their decisions about who should be listened to (who has a voice in these debates), their assumptions about normative sexuality (and gender), their privileging of certain theological points of view, and their selection of lenses through which homosexuality is viewed and their order of precedence within the report. In one sense, *Pilling* is a static text, published in November 2013, and emblematic of the date when it appeared; in another sense, its tentacles reach into the past, to Church of England reports on homosexuality from the mid to the late twentieth century, and forward, into the process that *Pilling* itself engendered: the Diocesan Shared Conversations and conversations at General Synod; Living in Love and Faith and its repercussions in debate in and out of General Synod.

Beyond these 'authorized' channels, the debate continued in churches, on blogs and on Facebook, and this work will ask whether these voices include those marginalized by the formal procedures of the Church and the rhetoric of church reports and quasi-academic discourse on theology and scripture, science and sociology, or whether these 'unauthorized' voices also embody white cisheteronormative (and often male) privilege. in both authorized and unauthorized forms.[20]

The Limits of Inclusion

There is an inspirational meme in circulation that, in an attempt to encourage generosity of spirit, suggests that if you have more than enough, you should build a longer table rather than a higher wall.[21] I have seen it used on social media in ecclesial contexts to support inclusiveness, a gesture to enfold the marginalized and the outcast, rather than to build hedges to keep them out of canonical spaces. But how inclusive is such an initiative? For who are the they – or the we – who are to build this longer table; which persons or organizations are the ones with the authority and power to do the constructing and inviting, and who made them/us the hosts? The problem with the very notion of inclusion is that the idea presupposes an elite caste able to invite others to the table. In the Western and Northern world, and in Australia and New Zealand, this elite is white, cisheteronormative and male. However much institutions, such as churches, aim to embrace inclusivity, the reality is that they are the ones doing the inviting and the invitees are invariably people of colour, transgender people, women, disabled people and queer people. The invitations are dependent not only on the hosts' generosity, but also upon the recognition that the marginalized deserve a place at the table. Unfortunately, not all organizations and churches believe that all of these categories deserve an invitation; and because churches in the UK are exempt from areas of equality legislation,[22] some still exclude people of colour, transgender people, women, disabled people, neurodivergent people and gay and bisexual people from full inclusion in their life and rites.

The Living in Love and Faith initiative (LLF) demonstrates – according to one of its participants' reflections on partaking in the LLF process and their observation on the inherent constructions of privilege and authority shown in the selection of contributors and authors that have been conveyed into the texts – that the systems that produced *Pilling* have remained unchanged. This is despite the 'radical new Christian inclusion' that Justin Welby promised as a prelude to the LLF initiative after the February 2017 General Synod refused to 'Take Note' of a Bishops' report on sexuality.[23] Alex Clare-Young, a transmasculine non-binary person, writes on what they perceive to be the skewed representation on the LLF Co-ordinating Group:

INTRODUCTION

The Co-ordinating Group (in its final, 2020, composition) was made up of 13 people, 8 of whom were Church of England Bishops. It was chaired by a male, cisgender, heterosexual Bishop of the Church of England. Just over half of the members were male. One member was an out transmasculine non-binary person. One member was an out gay person. In other words, as far as I know, 85% of the Co-ordinating Group was cisgender and heterosexual. There was no out female LGBTQ+ representation. While presenting identities may not fairly represent a person's authentic identity and experiences, it was clear that only myself and the out gay member of the co-ordinating group were able to speak openly from an LGBTQ+ perspective and, as a result, we were frequently asked to do so. I felt very strongly that the LGBTQ+ representation in the co-ordinating group was tokenistic. It also put a heavy burden on LGBTQ+ members to be a part of every single process and sub-group as an educator. This often meant that out LGBTQ+ members were expected to speak about our own experiences, from a position of vulnerability, whereas the significant majority of members were predominantly speaking about opinion or theory about LGBTQ+ people, from a position of power.[24]

Chapter 1 examines the hermeneutics of the report and queries the lenses – scientific, sociological and biblical – through which *Pilling* views the 'problem' of homosexuality. Here I ask the question: why are some lenses privileged over others? For instance, social science and science are used as epistemological tools before the *Pilling Report* turns to reflections on scripture. Does this pathologize homosexuality as a 'condition' to be dissected, and do Church of England reports examine homosexuality as an 'issue' rather than looking theologically at the lives and experiences of LGBTIQ+ people? And where those lives are considered in this report and its authorized afterlife, whose voices are chosen and who does the choosing? My interrogation of the report's epistemological framework and the framing of the Shared Conversations that were one outcome of *Pilling* reveals that ethical and theological canonicity is produced by those who hold authoritative power and privilege in the Church of England and that queer voices are inevitably marginalized by the processes that created this hegemonic normativity. Even when conversations and reflections are unauthorized by official bodies, they are constrained by the gatekeeping effect of electronic and epistemic access to quasi-academic – and often elite – white, male, discourses.

Chapter 2 looks first at the 'authorized' responses to the report – the regional Shared Conversations and the conversations at General Synod. I ask whose voices are included in these conversations, and are any particular viewpoints privileged? Do the 'authorized' contributions to the debate – those self-selected voices – have space for the liminal, or is this the discourse of an elite: those privileged by education, knowledge, access to the internet, and access to ostensibly open, but, perhaps, intimidating or inaccessible spaces? The last section of the chapter is a reflection on two Synod debates from 2023 on the reception of the *Prayers of Love and Faith* proposed by the bishops.[25] This serves as an addendum to reflections on the hermeneutics of authority in the post-*Pilling* process.

Chapter 3 reviews some of the unauthorized afterlives of *Pilling*, critically examining a blog that regularly canvasses ecclesial issues, often those that touch upon sexual and gender identity in the Church of England, and offering a brief reflection on social media discussions on sexuality and the Church of England. Here I examine whether these unofficial channels can accommodate abject lives and non-privileged experiences or whether these discourses are also 'disembodied practices of textual analysis'.[26]

Chapter 4 reflects on the ways in which the hermeneutics of *Pilling*, both as text and as process, may be queered in the venture to disrupt the normative premises that underpin the construction and aims of the report. Here I consider different ways in which the hermeneutics that *Pilling* deploys could have been disrupted by taking paths that are already in the Church's traditions, but have been routinely not taken in contemporary ecclesial contexts. These include, as conversation partners, theologians and biblical scholars who have taken what appear to be non-normative or transgressive approaches to scripture and tradition. The queering here is that of looking through what may seem, to the writers of church reports, strange lenses: ones that not only offer a different perspective but themselves challenge the constructions of power, privilege and normalcy that the authors of such reports and the begetters of such processes apparently regard as unexceptionable.

Chapter 5 aims to deconstruct church discourses both as text and process and to ask in what ways could it be queerer: not merely 'allowing' space for the liminal, the queer and the non-normative, but razing the notion of an 'us' who gets to decide which of the 'them' deserves inclusion in the full life and rites of the Church. I suggest that the Church of England should dwell for a time in the 'queer temporality' of Holy Saturday, reflecting on what constitutes failure and without looking too assuredly and prematurely for the certainties and the success of the resurrection. Holy Saturday time is too often merely a theological pause because, of course, we know the certainty of the resurrection. The original inhabitants of Holy Saturday did not. I will have looked in earlier chapters at the idea of 'deserving queers' who might merit a place in the Church versus 'undeserving queers' who are deemed beyond the bounds of ecclesial spaces. Here, I reflect upon how queer some Christian LGBTIQ+ people want their spaces to be or to become. For some secular queer people,[27] the desire for the goods of marriage and parenthood are the signs of an undesirable assimilation that is a capitulation to neoliberal cisgender, heteropatriarchal norms. For others, many Christian men and women among them, the telos of vowed, covenantal sexual relationships is one that they wish to share with their cis, straight siblings; they do not want to drink from a different water fountain. Does this desire for a state that is culturally normative in both secular and religious contexts curtail the very concept of disrupting the basis and structure of *Pilling*'s text and afterlife? Or is there still queer space for questions about the inviolability of those very norms and the constructions of power and privilege that undergird their genesis and continuity?

Que(e)rying Conversations

In Chapters 4 and 5 I am in dialogue with conversation partners from the fields of queer theology, queer theory and queer biblical studies. These include Halvor Moxnes, who writes about Jesus entering queer space in Matthew 19;[28] Robert Song, who argues that both celibacy and (unprocreative) covenant partnerships are fruits of the new eschatological age in which the coming of Christ has relativized the sexual ethical norms of the Genesis edicts;[29] Lee Edelman, whose *No Future: Queer Theory and the Death Drive* queries procreative norms that attach ethical value to investment in the future and in 'the Child' and provocatively offers a non-eschatological eschatology;[30] Karen Bray, who writes of the 'queer temporality' of Holy Saturday as a time of abjection;[31] and J. Halberstam, whose *The Queer Art of Failure* suggests too that inaction (the subversion of the productivity invoked by neoliberal norms) may produce 'generative models of failure'.[32] My dialogue with these scholars aims to open up the queer spaces that the authors of *Pilling* choose to disregard in their valorization of canonical sexuality and normative scholarship. In Chapter 4 I engage with Robert Song, Halvor Moxnes and Lee Edelman as participants in a conversation about queering the so-called creation ordinances of the Genesis narratives. Song, one of the authors of *Pilling*, has written a provocative book that argues that in the new age inaugurated by the coming of Christ the command to 'be fruitful and multiply' (Gen.1.28) has been relativized such that the good of procreation is not (or need not be) the primary good in marriage. Marriage now can be non-generative (in a biological sense and thus open to same-sex couples), while procreative partnerships could be re-categorized as 'covenant partnerships'.

Song's Christological re-reading of Genesis subverts the more normative readings of the creation ordinances, such as those found unexamined in *Pilling*, but I would argue that it stops short of interrogating both those ordinances and what it perceives as the unchanging definition and nature of marriage itself.

My second conversation here is with Moxnes, whose reading of the Matthean eunuch sayings is an unapologetically queer exegesis of a text that, he argues, figures a queer Jesus in a queer space. Ignoring, for once, Marcella Althaus-Reid's admonition that queer theology should not move from the margins to the centre,[33] I see this disclosure of Jesus' mission as unexceptional; that is, not queer in the sense of being strange or subversive. It has a 'distinctive hermeneutic' in that it is original and timely, but not, perhaps, in the way in which *Pilling* uses this term, to refer to scholarship that uses queer or other non-mainstream methodologies.[34] Moxnes' Jesus is, however, disrupting expectations (both the disciples' and ours) by repurposing a slur – eunuch – as an owned identity marker, much as 'queer' has been reclaimed (by some) as an adjective that bestows dignity and self-worth. And yet, it is a reading of this Matthean text that has so often been elided by more normative, spiritualizing readings.

Lee Edelman may seem a 'queer' partner in a conversation about theology. Yet his resistance to reproductive futurity in the telic symbol of the Child has, for me, profound echoes in the valorization of the barren and the eunuch/ascetic in Matthew's Jesus, in Song's eschatological rewriting of the procreative goods of marriage, and in my own reflections on the contingency of marriage and reproduction in the biblical and Christian tradition. These voices speak of the alternative queer spaces that await further exploration, but that have been elided by the authors of *Pilling* (except for Song, whose reflections were published soon after the report) and by those who have orchestrated the processes – conversations and texts – that *Pilling* initiated.

It is entirely possible to look at *Pilling*, perhaps through Halberstam's 'queer art of failure', and conclude that it has done little, if anything, to fix the mind of the Church of England on the discourse of homosexuality. Indeed, the very concept of fixing the mind – of attaining consensus and harmony that will satisfy all 'interested parties' or on 'winning' the debate on sexuality– owes much to the neoliberal ideals of progress and productivity that have tended to shape much of the Church's reflections. A queer proposal might be to abandon all such striving altogether and to accept a kind of apophatic state that acknowledges uncertainty and provisionality as the only possible telos to this discourse. However, I am concerned with how queer Christians can effect, in Judith Butler's words, a 'livable life' within a church that has often rejected their bodies and their lived experiences.[35] There should, I argue, be a movement towards a tentative resolution that offers some hope of redemption from hegemonic normality and compulsory heterosexuality. Karen Bray (who also draws on Shelly Rambo's work on trauma) and J. Halberstam are my interlocutors in my final chapter on the redemptive potential of failure. Bray's writing about the Wordlessness and inaction of Holy Saturday as a place of trauma and queer temporality suggests to me a kind of resolution to the neoliberal optimism of *Pilling*, which offers the possibilities of unbeing and undoing of hegemonic epistemologies and privileged constructions of virtue, canonicity and normativity. The acceptance of alterity, abjection and failure is Halberstam's[36] contribution to this negative quest for a life beyond cisheteronormativity's boundaries and a move beyond the 'narrative of hope' that informs Church of England reports.[37]

Reflexivity

Because I am writing about Church of England reports that study human sexuality – in particular, what they term the 'problem' or 'issue' of homosexuality, which is an orientation/identity/experience I do not share – it is necessary to locate myself within this debate; to try to determine how my own beliefs and experiences have informed my approach towards sexuality and to indicate for the reader what these views might be and how they may have been formed. I use provisional terms about my view and approach to this topic because I can only construe what my motives are, and each reader may infer something different from the evidence presented here. I am not a queer theologian, if that adjective denotes someone whose identity is queer: gay, trans or with the characteristics of Differences in Sexual Development (DSD)/intersex people. I do not aim, or wish, to colonize others' experiences and identities; I deploy queer hermeneutics as a rich, playful and grave means of interrogating the white cisheteronormative epistemologies of the Global North that underpin the construction of ecclesial reports and the discourses that they create.

I am a heterosexual, cisgender, middle-class, married, white woman: which conjures an instant stereotype – a typical, cultural British 'norm' – although this may tell the reader only how I self-identify, not what I am likely or unlikely to believe. Although I attempt to read texts with critical detachment, I know that I cannot be free from the bias of my privilege and my particular ethical commitments and that I cannot help but read them from a confessional perspective. With these particular texts I am aware that I can only read them with the premise that the experience of gay and lesbian, bisexual, transgender, queer and intersex Christians is as valid and authentic as that of heterosexual, cisgender Christians; that voices that have been muted can be as credible and real as voices that are sanctioned; and that homosexual partnerships may be as holy (or not) as heterosexual ones. This must affect my reactions, not only to the conclusions of these reports, but also to their methodologies and their hermeneutics.

I believe in equality for LGBTIQ+ people, not simply because many have experienced bigotry and hostility from both the institutional Church and individual churches, but because I believe in a generous and egalitarian gospel in which everyone is able to participate fully regardless of gender, sexuality, ethnicity, ability or monetary worth. In Christ we are a new creation (2 Cor. 5.17) and we are all one (Gal. 3.28). My purpose, therefore, is to see people (especially those outwith the cisheteronormative mould) not as victims whose agency is compromised by their vulnerability; the risk of advocacy on behalf of others is that it can buttress one's own privilege. In analysing the hermeneutics of texts, such as *Pilling*, and in attempting to discern which voices they endorse and which they suppress or mute, I am aware that I am speaking of (and maybe for) people whose experience I cannot share.

I assent to the belief in a fallen creation, but not to the view that homosexual desire, gender dysphoria or being intersex[38] is a sign of singular fallenness, a peculiar flaw that marks those who do not share what is perceived as the primal and God-given binary and complementary nature of humankind. This is the cultural context in which I work; developing knowledge about the human mind and body and about how bodies have been written and read at different times and in differing cultures, informs the way in which I read scripture and, indeed, every text, everything drawn and inscribed and shaped, every piece of music. I cannot dissent from this knowledge and wisdom and, having encountered it, it cannot be unlearnt. Biblical scholarship and theological reflection can never be pure, untainted by culture or by the perceptions of the scholar and reflector. Even the attempt to uncover the 'original meaning' of a text, as if centuries of mediated grime could be swept away by the cold, dispassionate eye of the scholar, is a Sisyphean task. Dale Martin calls this attempt to recover the ancient meaning of the text, to determine the author's original intention, 'the sin of Christian textual foundationalism' and he argues that much historical scholarship assumes that this primal meaning must be the authentic meaning of the text.[39] Of course, like all scholars, Dale Martin was partisan. He had the preconceptions of a liberal, postmodern American gay man. But he did dispel the 'myth of textual agency', to note the rhetorical skirts behind which some of his peers hide, and to explore the allegorical and analogical interpretations of scripture that early commentators freely canvassed but began to be lost in the West after the Reformation. Once read, the work of other commentators inscribes itself in the mind and informs interpretation, belief and judgement.

Discourses of Power and Privilege

> The knowledge which a discourse produces constitutes a kind of power, exercised over those who are 'known'. When that knowledge is exercised in practice, those who are 'known' in a particular way will be subject (i.e. subjected) to it.[40]

The *Pilling Report* is a discourse created by and for the Church of England on the 'topic' of 'human sexuality'. I have borrowed this use of the term 'discourse' from the cultural theorist Stuart Hall, himself employing Foucault's theory of discourse as ideology. Hall writes, '[w]hen statements about a topic are made within a particular discourse, the discourse makes it possible to construct the topic in a certain way. It also limits the other ways in which the topic can be constructed.'[41] It is my contention here that, although *Pilling* suggests its own provisionality as the first step in a process of conversations and discernment, it is conceived by those whose ecclesial power and privilege bestow a canonical authority on their deliberations and judgements which necessarily limits the ways in which this topic can be constructed. Thus, the Working Group that produced the report construes heterosexuality (and cisgender identities) as 'natural' and unmarked, hence normative and orthodox. Behind the report's discussions of what kinds of sexualities are licit within the life of the Church lies the assumption that sexuality is not contingent and that, therefore, homosexuality is in some ways aberrant, even if or when it is to be tolerated or even 'welcomed'. The telic disposition of hegemonic heterosexuality as the norm for humanity is never interrogated, while sexualities outside the hetero/homosexuality binary and gender diversity – transgender people and those with Variations in Sexual Characteristics (VSCs)/DSDs – are touched on only very briefly in the Introduction. The authors write that the Church of England needs to address these as 'important theological and pastoral issues' but they refer their readers to a chapter in *Some Issues in Human Sexuality*, published ten years earlier.[42]

Pilling deploys particular hermeneutical lenses and epistemological tools to construct an understanding of 'human sexuality' (and binary gender identities) as naturally cisheteronormative and located within a patriarchal structure, thereby 'othering' all other variant sexualities and gender identities. David Halperin, in *Saint Foucault*, argues that this reification of heterosexuality is inevitably homophobic since it pathologizes homosexuality:

> The heterosexual/homosexual binarism is itself a homophobic production, just as the man/woman binarism is a sexist production. Each consists of two terms, the first of which is unmarked and unproblematized – it designates the category to which everyone is assumed to belong (unless someone is specifically marked as different) – whereas the second term is marked and problematized: it designates a category of persons whom *something differentiates* from normal, unmarked people ... Heterosexuality defines itself without problematizing itself, it elevates itself as a privileged and unmarked term by abjecting and problematizing homosexuality.[43]

Thus, heterosexuality is figured as both normal and natural, while at the same time being a site of vulnerability and instability that can be threatened by gay temptation in the form of role models or teachers, adolescent seduction or hearing homosexuality spoken of too often, and so must be constantly safeguarded. Halperin describes the methodology whereby heterosexuality is constructed as the disinterested and privileged subject that 'others' homosexuality as an 'object of enquiry' but one that is never allowed a legitimate or authorized voice except as 'an already discounted and devalued subcultural minority'.[44]

This, I will argue, is the methodology that the authors of church discourses adopt – maybe unwittingly – to privilege heterosexuality as *the* canonical sexuality, although here it is the unmarked category not only because it is regarded as normal, but also because it is presented as being divinely ordained. In a brief chapter on 'Homophobia' in *Pilling*, the Working Group rejects homophobic bullying and admits that the Church of England has not always combatted prejudice and bigotry against gay people.[45] Yet this assurance is hedged with caveats that seek to exculpate the Church from charges of homophobia, claiming that the term 'has been used in ways which tend to foreclose rational argument rather than to pursue it', and asserting that the Church's 'traditional' teaching on sexuality is not homophobic.[46] *Pilling* frames its topic as a debate, not between contested sexualities but on whether homosexuality has any place in the life of the Church, without acknowledging that 'rational argument' is not, perhaps, an appropriate tool for investigating people's identities, orientations, experiences, proclivities and desires.[47] This equivocation on the concept of homophobia as a problematic concept for the Church is buttressed by the statement that:

INTRODUCTION

> Power relationships within any institution are complex and those who are perceived as powerful by some may themselves feel marginal and misunderstood. We believe that, notwithstanding the continued 'outsider' status felt by many gay and lesbian people in the Church, some (perhaps many) are confident enough in their theology and relationships, and in their new-found position of affirmation in society, for us to propose that they too might listen carefully and prayerfully to those who hold firmly to the Church's traditional teaching.[48]

The observation that institutional power relationships are complex obscures the asymmetrical relationship between the author(itie)s behind *Pilling* – who are the keepers of knowledge and orthodoxy – and the targets of the report's investigation. This belief that Britain is inherently affirming of LGBTIQ+ identities is clearly unnuanced, although intolerance and violence, or at least the reporting of those incidents, have risen since *Pilling* was published. The alterity of the homosexual object creates, in Halperin's terms, a discourse that is implicitly homophobic because heterosexuality and homosexuality are not an equal pair but exist in a hierarchy where the latter's abjection demonstrates the superiority of the former. The work of transcending this institutional homophobia, then,

> [m]ight be to expose ... the operations of homophobic discourses, to reveal the strategies by which the discourses of medicine, law, science, and religion deauthorize lesbians and gay men, to subject those discourses to a political critique, and thereby to find ways of frustrating the political strategies immanent in their deployment, of delegitimating their claims to authority and dismantling their institutional base.[49]

Halperin's strategies quoted above are those that I wish to claim in order to delegitimize the cultural and religious constructs and to que(e)ry the power and privilege that undergird them created by institutions such as the Church (here, particularly, the Church of England, whose established status gives it an actual authority in England).[50]

This book is a counter to the discursive constructions of church reports in that it seeks to find a lens (or lenses) that would enable bodies like the Church of England to adopt queer methods of transformation. These methods would involve the undoing of dominant theological and cultural precepts that have resulted – whether inevitably or contingently – in a sexual (and non-cisgender) precariat and would expose church institutions to the experiences of abjection, of powerlessness, and of irresolution. They would attempt this, first, by challenging the hermeneutic and epistemological lenses that 'other' and pathologize sexual behaviours and identities that are construed as aberrant. Second, they would make a suggestive move towards queer transformations in particular discourses and practices where intersectionality and multiple identities are not only acknowledged, but also valued, as part of the democratic and diverse voices of experience within the body of the Church of England. And, in the final chapter, I explore ways in which transformation may be realized through the precarity of non-resolution to reach a 'solution'[51] that recognizes and lives with unknowing and undoing – what Halberstam terms 'the queer art of failure'.[52]

So, What is Queer?

It is not possible here to explore the vast – and sometimes contested – discourses of queer theory, but I must offer a brief explanation of what I understand by this concept, how I aim to use it in this book, and what I believe the relationship between queer theory and queer theology to be. Sara Ahmed writes that 'queer theory has been defined not only as anti-heteronormative, but as anti-normative',[53] arguing that heterosexuality is more than simply a norm – it is a regulatory norm that is sanctioned by marriage, reproduction, and the production of good citizenship:

> In this way, normative culture involves the differentiation between legitimate and illegitimate ways of living whereby the preservation of what is legitimate ('life as we know it') is assumed to be necessary for the well-being of the next generation. Heteronormativity involves the reproduction or transmission of culture through how one lives one's life in relation to others.[54]

I find this definition helpful because it describes the ways in which *Pilling* regards heterosexual marriage as a regulatory norm, since it is read as a creation ordinance that authorizes marriage as the ideal state, the standard by which all other 'lifestyles' – even celibacy – must be measured. This is what I mean when I use the term canonical to describe the place of heterosexuality and marriage for the writers of these reports. It is this construction of canonicity that I wish to que(e)ry here and, further, to interrogate the constructions of power and privilege whose authority is invested in enforcing the regulatory norms that appear unimpeachable to those producing them.

The term 'queer theory' was coined by Teresa de Lauretis in 1991 in a special, edited issue of the feminist cultural studies journal *differences*, 'Queer Theory: Lesbian and Gay Sexualities'. She defined it as a

INTRODUCTION

refusal of heterosexuality as normative, an interrogation of the assumption that lesbian and gay studies represent a homogeneous topic, and as focusing on the ways in which race shapes sexual subjectivity. This refusal of normativity and que(e)rying of the ways in which sexes and genders are construed developed from the work of mid-twentieth-century deconstructionists and post-structuralists such as Jacques Lacan, Jacques Derrida and Michel Foucault. Two of Foucault's works are particularly key to the development of queer theory: *Discipline and Punish*, in which he contends that power produces knowledge and that people adjust their own behaviours according to the perceived perceptions of others; and the four-volume *History of Sexuality*, where what he terms *Scientia Sexualis* makes sexuality a subject of scientific disciplines. Thus, he argues, sexuality in the nineteenth century, far from being repressed, was the object of new kinds of discourses aimed at telling us the scientific truth.[55] These discourses are also key, I will argue, to the constructions of knowledge in the *Pilling Report* where heteronormative understandings and scientific explanations of sexuality are privileged as unexceptional and authoritative. Queer theory had foremothers too in feminist and womanist scholars such as Audre Lorde, Monique Wittig, bell hooks, Adrienne Rich and Gayle Rubin, whose work aimed at undoings of gender and sexuality.[56] Writing as a lesbian and as part of what she described as 'the lesbian continuum', Rich wrote about 'compulsory heterosexuality' in 1980, creating a term that would inform queer theory and, later, queer theology, to critique heterosexuality as a site of power.[57]

Two other pivotal foremothers, who would later be categorized as queer scholars, produced significant and formative books in the year before de Lauretis's coinage: Eve Kosofsy Sedgwick's *Epistemology of the Closet* and Judith Butler's *Gender Trouble*. In Butler's contention that gender – and, indeed, sex – is performative lies one of the influential tenets of queer theory: that identity is not immutable but provisional and historically determined. Butler is, however, here interrogating '*regulatory practices* of gender formation and division';[58] as she argues in her later work *Undoing Gender*, '[a] life for which no categories of identity exist is not a livable life'.[59] Indeed, those queer people seeking a 'liveable life'[60] have often sought it in the activism of 'identity politics', construing 'queer' as an identity resistant to 'compulsory heterosexuality' and with slogans such as 'We're here, We're Queer, Get used to it!'[61] And there persists, as I shall argue in my concluding chapter, a division between LGBTIQ+ people who wish to be quietly assimilated into the norms of heterosexual culture and society, and those who resist, in Muñoz's criticism of homonormativity, 'inclusion in a corrupt and bankrupt social order'.[62]

Queer theory has grown and developed in the three decades since de Lauretis's journal edition and, although it is embedded in the Academy and, to some extent, in popular discourse, it remains both a fluid, or non-essentialist, concept and a contested one.[63] Queer is better figured, perhaps, as a verb rather than as a noun; a doing rather than a being. Since queer theory is disruptive, transgressive and troubling, it can have no definitive logic, discourse or end. Halperin apprehends queer's slipperiness in his statement that the concept owns no stable reality:

> Queer is by definition *whatever* is at odds with the normal, the legitimate, the dominant. *There is nothing in particular to which it necessarily refers.* It is an identity without an essence. 'Queer', then, demarcates not a positivity but a positionality vis-à-vis the normative – a positionality that is not restricted to lesbians and gay men but is in fact available to anyone who is or who feels marginalized because of her or his sexual practices; it could include some married couples with children, for example ... it describes a horizon of possibility whose precise extent and heterogeneous scope cannot in principle be delimited in advance.[64]

This is a helpful observation for a scholar who is a cisgender married heterosexual and, thus, a theologian who utilizes queer theory rather than a queer theologian (see above for further reflections on positionality in this discourse). This definition is also key to this project of interrogating the dominant norms, the hegemonic epistemologies, the assumptions of authority, and the constructions of power and privilege, both implicit and explicit in church bodies and church reports, although in limiting the concept of queer to sexual practices Halperin hobbles its usefulness as a deconstructing discourse.

Next, I want to explore, again briefly, the intersections of queer theory and queer theology and to position this work somewhere in the interstices between the two. As Susannah Cornwall argues in *Controversies in Queer Theology*, queer theologians are not, necessarily, the inheritors of methodologies from secular queer theory:

> Interestingly, queer theologians have not often engaged explicitly in their writing with Butler, Foucault and the other theorists whose work underlies queer theory. In some cases this lack of acknowledgement of critical theory may be motivated by a desire to make queer theology more accessible than queer theory has often been even while retaining its emphasis on praxis (albeit not always realized) and resistance. However, it also seems that the use of the term queer within theology is much broader than within queer theory itself, and that in fact not every queer theologian is even familiar with queer theoretical discourse.[65]

INTRODUCTION

One significant criticism of queer theology is that, in attempting to find feminine or queer attributes for the divine or in searching for queer or female role models in scripture and tradition, it reinscribes the hegemony of cisgender patriarchal heteronormativity rather than undoing it. What is feminine/female or queer is always the marked – and subordinate – category measured against the unmarked heterosexual and patriarchal norm, even when the male bride imaged in the Church is, for example, rendered as female/feminine. Marcella Althaus-Reid wrote that 'dyadic oppositional systems such as God-Father and God-Mother'; or discourses about 'the feminine side of God' (which assumes that the core of God's identity is heterosexually male, and femininity is just a side or an extra point of view) do not undo patriarchal theology.[66] Instances of these kinds of queering include foregrounding imagery that depicts Christ breastfeeding the believer and the retrieval of maternal language for God.[67]

Linn Marie Tonstad critiques three issues that she finds in some inclusive queer theologies.[68] The first is the depiction of Jesus as a radically inclusive universalist contrasted with the legalistic, works-righteous, ethnocentric Jew, an interpretation that is inherently antisemitic and problematically supersessionist.[69] Her second concern is that inclusivity can result in theology that becomes unqueer, since queering as a repetition – rather than as a dismantling of norms and of the failure to pay attention to the 'affective life of binaries' – results in

> [v]alorizations of fluidity that ignore the affective life of binaries [which] assume that fluidity's generative aspect is that male-bodied and female-bodied persons move between sexed positions in symbol systems without their bodied identifications determining their symbolic locations. But on the symbolic level, male and female, man and woman, are not two indifferent instances of a generic category. This is especially true in the symbolic order of the Christian imaginary, where the designations 'God' and 'creation' often map onto the symbolic positions 'male' and 'female'. As a result, the movements of actually existing humans between positions in a symbol system may have little effect on the stability of the symbol system itself.[70]

According to Tonstad, troubling fixed gender categories in a hierarchical system results not in their undoing, but in their reinforcement. Her third contention is that some queer readings employ 'flat literalism and reductive presentist assumptions' that, ironically, valorize sexual normativity. Thus, Jesus is presented as a man who must have had sexual impulses – erections and orgasms – whether directed to his female or male disciples, in order to be fully human. A 'healthy' sexuality is seen as an incarnational imperative, thus rendering Jesus as 'normal' and very 'unqueer':

> But if queerness disturbs identity, in Edelman's terms, or is an 'identity without an essence,' in Halperin's, or even if queerness is defined by fluidity and inclusivity, as in many of the theologians discussed here, then producing normative visions of humanity (beyond a general recognition of the plasticity of the human person) is fundamentally anti-queer as well as false.[71]

The aspiration for inclusion through attempts both to destabilize conventional or modern readings and to recover textual denotations and connotations is wholly understandable for people who have been othered and damaged by the culturally normative readings of scripture and tradition of the Global North. Tonstad's prescription lies in an Edelman–Althaus-Reid[72] nexus where the latter's insistence that queer theology is always done in the first person intersects with Edelman's refusal of the ideal of human flourishing (through reproductive futurity) that 'serves as a site of constraint rather than possibility'.[73] Both Edelman and Althaus-Reid will reappear as conversation partners later and I ground some of this project of queering *Pilling* (and the conventions of church reports on homosexuality) on their theological and teleological perceptions. However, liveability or what Ahmed describes as 'comfort'[74] – to be at ease in the world – is requisite for those whose queer lives and loves do not conform to canonical norms. Ahmed is as dismissive of queer assimilation to the telos of compulsory heterosexuality as Muñoz, writing:

> it is hence important that queer lives do not follow the scripts of heteronormative culture ... Such lives would not desire access to comfort; they would maintain their discomfort with all aspects of normative culture in how they live.
> Ideally, they would not have families, get married, settle down into unthinking coupledom, give birth to and raise children, join neighbourhood watch, or pray for the nation in times of war. Each of these acts would 'support' the ideals that script such lives as queer, failed and unliveable in the first place. The aspiration to ideals of conduct that is central to the reproduction of heteronormativity has been called, quite understandably, a form of assimilation.[75]

And yet, Ahmed develops this critique of assimilation into a recognition that queer families do not merely reproduce heteronormative scripts but rework and, perhaps, transform them. This transgression of norms may not be deliberate or consciously political, but it comes about through the 'queering' of space:

> comfort is the effect of bodies being able to 'sink' into spaces that have already taken their shape. Discomfort is not simply a choice or decision – 'I feel uncomfortable about this or that' – but an effect of bodies inhabiting spaces that do not take or 'extend' their shape. So the closer that queer subjects get to the spaces defined by heteronormativity the more *potential* there is for a reworking of the heteronormative, partly as the proximity 'shows' how the spaces extend some bodies rather than others. Such extensions are usually concealed by what they produce: public comfort. What happens when bodies fail to 'sink into' spaces, a failure that we can describe as a 'queering' of space?[76]

Transformation through the que(e)rying of time and space is something to which I will return in the final chapter.

It may also be transformative for LGBTIQ+ people to derive 'comfort' from queer theologies in which they find reflections of their own lives and desires, in those narratives that speak of liminality and queerness, or in which transgressive ancestors may be traced. Indeed, for anyone who finds the '"surly bonds" of compulsory heterosexuality' irksome, the confession that '[t]heology is a queer thing. It has always been a queer thing'[77] offers the possibility of a place of ease and the loosening of constraint. For Gerard Loughlin, theology is a strange undertaking in the contemporary, neoliberal West, but, he maintains, it has always been strange in that it deals with unknowability, with mystery and with what is beyond human comprehension. When it affects to understand this mystery, theology becomes idolatrous. Queer is also a slur repurposed as a badge of pride that has always been there in the dominant heterosexual cultural narrative: in the songs of Cole Porter, and the fiction of Henry James, who, in 1914, declared, 'I am the queer monster, the artist, an obstinate finality, an inexhaustible sensibility.'[78] Queer theology, argues Loughlin, is 'oddly central' to Christian thought and culture: 'it finds itself to be the disavowed but necessary condition for the Christian symbolic; and not simply as that which is rejected in order to sustain its opposite, but upfront ... playing in the movement of stories and images that constitutes the Christian imaginary'.[79] Orthodox theologians, such as Gregory of Nyssa, St John of the Cross and Hans Urs von Balthasar, turn out to be the queerest of all.[80]

Theology's capacity to provide, in Halperin's words, a 'social space for the construction of different identities',[81] could be the means of exploring a queer eschatology in which the Kingdom is inaugurated proleptically through a call to new ways of living and being that have not been found in 'the surety of heteropatriarchal Christianity'.[82] There is, as I have noted elsewhere, a risk in bringing queer (theology or theory) in from the margins to the centre in that it can become an identity rather than a positionality, but Loughlin's view that queer was always already there has the capacity for comfort. His perception is that God is also queer, for Godself is (in Halperin's phrase) an 'identity without an essence'; we can know the unknowable God only though their effects. For queer people in the Church whose vulnerability is often predicated on their marginal status in a cisheteronormative culture, the knowledge that their lives and loves are already threaded into the narratives of Christianity may secure a more liveable life.

This book does not attempt to examine all the biblical and theological arguments that the authors of church reports present, nor to queer all the biblical material presented. The focus instead is on undoing the hermeneutic lenses and hegemonic epistemologies that underpin church discourses, and for this purpose I am utilizing queer methodologies to attempt an interrogation of *Pilling*'s ontology and its construction of authority and canonicity; and a suggestion of ways in which the dominance and normativity of church reports might be transformed through the abjection of experiencing the queer temporality of Holy Saturday. Halperin's observation that queer is '*whatever* is at odds with the normal, the legitimate, the dominant' (emphasis original) has become *my* lens through which to view the normative constructions of church report writing. His expansive definition of queer is supplemented and nuanced through engagement with Butler, Edelman, Althaus-Reid, Halberstam, Song, Moxnes and Bray.

Two quotations, one from Althaus-Reid and the other from Jose Esteban Muñoz (a more optimistic queer theorist than Edelman), frame this proposal:

> Queering theology does not leave theology intact in its systematic structures, traditional positions or ecclesiologies, but uses its own sexual ways of knowing to question the sacred as a heterosexual assumption. That is, of course, high sexual revolt in theology. If the theologian puts her hands under the skirts of God, she is establishing a different pattern of dialogue with the sacred and with herself and her community of resistance. This heralds the end of unnecessary transcendence and the beginning of sensual concretization in theology.[83]

> Queerness is also a performative because it is not simply a being but a doing for and toward the future. Queerness is essentially about the

INTRODUCTION

rejection of a here and now and an insistence on potentiality or concrete possibility for another world.[84]

Is there a conclusion to this project beyond the pragmatic realization that even when inhabiting queer temporality there must be a space in which to pause and reflect and to draw a tentative line under this particular venture at queering an ecclesial project? There are and will be further church resources that require disrupting and que(e)rying. This book suggests that que(e)rying the assumptions, strategy, structure and processes of church discourses, in an attempt to disrupt the givenness of such assumptions and constructions, could hear the many and various voices of non-normative people (particularly those of LGBTIQ+ folk) without deciding first who the hosts are to be, how long the table should be, and to whom to issue the invitations.

Notes

1 J. Halberstam, *The Queer Art of Failure* (Durham, NC: Duke University Press, 2011), 89.

2 The Archbishops' Council, *Report of the House of Bishops Working Group on Human Sexuality* (London: Church House Publishing, November 2013), chaired by Sir Joseph Pilling and – hence – popularly termed the *Pilling Report*.

3 *Living in Love and Faith: Christian Teaching and Learning about Identity, Sexuality, Relationships and Marriage*, https://www.churchofengland.org/resources/living-love-and-faith (accessed 15.2.24).

4 Neoliberalism – as an academic, economic, political or philosophical ideology – is a contested term. The following quotation, however, provides a mainstream definition of how the concept is generally understood: 'Neoliberalism is ... a theory of political economic practices that proposes that human well-being can best be advanced by liberating individual entrepreneurial freedoms and skills within an institutional framework characterized by strong private property rights, free markets, and free trade.' David Harvey, *A Brief History of Neoliberalism* (Oxford: Oxford University Press, 2005), 2. When I describe the Church of England as a neoliberal institution, as I do throughout this book, I am using the term, in a similar way, to describe an organization which has adopted the free market ideologies of late capitalism which construe individuals as resilient and productive consumers.

5 J. Halberstam, *The Queer Art of Failure*, 88.

6 J. Halberstam, *The Queer Art of Failure*, 147–148.

7 J. Halberstam, *The Queer Art of Failure*, 23.

8 J. Halberstam, *The Queer Art of Failure*, 25

9 Holy Saturday, in the Christian liturgical calendar, is the day between Great/ Good Friday and Easter Sunday – a day in which Jesus Christ remains in the tomb or harrows Hell rescuing the righteous dead from Adam onwards.

10 The idea of Holy Saturday as a site and state of 'queer temporality' is borrowed from Karen Bray, *Grave Attending: A Political Theology for the Unredeemed* (New York: Fordham University Press, 2020).

11 The Archbishops' Council, *Marriage: A Teaching Document from the House of Bishops of the Church of England* (London: Church House Publishing, 1999).

12 The General Synod is the national assembly of the Church of England. It came into being in 1970 under the Synodical Government Measure 1969, replacing an earlier body known as the Church Assembly. Synod considers and approves legislation affecting the whole of the Church of England, formulates new forms of worship, debates matters of national and international importance, and approves the annual budget for the work of the Church at national level. It has 483 members divided into three houses: House of Bishops, House of Clergy, House of Laity, *The National Assembly of the Church of England: General Synod*, https://www.churchofengland.org/about/leadership-and-governance/about-general-synod (accessed 15.2.24).

13 The Baughen Amendment to the Higton motion passed at the 1987 General Synod, quoted in Jeremy Pemberton, 'Deadly Pressure', *From the Choir Stalls, Reflection and Comment from a Priest Musician: Deadly Pressure*, https://jeremypemberton.wordpress.com/2020/10/23/deadly-pressure/ (accessed 15.2.24).

14 'Queer' is used here both to encompass gay and bisexuality (or, indeed, all sexuality and gender identities that are not heterosexual or identify with the gender assigned at birth) and to denote those epistemologies that seek to disturb the notion of a stable reality, including sex and gender norms, but also other normative constructions, to which society must conform.

15 Theologically, 'taint' is the belief in a male-only priesthood that secures its authenticity through eschewing the oversight of bishops who have ordained or been ordained by women. I am borrowing the term to denote any identity which appears aberrant to a church invested in the norms of canonical gender expression and sexuality.

16 Cf. n. 18.

17 An umbrella term for those who identify as gay, lesbian, bisexual, transgender, non-binary, those with Differences in Sexual Development (also known as intersex). There are other identities, such as pansexual or asexual, which are sometimes added to the acronym; here I use the + sign to denote all the further varieties of human identity and experience. The acronym is not uncontested since some gay people do not want to be included with those who identify as trans and some intersex people do not believe that their experience allies them to the LGBT identities on this spectrum.

18 Cisheterosexual is the experience of being heterosexual (straight) and identifying with one's gender as assigned at birth (cis). Again, this is a not uncontested term since some people who see themselves as 'gender critical' reject the label 'cis'.

19 For example, Gustavo Gutiérrez, 'Liberation Praxis and Christian Faith', in *Frontiers of Theology in Latin America*, ed. Rosino Gibellini (New York: Orbis Books, 1979); Jenny Daggers, *Postcolonial Theology of Religions: Particularity and Pluralism in World Christianity* (Abingdon: Routledge, 2013); Wilda C. Gafney, *Womanist Midrash: A Reintroduction to the Women of the Torah and the Throne* (Louisville, KY: Westminster John Knox Press, 2013); Chine Mc Donald, *God Is Not a White Man* (London: Hodder and Stoughton, 2021); Jarel Robinson Brown, *Black, Gay, British, Christian, Queer: The Church and the Famine of Grace* (London: SCM Press, 2021).

20 'Authorized' forms are those initiated by the Church: official publications and discussion groups in churches and at Deanery Synods. 'Unauthorized' forms are discussions on social media such as Facebook and blogs.

21 There are various illustrations of this meme: Average Advocate, 'When you have more than you need, build a longer table not a higher wall', https://averageadvocate.com/?s=build+a+bigger+table (accessed 15.2.24).

INTRODUCTION

22 There are religious exemptions to the Equality Act of 2010; under certain circumstances it is lawful for a religious organization to discriminate against someone on the grounds of sex/gender, sexual orientation, or belief: Citizens Advice, *Religious Organisations and Charities – When Discrimination is Allowed in the Provision of Goods or Services*, https://www.citizensadvice.org.uk/consumer/discrimination-in-the-provision-of-goods-and-services/discrimination-in-the-provision-of-goods-and-services1/goods-and-services-what-are-the-different-types-of-discrimination/what-doesn-t-count-as-unlawful-discrimination-in-goods-and-services/religious-organisations-and-charities-when-discrimination-is-allowed-in-the-provision-of-goods-or-services/ (accessed 15.2.24).

23 This is discussed further in Chapter 2 on the authorized afterlife of *Pilling*, General Synod – Take Note Debate on GS2055, 15 February 2017 (YouTube), Welby speaks at 1.59.17, https://www.youtube.com/watch?v=Oyj5xfSCzMY (accessed 15.2.24).

24 Alex Clare-Young, '"Living in Love and Faith"? The Construction of Contemporary Texts of Terror', *Theology and Sexuality*, 27, nos. 2–3, 5 August 2021, 118–120, https://www.tandfonline.com/doi/full/10.1080/13558358.2021.1954864?scroll=top&needAccess=true (accessed 15.2.24).

25 The Church of England, *Prayers of Love and Faith* (final version), https://www.churchofengland.org/sites/default/files/2023-01///final-draft-prayers-of-love-and-faith.pdf (accessed 15.2.24).

26 Natalie Wigg-Stevenson, *Ethnographic Theology: An Enquiry into the Production of Theological Knowledge* (London: Palgrave Macmillan, 2014), 117.

27 'Against Equality is an online archive, publishing, and arts collective focused on critiquing mainstream gay and lesbian politics. As queer thinkers, writers and artists, we are committed to … challenging the demand for inclusion in the institution of marriage, the US military, and the prison industrial complex via hate crimes legislation … Gay marriage apes hetero privilege … In their constant invoking of the "right" to gay marriage, mainstream gays and lesbians express a confused tangle of wishes and desires. They claim to contest the Right's conservative ideology yet insist that they are more moral and hence more deserving than sluts like us', https://www.againstequality.org/about/marriage/ (accessed 15.2.24).

28 Halvor Moxnes, *Putting Jesus in His Place: A Radical Vision of Household and Kingdom* (Louisville, KY: Westminster John Knox Press, 2003).

29 Robert Song, *Covenant and Calling: Towards a Theology of Same-Sex Relationships* (London: SCM Press, 2014).

30 Lee Edelman, *No Future: Queer Theory and the Death Drive* (Durham, NC: Duke University Press, 2004), 4.

31 Karen Bray, *Grave Attending: A Political Theology for the Unredeemed* (New York: Fordham University Press, 2020).

32 J. Halberstam, *The Queer Art of Failure* (Durham, NC: Duke University Press, 2011), 120. There are also numerous other voices with whom I engage, among them: Marcella Althaus-Reid, Linn Marie Tonstad, Karen O'Donnell, Gerard Loughlin, Susannah Cornwall, Louise Lawrence, Sara Ahmed, Lauren Berlant, Chris Greenough, Judith Butler, David Halperin, Ed Shaw and Ian Paul.

33 Marcella Althaus-Reid and Lisa Isherwood, 'Thinking Theology and Queer Theory', *Feminist Theology*, 15, no. 3, 2007, 304, https://journals.sagepub.com/doi/pdf/10.1177/0966735006076168 (accessed 15.2.24).

34 *Pilling*, 68.

35 Judith Butler, *Undoing Gender* (Abingdon: Routledge, 2004), 8.

36 Halberstam works in the secular discipline of queer theory but his work in

The Queer Art of Failure has been recognized as having theological resonances and theologians have been in dialogue with him about 'what comes after hope', in Silas Morgan, Kate Ott, Ellen Armour, Lisa Isherwood and Ashon Crawley, 'The Queer Art of Failure', *Syndicate Symposium*, 6 August 2015, https://syndicate.network/symposia/literature/the-queer-art-of-failure/ (accessed 15.2.24); and Hollis Phelps and Silas Morgan, 'Special Issue: Jack Halberstam's *The Queer Art of Failure*', in *The Other Journal: An Intersection of Theology and Culture*, 29 May 2015, https://theotherjournal.com/2015/07/29/special-issue-jack-halberstams-the-queer-art-of-failure/ (accessed 15.2.24).

37 Renewal and Reform is 'an ambitious programme of work, which seeks to provide a narrative of hope to the Church of England in the 21st century. It is rooted in a sense of Biblical hope and an understanding of Christ's call to us to pray that the Lord of the harvest will send out workers into the harvest field', in The Church of England, *Renewal and Reform: Helping Us Become a Growing Church for All People and All Places*, https://www.churchofengland.org/about/renewal-reform (accessed 15.2.24).

38 Although the term 'intersex' is still used, many in the intersex community now prefer the descriptors DSD or Variations in Sexual Characteristics (VSC).

39 Dale B. Martin, *Sex and the Single Savior* (Louisville, KY: Westminster John Knox Press, 2006), 2.

40 Stuart Hall, 'The West and the Rest: Discourse and Power', *Essential Essays, Volume II: Identity and Diaspora* (Durham, NC: Duke University Press, 2018) 89, https://books.google.co.uk/books?hl=en&lr=&id=oCJIDwAAQBAJ&oi=fnd&pg=PA85&dq=west+and+rest&ots=qK-FCSJRiK&sig=IAQA_7Hra8IdSWJXwp-Zhc_paHA#v=onepage&q=west%20and%20rest&f=true (accessed 15.2.24).

41 Stuart Hall, 'The West and the Rest: Discourse and Power', 86.

42 *Pilling*, 9.

43 David M. Halperin, *Saint Foucault: Towards a Gay Hagiography* (Oxford: Oxford University Press, 1995), 44, emphasis original. In this extract Halperin also cites Janet E. Halley, 'Misreading Sodomy: A Critique of the Classification of "Homosexuals" in Federal Equal Protection Law', in Julia Epstein and Kristina Straub, eds, *Body Guards: The Cultural Politics of Gender Ambiguity* (New York: Routledge, 1991).

44 David M. Halperin, *Saint Foucault*, 47.

45 The authors cite the *Don't Throw Stones* initiative that was presented to the Anglican Primates in 2007 and adopted by the Anglican Consultative Council and the Standing Committee of the Anglican Council in 2009, 58–59.

46 *Pilling*, 54.

47 The uses of rational argument to interrogate lived experience – the notion that investigating identities is a 'two-sided debate' – is explored in later chapters.

48 *Pilling*, 20.

49 David M. Halperin, *Saint Foucault*, 52.

50 Twenty-six bishops, plus retired archbishops, have seats in the House of Lords, and, thus, wield real legislative power, rather than soft persuasive power.

51 A solution is not just a means to solving a problem, but also a mixture in which other components are dissolved in the solvent. Dissolution seems, perhaps, a more appropriate metaphor for non-resolution than the solving of problems.

52 J. Halberstam, *The Queer Art of Failure*.

53 Sara Ahmed, 'Queer Feelings', in *The Cultural Politics of Emotion* (Edinburgh: Edinburgh University Press, 2004), 150, https://law.unimelb.edu.au/__data/assets/pdf_file/0003/3453618/ahmed_2014_queer-feelings-in-the-cultural-politics-of-emotion.pdf (accessed 15.2.24).

INTRODUCTION

54 Sara Ahmed, 'Queer Feelings'.

55 Michel Foucault, *Discipline and Punish: The Birth of the Prison* (New York: Random House, 1977); *History of Sexuality* (London: Penguin Classics, 1976–2018).

56 This list is taken from Chris Greenough, *Queer Theologies: The Basics* (Abingdon: Routledge, 2020), although he also includes Judith Butler as a precursor rather than as a queer theorist.

57 Adrienne Rich, 'Compulsory Heterosexuality and Lesbian Existence', *Signs: Journal of Women in Culture and Society*, 5, no. 4, summer 1980, 631–660, https://law.unimelb.edu.au/__data/assets/pdf_file/0003/3453618/ahmed_2014_queer-feelings-in-the-cultural-politics-of-emotion.pdf (accessed 15.2.24).

58 Judith Butler, *Gender Trouble: Feminism and the Subversion of Identity* (Abingdon: Routledge, 1990), 23, emphasis original.

59 Judith Butler, *Undoing Gender* (Abingdon: Routledge, 2004), 8.

60 My preferred spelling.

61 Caitlin Donohue, 'When Queer Nation "Bashed Back" Against Homophobia with Street Patrols and Glitter', *KQED*, 3 June 2019, https://www.kqed.org/arts/13858167/queer-nation-lgbtq-activism-90s (accessed 15.2.24).

62 Jose Esteban Muñoz, *Cruising Utopia: The Then and There of Queer Futurity* (New York: NYU Press, 2009), 20.

63 For example, the film producer Malcolm Clarke, whose Twitter biography proclaims: 'Made shows with Hawking, Dawkins, Jesse Jackson and Gorbachev so your silly "queer" theory doesn't scare me', https://twitter.com/TwisterFilm (accessed 15.2.24). See also William Fisher's response to my use of the term 'queer' on the Psephizo blog, https://www.psephizo.com/life-ministry/how-to-simply-grow-the-church/#comment-396396 (accessed 15.2.24).

64 David M. Halperin, *Saint Foucault*, 62, emphases original.

65 Susannah Cornwall, *Controversies in Queer Theology* (London: SCM Press, 2011), 24.

66 Marcella Althaus-Reid, 'Queer I Stand: Lifting the Skirts of God', in Marcella Althaus-Reid and Lisa Isherwood, eds, *The Sexual Theologian: Essays on Sex, God and Politics* (London: T&T Clark, 2004), 100.

67 Karen O'Donnell cites examples, from scripture and the Church Fathers, of milk as a Eucharistic element (milk in late antiquity was believed to be frothed or heated blood), including images of Christ nurturing believers with breast milk in *Broken Bodies: The Eucharist, Mary, and the Body in Trauma Theology* (London SCM Press, 2019), 33–47. O'Donnell sites this not as a queering of the Eucharistic elements but as an incarnational, rather than a cruciform, theology of the Eucharist.

68 Linn Marie Tonstad, 'The Limits of Inclusion: Queer Theology and its Others', *Theology and Sexuality*, 21, no. 1, 2015, https://www.tandfonline.com/doi/full/10.1080/13558358.2015.1115599?needAccess=true (accessed 15.2.24).

69 See also, James Crossley, 'Jewish … But Not *That* Jewish', in *Jesus in an Age of Terror: Scholarly Projects for a New American Century* (London: Equinox, 2008), 179–180, for another critique of a proto-Christian Jesus who was Jewish, but who radically subverted at least one of the key concepts of Jewish identity, at least according to the constructions of contemporary scholarship, 173–194. Of course, not all theologians and biblical scholars who present a Jesus who is at once Jewish and radically transformative of Jewish conventions are 'queer'; Crossley cites several decidedly 'unqueer' biblical scholars, including N. T. Wright.

70 Linn Marie Tonstad, 'The Limits of Inclusion: Queer Theology and Its Others', 9.

71 Linn Marie Tonstad, 'The Limits of Inclusion', 12.

72 Lee Edelman is an American literary critic, queer theorist and academic; the late Marcella Althaus-Reid was a pre-eminent liberation and queer theologian.

73 Linn Marie Tonstad, 'The Limits of Inclusion', 16–17.

74 Sara Ahmed, 'Queer Feelings', 148.

75 Sara Ahmed, 'Queer Feelings', 150.

76 Sara Ahmed, 'Queer Feelings', 153–155. Ahmed does acknowledge that the foundation of queer families may other queer people who do not belong, nor wish to belong, to something resembling a normal or conventional family unit: 'There remains a risk that "queer families" could be posited as an ideal within the queer community ... The word "families" may allow some queers to differentiate between their more and less significant bonds, where significance is not assumed to follow a form that is already given in advance. For others, the word "families" may be too saturated with affects to be usable in this way. Eve Kosofsky Sedgwick's vision of the family, for instance, is "elastic enough to do justice to the depth and sometimes durability of non-marital and/or nonprocreative bonds, same-sex bonds, nondyadic bonds, bonds not defined by genitality, 'step'-bonds, adult sibling bonds, nonbiological bonds across generations, etc"' (Sedgwick 1994, 71).

77 Gerard Loughlin, ed., 'Introduction', in *Queer Theology: Rethinking the Western Body* (Oxford: Blackwell, 2007), 7.

78 Gerard Loughlin, 'Introduction', 8. See also Eve Kosofsky Sedgwick, *The Epistemology of the Closet* (London: Penguin, 1994), 182–212.

79 Gerard Loughlin, *Queer Theology*, 9.

80 There are chapters on the queer thought of these three theologians in the section 'Queer/ing Tradition' in Loughlin's edited volume.

81 Quote in Gerard Loughlin, *Queer Theology*, 10.

82 Gerard Loughlin, *Queer Theology*, 10.

83 Marcella Althaus-Reid, 'Queer I Stand: Lifting the Skirts of God', 102.

84 Jose Esteban Muñoz, *Cruising Utopia: The Then and There of Queer Futurity*, 1.

I

The Hermeneutic Lenses of Church Discourses

What kinds of rewards can failure offer us? Perhaps most obviously, failure allows us to escape the punishing norms that discipline behavior and manage human development with the goal of delivering us from unruly childhoods to orderly and predictable adulthoods. Failure preserves some of the wondrous anarchy of childhood and disturbs the supposedly clean boundaries between adults and children, winners and losers.[1]

The *Pilling Report*[2] acknowledges that failure might be the outcome of attempting to solve the Church of England's issues in its selection of hermeneutical lenses through which to view (homo)sexuality. None of them – cultural, scientific, biblical – offers an unambiguous solution to either the aetiology of homosexual orientation or the probity of homosexual relationships for Christians. But nowhere in the report and its afterlife is failure suggested as an art, still less a 'queer art', which can offer new ways of being and a different telic resolution. Despite the provisionality and uncertainty of some of its conclusions and findings, *Pilling* does not seem to regard failure as a valid outcome. Provisionality is often foreclosed by magisterial statements such as: 'we can say with confidence that the created nature of humanity as male and female is built into that [the creation narratives'] natural order'[3] and 'at the level of declared doctrine, we are agreed that there is not sufficient consensus to change the Church's teaching on human sexuality'.[4] The authors of *Pilling* write about the Church's calling to be countercultural,[5] but then fail to see the possibility of failure as 'an opportunity ... to poke holes in the toxic positivity of contemporary life'.[6]

This chapter que(e)ries the hermeneutical lens through which *Pilling* examines the issue of (homo)sexuality much on the terms of the report itself, analysing the sources of outside authority that are appealed to in order to buttress the report's findings. The lenses are examined in the order in which they appear within the report. I assume some thought was given by the authors to this order of precedence and that there is a reason why social and cultural and scientific considerations are viewed before the evidence of scripture. An order of precedence is not necessarily an indicator of priority or importance for the authors of the report, but it does suggest that they wanted their readers to engage with social and scientific data and reflections about LGBTIQ+ people before turning to the biblical material. By choosing to direct their readers in these ways, the authors of *Pilling* are constructing an authoritative hermeneutic focus through which the material they choose to include (and that which they reject) would be viewed. Selecting some hermeneutic and epistemological lenses and ignoring (or disallowing) others creates a space in which certain voices predominate and, thus, certain views are granted influence and power.

The Social and Cultural Lens: 'the overwhelming change of cultural hinterland'

The first hermeneutical lens that *Pilling* deploys to examine issues of 'human sexuality' is that of the contemporary cultural and social context, reflecting perhaps an awareness that the Church of England is seen as increasingly out of step with the ethics of secular culture. *Pilling* quotes Justin Welby speaking at the 2013 General Synod: 'The cultural and political ground is changing. There is a revolution.'[7] The Archbishop was referring here to the overwhelming support for same-sex marriage, which he had observed throughout the debate on the Marriage (Same Sex Couples) Bill in the House of Lords, and he noted a corresponding hostility to the view of the churches that, largely, opposed the Bill.[8]

Pilling opens with a brief introduction to the Working Group and its remit and then considers the current social attitudes that the members of that Group encountered during the 'listening exercise' that it undertook:

> the Working Group heard directly from gay and lesbian people during the evidence days in which a variety of different groups and individuals were invited to give evidence to the Working Group.[9] These respondents spoke from a variety of different theological and personal perspectives ... they were not chosen from among the lobby groups – and represented a diversity of people, lay and ordained.[10]

The report then foregrounds some of the 'most significant and telling points' that emerged from these meetings.[11] The Working Group felt that from these encounters they had learnt that the debate about sexuality is not theoretical but 'about real people facing real situations [and] that it was important to avoid any sort of stereotyping of gay, lesbian, bisexual and transgendered [sic] people'.[12] Furthermore, the Group 'noted that they had been impressed by the quality of the relationships of the people they had met during the exercise and felt that this needed to be taken into account in any theological reflection on such relationships'.[13] But shouldn't any discussion of these 'issues' focus on the lived experience of those in the discussion and avoid stereotyping? Or is there an underlying assumption here that *theological* debate and reflection can disregard lived experience and appeal wholly to divine revelation, which, it could be argued, has itself been mediated through fallible human beings and a fallible church? It is also telling that the Group notes that this is a '*debate ... about* real people',[14] rather than a '*conversation with*'. The model of a debate rather than a discussion or a conversation is adversarial and the use of the adverb 'about' rather than the preposition 'with' relegates those who engaged in the meetings with the members of the Working Group; they have become the 'other' in relation to the normative group – a group of mainly white, middle-aged and middle-class males, four of whom were bishops. And there appears a faint element of surprise when the report comments on the quality of the relationships encountered, as if the assumption had been that any relationships that were not heterosexual would not embody 'quality', whatever that word means in this context.[15] The Working Group concluded that this exercise of listening and encounter was one that they wanted 'to recommend strongly to the Church [of England] as a whole'[16] and in their 'Findings and Recommendations' they suggest a series of national and diocesan 'facilitated conversations' (subsequently re-named 'Shared Conversations', which were undertaken regionally, with each region incorporating several dioceses).[17] 'Such encounters', they write 'are not about persuasion or endeavouring to reach a place of consensus ... It is about each person being willing to contemplate carrying a few more question marks ... while at the same time maintaining the integrity of their own convictions about what it means to be a faithful disciple of Jesus Christ.'[18]

The final 'Findings and Recommendations' of the report uphold 'the Church's traditional teaching on human sexuality', while encouraging 'the Church to continue to engage openly and honestly and to reflect theologically on the circumstances in which we find ourselves to discern the mind of Christ and what the Spirit is saying to the Church now'.[19] These two aspirations appear to be incompatible: the Church cannot adhere to traditional teaching while remaining open to the promptings of the Spirit; the latter must be potentially disruptive of the former. In summary, the report seems to be confused about what the insights of social science might offer the process of theological reflection on the issue of homosexuality, either for the conclusions of the report itself or for the teaching of the Church. We are told that engagement with the social context appears to effect a claim that the doctrine of the Church cannot be changed without reaching a consensus, yet that a consensus will not result from a 'listening exercise' or 'facilitated conversations', and, meanwhile, that we should abide by the current teaching of the Church which the Working Group admits is probably out of date and does not command universal agreement, while trying to discern the mind of Christ. The incommensurability of these positions could offer a queer resolution in embracing a failure to accomplish all this as an art that comprehends the affective negativity of unknowing and unbecoming, and recognizes the interim as a site of queer restoration. But *Pilling*'s recommendations do not provide any guidance either on how it might be possible to resolve these apparently irreconcilable objectives or on how to embrace the provisionality of their messy incongruence.

The following section of the report on 'a rapidly changing context' is the one from which the Archbishop of Canterbury's observation to General Synod is drawn. It touches upon the passage of the Marriage (Same Sex Couples) Act 2013, which was not even on the radar when the Working Group was convened and claims that this 'issue' affects the social understanding of all marriages.[20] Some commentators, both Christian and non-Christian, have, indeed, claimed that this Act 'redefines' marriage and in some ways changes either the fundamental nature of marriage or its identity as a cultural norm (or both).[21] However, the report does not clarify what the 'social understanding' of marriage might be and in what ways same-sex marriage may affect this, although it does assert twice that some 'liberally minded' Christians opposed same-sex marriage because it 'represented a confused understanding of equality and could be prejudicial to the meaning of marriage in society in general'.[22] No evidence – anecdotal or otherwise – is provided to support this assertion. The report observes that those churchmen (and those who were prominent in the debates were indeed men) who supported the decriminalization of homosexuality saw this as a civil matter that in no way lessened their belief that homosexual acts were gravely sinful. It may be that not all senior church people today – or even in the last fifty years – would regard homosexual relationships as always wrong, yet in 1987 the Bishops all voted for the 'Higton' motion, even though some of them, such as the then Archbishop of Canterbury, Robert Runcie, and the former Bishop of Durham, David Jenkins, had purportedly ordained openly gay men.

The growing acceptance of homosexuality in English society (of which the Church is, of course, a part) for over fifty years is rather more nuanced than a continuous advancement towards increasing permissiveness and 'tolerance'. Opinion polls show that the AIDS crisis of the 1980s probably caused the blip in which, for a while, attitudes became 'less tolerant'.[23] One possible outcome of that blip was the Conservative Government's Section 28 amendment to the Local Government Act 1988[24] which proscribed the promotion of homosexuality or of 'homosexuality as a pretended family relationship' by local authorities.[25] The main section in the report that deals with social attitudes towards homosexuality is headed 'Sexuality and social trends'. This section examines three questions: 'the prevalence of homosexuality in the population at large, current attitudes ... and the ways in which attitudes towards homosexuality have changed over time, including in the Churches'. The first is, in many ways, the most enigmatic question, although it is one that is asked often in theological reflections on the nature of homosexuality. It is puzzling that the Working Group and the writers of previous reports feel the need to ask this for it implies that the prevalence of homosexuality has some theological import. Might this suggest that if LGBTIQ+ people could be shown to be only a small minority of the population, then any attempt to work towards equality could be correspondingly modest? Do numbers carry some theological freight?[26] *Pilling* does not extrapolate anything from the data it cites, and it observes that the figures quoted for homosexual and bisexual people (of 1.5 per cent) are only a snapshot from when the survey was taken, so it seems odd to record the figures here.[27] If the numbers are not held to have theological significance, perhaps this research is cited to add further scientific weight to the social studies of attitudes towards homosexuality that follow. This, in turn, raises the question of whether scientific analysis is seen as adding gravitas to these reports, or whether homosexuality is here being pathologized, seen as a 'condition' that can be studied dispassionately and 'scientifically', rather than being the lived experience of members of the Church.

This section of *Pilling* then cites three studies that examined attitudes toward homosexuality in general and same-sex marriage in particular. The first, a YouGov poll from 2012,[28] records that 47 per cent of respondents believed that the Church of England was right to defend marriage as being solely for heterosexual people.[29] Only a year later, just as *Pilling* was being published, another YouGov poll, commissioned for the Westminster Faith Debates,[30] found that 44 per cent of Anglicans supported same-sex marriage, with 43 per cent opposing it.[31] That this survey (not cited in *Pilling*) canvassed 2,381 Anglicans, whereas the former had 1,707 (unspecified) respondents, suggests that the 2013 poll was more representative of the mind of the Church, or, at least, churchgoers' opinions.

The next survey, by Ben Clements from the University of Leicester,[32] reviewed attitudes towards homosexuality and, specifically, same-sex marriage among Anglicans. The results show that the proportion of Anglicans who thought that same-sex relationships were wrong had fallen from 69.7 per cent in 1983 to 37.4 per cent in 2010, and that Anglicans were less likely than all respondents to believe that same-sex relationships are as valid as heterosexual ones, although a majority did think that homosexual and heterosexual relationships are equally valid. Around two-thirds of Anglicans supported the Church's position on same-sex marriage while a quarter of those surveyed disagreed. Interestingly, Clements' research shows that the YouGov survey of 2012 recorded that 52.4 per cent of Anglicans believed that same-sex relationships were as valid as heterosexual – with 37.5 per cent believing that they were not as valid – which appears to contradict the YouGov findings on the Church's right to 'defend' marriage quoted in *Pilling*.

Although the questions posed are different, it may still be possible for 47 per cent of respondents (presumably not all Christian or churchgoers) to believe that the Church of England is right to defend 'traditional' marriage, while over 52 per cent of Anglicans thought that same-sex and heterosexual relationships were equally valid. The last survey is that of Crockett and Voas,[33] which finds that 'British attitudes to homosexuality have changed with astonishing rapidity over recent decades ... The Christian Churches ... have been finding it increasingly difficult to adjust to the new environment.' As the Working Group notes, the survey was already ten years old at the time of the report's publication, and the research on which it is based was even older, with the most recent sample being 2000–2001. With the advent of civil partnerships[34] and equal marriage, it is now likely that both secular and church (as in church 'membership' rather than church 'hierarchy') attitudes have changed further.[35]

In 'Reflecting on the evidence' there are a further few paragraphs on the significance of scientific evidence and social surveys. Here, the Working Group observes that 'the data from single opinion polls may lack robustness and that the way the question is framed can have a significant influence on the response it elicits'.[36] This rather more nuanced approach was not reflected in *Pilling*'s own earlier review of the social attitudes surveys. Once again, there is confusion in the report about what the insights of social analysis and the 'listening exercise' might have to offer the Church. On the one hand, there is an acknowledgement that the Holy Spirit can speak through society as well as through the Church and through 'real people's lives'. Yet, 'mission is not about conforming to culture', and 'there is not sufficient consensus to change the Church's teaching on human sexuality'.[37] The Working Group seems to be hedging their bets as if the relationship between 'tradition' and 'revelation' was one of competition. The *Pilling Report* has foregrounded changing social attitudes, implying that these will have some influence on the teaching of the Church, but it seems unsure if, and how, such opinions should form church policy. The report appears to argue that a majority cannot determine doctrine, that consensus (in many areas) is impossible and, yet, that consensus (although between whom is not specified) is necessary for an authoritative change in church teaching on the validity of same-sex relationships and the place of LGBTIQ+ people in the Church.

Church reports are written by people who are a part of society when the reports were produced and who are inevitably influenced by cultural trends, whether in reaction against them or in a modified approval of some of them. But the authors are not merely participants in a society whose norms they share or resist, they are constructors of authority in a particular sphere of that society – the Church of England – and one that has a real, if perhaps declining, influence. The working parties that produced these reports are arbiters of a canonical authority that sometimes listens to or engages with the 'other', but always on the party's own terms; the welcome is conditional, the invitation to the table dependent upon conformity to certain cultural and ecclesial norms. Moreover, *Pilling* criticizes only the permissiveness or the individualism of secular society and culture; it does not challenge the neoliberal ethos of the Global North, despite the authors' claims about the countercultural nature of the Church.[38] Hegemonic cultures are occasionally disparaged but the authors seem uninterested in their subversion or queering; they appear to be invested in the neoliberal secular structures of which they are both supporter and critic. The authors' goals, then, align with those of the surrounding societies: they are orientated towards progress, success and consensus, or at least towards 'good disagreement'.[39] It seems that while disagreement is licit, outright failure to conform to progressive epistemologies is to be resisted by working parties and by the House of Bishops. 'Heteronormative commonsense'[40] is the hallmark of church reports. Failure, as a queer art, offers alternative goals, different ways of imagining culture and society and, maybe, of being church. As Halberstam writes: 'the queer art of failure … quietly loses, and in losing it imagines other goals for life, for love, for art, and for being.'[41]

The Scientific Lens: 'can they help it?'[42]

For the authors of *Pilling*, science, it seems, has replaced theology as the queen of the sciences for they accord it priority over theological and scriptural reflection in their report. They are, whether wittingly or not, constructing a framework in which culture and science are viewed as incontrovertible material realities that may be flawed but are necessary to the neoliberal project. The report does not que(e)ry their authority, nor interrogate their enduring control, especially in areas – ecclesial discourse and theological reflection – where bowing to the alloyed good of science and society might appear idolatrous. Here I interrogate *Pilling*'s search for a solution to the problem of homosexuality in the apparently disinterested endeavours of science to provide answers to questions such as the aetiology of gay identity and desire and I ask how biological origins can provide solutions to the ethics of desire and orientation. Working parties are pursuing solutionism; searching for the key (or keys) that will unlock these intractable issues with a positivity that neglects the possibility that failure – of their quest or of solutionism itself – is also an alternative response. Negativity, falling away from the anxious search for certainties and progress and inhabiting sites of queer temporality may not only provide respite but also point the way to a tentative redemption in the abjuring of the gods of productivity and success and in the recognition of the paradoxical fruitfulness of failure.

Pilling privileges science by looking 'at the evidence surrounding some of the key scientific controversies relating to homosexuality'.[43] No other human sexualities are submitted to interrogation by science, and science's failure to provide answers must be inferred from the varying findings on the aetiology of homosexuality and science's agnosticism about providing a moral framework. But science, particularly biological science, is utilized here because it is clear that, for the Working Party, homosexuality (as well as transgender and intersex, which are touched on briefly) is regarded as a disorder, a phenomenon that disrupts the natural, binary, created order of men and women who are exclusively attracted to each other. Foucault's observation on the pathologization of the 'homosexual'[44] informs the Working Party's anthropological view that gay orientation is not morally neutral, but rather is an anomaly for which people might reasonably seek help.

> The nineteenth-century homosexual became a personage, a past, a case history, and a childhood, in addition to being a type of life, a life form, and a morphology, with an indiscreet anatomy and possibly a mysterious physiology. Nothing that went into his [*sic*] total composi-

tion was unaffected by his sexuality. It was everywhere present in him: at the root of all his actions because it was their insidious and indefinitely active principle; written immodestly on his face and body because it was a secret that gave itself away. It was consubstantial with him, less as a habitual sin than as a singular nature.[45]

In order to explore this 'singular nature' through the lens of science the authors write that they have received submissions from a large number of organizations and individuals that touch on scientific issues. They also received evidence from the Royal College of Psychiatrists, the Core Issues Trust, and the Society of Ordained Scientists, in addition to two presentations by the Revd Dr John Hare and Professor Glynn Harrison. The Working Group also consulted a copy of 'The Witness of Science' by David De Pomerai and Glynn Harrison from *The Anglican Communion and Homosexuality*, edited by Phil Groves.[46] Pathologizing homosexuality – considering it as a medical condition with a distinctive aetiology – deems it non-normative. It is then seen as 'other', atypical, diverging from, and perhaps even inimical to, a heterosexual norm. Heterosexuality thus becomes not merely the majority orientation, but also the canonical one: the rule by which all other varieties of sexual 'being' may be judged. This canonical view of heterosexuality can then map onto the human creation account in Genesis 2, which is seen as God's true plan: a creation ordinance in which Man and Woman form an 'opposite' and 'complementary' pair.

Two key submissions are assessed, in a rather summary fashion: one from the Royal College of Psychiatrists and the other from the Core Issues Trust. Although the Royal College of Psychiatrists has a clear advocacy role, as a professional body, it has no particular religious, social, political or secular bias. It exists to serve the professional psychiatric community and to promote and encourage better outcomes for those with mental health issues. The Core Issues Trust is a religious lobby group that seeks to support men and women with homosexual 'issues' who voluntarily seek to change their sexual preferences and expression. The Trust's 'Statement of Belief' is a recapitulation of the beliefs that underwrite its work in striving to affirm particular biblical, ethical and theological precepts and in seeking to change unwanted sexual orientation. The Statement declares

> that the Scriptures clearly teach both that sexual relationships outside of marriage between a man and a woman fall short of the will of God, and that that marriage is between one man and one woman; [and] that the Church of Jesus Christ, when true to the Scriptures, properly provides

a spiritual home and sensitive support for believers and seekers who struggle with issues of sexual brokenness, including homosexuality.[47]

This represents Christianity of a particular stamp, most commonly known as conservative evangelical. Christians from other 'traditions' in the Church do not all agree that 'the Scriptures clearly teach' that marriage is, invariably, between one man and one woman, nor that homosexuality is a sign of sexual brokenness – except insofar as a belief in the Fall suggests that all human sexuality, and not a specific orientation, is imperfect. It is, of course, quite proper that a Working Party reflecting on the theological and ethical implications of homosexuality in the Church should seek and receive submissions from Christian organizations and lobby groups with various perspectives on (homo)sexuality. Lobby groups exist to promote their objectives. Submissions have been received from other organizations, some of which are listed in Appendix 2; these include Accepting Evangelicals, Sybils,[48] the Evangelical Group on General Synod (EGGS) and Modern Church. However, these groups have not, unlike the Core Issues Trust, been given parity with the Royal College of Psychiatrists; indeed, the Trust is further privileged in that it is given space to critique the evidence submitted by the College, but no interrogation of the Trust's own aims and methodologies appears in the report. A visit to the Trust's website will confirm that its primary commitment is to reparative therapy that seeks 'to change [people] from a "gay" lifestyle to a gender-affirming one'.[49] The Professional Standards Authority, the Royal College of Psychiatrists and the Association of Christian Counsellors are all opposed to reparative therapy and members of the latter two bodies may not offer counselling that seeks to change sexual orientation. The Trust's criticism of the College's scientific integrity includes some rather questionable scientific assertions, such as:

> Core Issues Trust does not believe that people who experience same-sex attraction were 'born gay' … Science suggests that most of them 'became that way' as a result of real or perceived traumatic experiences in early life. The Church should treat them with love and understanding … encouraging them to try to live their lives in accordance with Biblical principles. The Trust … upholds the right of individuals to seek professional assistance in attempting to reduce or eliminate unwanted sexual feelings and patterning.[50]

Here LGB desire and orientation are presented as a 'disorder' – caused by trauma and needing to be healed – a clear contradiction of the College's position:

The College wishes to clarify that homosexuality is not a psychiatric disorder. In 1973 the American Psychiatric Association (APA) concluded there was no scientific evidence that homosexuality was a disorder and removed it from its diagnostic glossary of mental disorders. The International Classification of Diseases of the World Health Organization followed suit in 1992.[51]

In this comparison of the aims, standards and conclusions of the Royal College and the Core Issues Trust, outside of their respective submissions in *Pilling*, I contend that, in granting the College and Core Issues equivalence, the Working Party has demonstrated a seriously flawed methodology that undermines the scientific conclusions that are drawn in the report from the evidence given. In every case where the submissions from the two bodies are compared, such as the questions of whether homosexuality is harmful or whether homosexual relationships are inherently unstable, the authors can decide that the evidence is inconclusive because the findings of the parties offer no consensus. This enables the Working Group to sit on the fence and is disingenuous, for there is no attempt to interrogate this evidence. For example, the conclusion that same-sex unions might be inherently less stable is based on balancing opinions from the College and from Core Issues with a reference to a study of the stability of same-sex marriage and cohabitation in Norway and Sweden. The report does not acknowledge that a longitudinal study of the stability of civil partnerships (since their inception in 2005) of gay people in England, with a comparison to heterosexual relationships, is lacking here.

In privileging the views of the Core Issues Trust, the authors, as authorities, have accorded hermeneutical canonicity to a 'lobby group', and to one that supports psychiatric interventions that most professional bodies in the field deem harmful. Throughout the report, the Working Party constantly makes judgements on what is canonical and what is seen as a 'distinctive' hermeneutic (for example, in the sections about scripture). This has the effect of presenting some views as normative while 'othering' differing views and perspectives. But here, a group whose views might reasonably be regarded as 'distinctive' is treated as though it is a disinterested 'authority'. While placing a high value on the insights of science, *Pilling*'s summaries of the scientific evidence are cursory: claiming, for example, that in studies where homosexuality is seen as having a biological cause there are 'some seeing it as genetic and others seeing it as hormonal'.[52] A summary of research on the biological factors involved in homosexual orientation (published in a 2008 collection) is cited, although the authors do not acknowledge in the text that the collection of essays was written from a confessional perspective for the Anglican Communion.[53] This does not necessarily make the essays less rigorous, but it does mean that its conclusions are not disinterested and their bias is elided by this omission.

There is no reference to other studies on the biological factors that may influence sexuality, nor to studies that question the propriety of doing research that may show homosexuality to have a genetic or otherwise 'biological' source. The authors appear to be unaware both of the eugenic implications of the quest for a 'gay' gene and of the epistemological implications of such a search. *Pilling*'s authors do not discuss the theological and ethical implications that would arise from finding that being LGB was 'biological' and immutable. The question of whether the discovery of a 'gay' gene might make homosexuality more acceptable to the Church because the condition would then be seen as fixed and immutable (i.e. not the result of individual 'choice') is not addressed. If, however, homosexuality isn't aberrant and potentially immoral, the questions of its genesis and mutability are void, particularly since what is being examined here is identity rather than behaviour. What is being implied is that being gay (a term the report largely avoids) is, at best, a misfortune; being corrected or conformed to heterosexuality, at any time from the womb onwards, would be a rescue from a morally liminal existence. The telos of morally neutral hegemonic cisheteronormativity is presented not only as desirable but as the Creator's original intention for humanity.

Much of the research cited in this section does not come from disinterested voices. Professor Glynn Harrison made a presentation to the Working Party. He is also the author of the second part of 'The Witness of Science' chapter – from *The Anglican Communion and Homosexuality*, which the Working Party had consulted.[54] The title of his contribution, not noted in the report, is 'Unwanted Same-Sex Attractions: Can Pastoral and Counselling Interventions Help People to Change?' Professor Harrison is a consultant psychiatrist who believes in the efficacy of reparative therapy within certain safeguards.[55] The allusion to 'unwanted same-sex attraction' in the title of his essay gives some indication of his position; the phrase 'same-sex attraction' is invariably used by those who do not believe that sexual orientation constitutes an identity and that to be attracted to the same gender is aberrant, as indicated by the adjective 'unwanted'.[56] Another essay entitled 'Unwanted Same Sex Attraction', by Andrew Goddard and Harrison, is quoted in support of the value of reparative therapy. These voices articulating 'conservative' and 'traditionalist' ethical and theological perspectives should, of course, be heard in the debate, as should those whose theological and scriptural reflections have led them to different conclusions about sexuality and marriage. But the Working Party could have required that each voice declared an interest. Some of the evidence from groups and individuals with what might be described as a 'conservative' hermeneutic has been presented as though it were 'scientific' or disinterested. This privileging of certain voices – with the consequent 'othering' of dissenting voices – makes them appear normative. The Working Party has given unacknowledged canonicity and authority to particular views and made them representative of what the Church believes.

In the section 'Science, society and demographics', which reflects upon the evidence, the authors claim that they have only discussed a small amount of the material that they have examined. Nevertheless, they feel able to reach the conclusion that 'neither the medical nor the social sciences have arrived at any firm consensus that would impact decisively on the moral arguments'.[57] The Working Group claims to have taken the scientific evidence seriously, but the evidence has been partial and the conclusions have been drawn from the voices that the group itself has privileged: those scientific voices chosen as representative, and therefore authoritative, by *Pilling*'s authors.

In choosing these lenses, the authors of *Pilling* and the earlier reports give no indication that epistemic tools, such as scientific evidence and cultural discourse, are themselves social constructs. The provisionality of such tools and their dependence upon the epistemic norms of the Global North is never interrogated in the methodologies of these reports; the authors present selected 'insights of science' or cultural reflections as if they are neutral panes through which to view the phenomenon of homosexuality. After they have surveyed 'the arguments about science' and concluded that 'the idea that science can give us clear and unequivocal answers, even on its terms let alone in the field of morality, turns out to be over-optimistic',[58] *Pilling*'s authors do not pursue the potentialities of this. There appears to be no impetus to que(e)ry the hermeneutic lenses that they have chosen.

If the Working Party is seeking a solution to these 'issues' using tools such as science or scripture, an inability to reach consensus or to provide answers will be seen as some kind of failure. What is not contemplated here is the latency of failure as both a tentative and a creative opportunity for a kind of queer resolution. In my final chapter, I explore how, by abandoning the neoliberal quest for solutions delivered by epistemological tools, the art of 'failing, losing, forgetting, unmaking, undoing, unbecoming, not knowing may in fact offer more creative, more cooperative, more surprising ways of being in the world'.[59] It is possible to imagine spaces where the tools deployed by neoliberal organizations are laid aside to enable room for a queer temporality where the failure of 'arguments' about science or scripture are laid to rest.

The Biblical Lens: 'arguments about scripture'

> To be both dutiful and dissenting at once, as Martha seems to be, is to open a dialogue on just what is demanded of Martha and of discipleship more generally. To let Martha's emotions remain negative without redeeming them into secretly happy moods, is in fact to feel our way toward different readings and hearings. It is to open ourselves and Jesus up to a hearing of Martha's lament such that we can affirm that from within her knowledge of life and her material attention to the things of this world we find righteous reasons to be angry. It is, therefore, not just that Martha is tied to the material, but more so that she is worried for and pissed at the matter at hand that makes her a theologically potent member of an archive of affect alienation.[60]

The Bible, like science and the societies of the Global North, is also a cultural artifact, created over hundreds of years by numerous authors, writing from various viewpoints and in several languages. However, the crucial difference here is that for adherents of religions scriptures have a divine agency as well as being human creations. Biblical texts and narratives may be critiqued by both secular and religious readers, but for the latter they are intrinsic to the debates on ethical issues such as the morality of sexual relationships. What kinds of intimate relationships does the Bible mandate, allow or proscribe? Scripture might, like science, fail to provide convincing or perspicuous answers, but its relevance to theological and ethical reflection cannot be gainsaid. Que(e)rying biblical texts and narratives may trouble and disrupt the hegemonic hermeneutics that privilege white, male, cisheteronormative readings, but scripture's place at the table in any discussion of 'human sexuality' in a Christian context must be assured. However, my response to *Pilling*'s use of scripture might be framed as 'be more Martha'; the acts of being dialogical, being lamenting, being dissenting, being negative can also be dutiful and righteous.

The Church of England doctrine of the sufficiency of scripture and the ongoing debate about the biblical proscriptions of same-sex acts, which has underwritten the Church's teachings on the status of sexually active gay relationships, might suggest that the biblical record would be engaged with extensively.[61] Indeed, the chapter heading 'Arguments about Scripture' indicates that contention over the interpretation of biblical texts and narratives is regarded as key. However, *Pilling*'s discussion of scripture is sketchy, with much of the debate being consigned to two appendices that showcase contrasting hermeneutical views. In whatever ways the *Pilling* Working Group intended to construct and inhabit authority, it appeared to acknowledge that the study of scripture may result in a failure to reach consensus on the licitness of homosexual relationships in contemporary society. This is a significant admission, because it points tentatively towards the possibility that the commissioning of working parties, reports, resources and discussion groups will inevitably lead to failure. That reading of failure might seem like an anticipation of an altogether negative outcome and one that the Church of England would want to avoid at all costs. Failure, however, need not be coded as defeat but, as I have argued, as a 'queer art' that may allow for the undoing of the hegemonic epistemologies that the Church embraces as readily as does secular society, despite its claims to be *contra mundum*. The unqueer art of striving for progress and what may look like 'success' in a settlement on sexuality that would suit all 'parties' is a neoliberal project. It is not necessarily doomed to failure in the sense that a compromise may never be reached (although such is looking unlikely in an increasingly fissiparous Church), but I would suggest that the struggle toward success, figured as consensus or accord, is illusory. The 'queer art' of failure accepts the limitations and finitude of making headway; resistance to the canonicity of cisheterosexual norms can lie in rupturing their hegemony by drawing attention to their obsolescence. Subverting norms through the inability to take them seriously can be more radical than creating other canonical models to take their place.[62] I believe that, despite the provisionality of its approach to scripture, the *Pilling* process in its pursuit of a telic solution found in debate and 'listening' is focused on attainment, rather than on a failure that could contain within it the seeds of a queer resolution and encompass the interim, the liminal and the uncertain. Perhaps being 'pissed' involves laughter and silliness as well as anger and lament.

The *Pilling Report* includes a brief (eight-page) chapter on 'Arguments about Scripture' in its 'Summarizing the Evidence' section and a summary in 'Scripture and theology'. Attention is drawn to the fuller treatment of the subject in *Some Issues in Human Sexuality*, although that work was already ten years old at the time of *Pilling*'s publication.[63] The authors also note here the contributions of two opposing views from evangelicals which are both included in appendices. The first is the dissenting statement by a member of the Working Party, the then Bishop of Birkenhead, Keith Sinclair, who did not feel able to sign the 'Findings and Recommendations' of the report.[64] His statement in Appendix 3 is on 'Scripture and Same Sex Relationships', in which he argues that the biblical witness incontrovertibly forbids homosexual relationships. Appendix 4 was written by the Revd David Runcorn and is an 'including evangelical' perspective on same-sex relationships. That both are from the evangelical wing of the Church of England and hold very different views on the arguments from scripture is indicative of how unresolvable these arguments may prove to be – a position acknowledged in the Working Party's decision to include both appendices as examples of differing conclusions drawn from the study of the same texts by two people from the same 'tribe' of the Church of England. This is a revealing perspective, probably intentionally on the part of the Working Group, on how two people, who essentially share the same ecclesial perspective, can differ on their interpretation of scripture. Yet, because they are part of the published report they acquire a 'canonicity' which may have been unintended but gives all such contributions and reflections a certain imprimatur.

The 'relative paucity' of scriptural engagement in *Pilling* is explained by the observation that although much has been written on this topic there is little that shows a consensus position. Biblical scholars and theologians themselves inhabit different traditions and their readings are influenced by their assumptions about what the text will 'say' or 'mean'. Even scholars who are working from a non-confessional viewpoint have cultural expectations and presuppositions about the texts that they are interpreting; unbelief conditions readings as much as belief. Indeed, the report shows itself to be wary of 'focusing too quickly on the search for detailed agreement' in its comments on the differences in biblical interpretation in the two appended papers. To this end one of the recommendations of the report is that process of 'facilitated' conversations[65] which 'should continue to involve profound reflection on the interpretation and application of Scripture'.[66] Perhaps 'begin to' would have been more appropriate than 'continue to' here, since there is little evidence of profound reflection on scripture within *Pilling* itself.

'Arguments about Scripture'

The first section, 'Arguments about Scripture', reflects upon biblical scholarship and the biblical texts that examine 'human' sexuality and same-sex activity. It provides a rather cursory summary of two kinds of biblical scholarship: those that are described as having a 'distinctive hermeneutic', such as Dale Martin's *Sex and the Single Savior*,[67] and the 'less numerous ... attempt[s] to engage with differing views', citing 'The Witness of Scripture' and *Homosexuality and the Bible*.[68] Here 'distinctive' means, I would suggest, idiosyncratic; the members of the Working Group are signalling that some hermeneutics are marked as peculiar while those they regard as being mainstream are unmarked. It is the same tactic deployed in the earlier section on 'Arguments about Science' to suggest that science is disinterested and non-ideological. And it is also the strategy that codes (white/able) cisheteronormativity as unmarked, while other identities are marked as distinctive, because they do not conform to the canonical model. Nevertheless, despite acknowledging that different interpretations of scripture tend to generate different approaches to sexual ethics, the report appears to privilege one view of scriptural authority:

> One of the main reasons for the intensity of the arguments about sexual morality is that, for many, any deviation from, or modification to, what they see as the Bible's teaching would constitute an apostasy. A Church that made such a move would, in their view, have rejected the authority of the Bible and, thus, have turned away from the revealed word of God. This is why, for many, the question of sexual ethics is not a secondary issue but one of absolutely fundamental significance for any Christian Church. This view has been powerfully put by one member of our Working Group and the whole group has benefited from hearing that view put sympathetically and with deep personal commitment.[69]

Each sentence here raises the question of what being faithful to the scriptural witness means and about the ways in which we read texts. First, it is claimed that, for 'many', apostasy would result from any deviation from, or modification of, the Bible's teaching. Since the Church of England (and other denominations) today countenances many views and actions that are, ostensibly, contrary to biblical teaching (the re-marriage of divorcees is just one such example), this is clearly not accurate. Second, it reveals the unacknowledged reality that this 'faithful' view of scripture is, like all views, subjective: it is *what they see* as the Bible's teaching. There is no recognition here that others who 'see' the Bible's teaching differently also see themselves as faithful to scripture and might strongly object to being viewed as apostate. Third, it assumes that such a deviation or modification would mean a wholesale rejection of biblical authority and a turning away from revelation. Fourth, the writers' view that the question of sexual ethics is a primary issue 'for many' – presumably the same 'many' mentioned above – implies that those who don't share this particular hermeneutic, or who have a different view of biblical authority, do not also think that 'the question of sexual ethics is … one of absolutely fundamental importance'. This presupposes that apostatizing can only go one way: in a liberal, or affirming, direction and in one area

– sexuality. I would contend that the Church can apostatize not through accommodation to the secular values of a permissive sexual culture but by capitulation to the contemporary mores of neoliberalism that, it is sometimes argued, marginalize the weak, the vulnerable, the poor and the dispossessed.[70] Lastly, the assertion that these views were put 'powerfully' and with 'deep personal commitment' might suggest that other presentations – from the individuals and groups listed in the report's Appendix 1 – were not received as equally valid, powerful and authentic.

Translation problems

Pilling moves on, again briefly, to the question of the translation of those texts 'which clearly speak about same sex relationships'.[71] The very issue of translation (and a mention of diverse cultural contexts in the same paragraph) might have alerted the Working Party to the likelihood of there being few texts that 'speak clearly' and that those that do speak of samesex activity may have nothing to 'say' about contemporary same-sex relationships, especially the relationships of those who aim to live according to Christian ideals of fidelity and chastity. This kind of discourse is inclined to be disingenuous in that, while it acknowledges that there are a variety of hermeneutics, it elides the ambiguities and uncertainties that interpretation and translation seek to discover. The readers may then infer that there are texts in the Bible that are 'clear' and are about 'samesex relationships', a conclusion that many scholars would argue was a misleading appropriation of those texts.[72] After a very brief summary of the complexities of translating meaning from one cultural and linguistic context to another, a single problem in translation serves as exemplar: the meaning of the Greek word *arsenokoitai* found in the New Testament in 1 Corinthians 6.9 and 1 Timothy 1.10 (here *arsenokoites*), and translated as 'sodomite' in the New Revised Standard Version of the Bible (NRSV).[73] Again, the Working Party thinks that the 'general meaning is reasonably clear' since the word is a 'compound noun that combines *arsen* meaning "male" and *koites* meaning "bed"'.[74] However, although the authors note that this term is a neologism, they gloss over the juxtaposition of two elements, 'male' and 'bed', forming a word that has no 'meaning' outside its context. Indeed, since it is a neologism, even within its context in the New Testament, we cannot be certain what *arsenokoitai* signifies. In 1 Corinthians, it appears in a vice list that includes some sexual sins such as fornication and adultery, but also lists thieves, the greedy, drunkards, revilers and swindlers. Some scholars regard it as part of a pair with *malakoi*, which literally means soft and therefore, by extension, 'effeminate'. If a *malakos* is the effeminate partner, they argue, the *arsenokoites* must be the active partner – literally, the 'man-bedder'.[75]

This is the translation adopted by Robert Gagnon in *The Bible and Homosexual Practice*, arguing that the term is a conflation of the two separate words used in the LXX[76] of Leviticus 18.22 and 20.13, *arsenos* and *koiten;* for Hellenistic Jews, therefore, among them Paul, *arsenokoites* became the Greek term for the technical rabbinic expression for same-sex activity.[77] Dale Martin, however, argues that 'the etymology of a word is its history, not its meaning'.[78] From looking at vice lists that are not dependent upon 1 Corinthians and 1 Timothy, Martin concludes that the word has some connection with economic exploitation, perhaps especially sexual exploitation. He concedes that it '*could* be taken as a reference to homosexual sex', but that to see this as the natural meaning owes more to ideology than to philology.[79] My aim here is not to determine which argument is the more convincing and so to decide what the word really 'means', or what it meant to Paul and the writer of 1 Timothy, but to show that meaning is often fugitive and provisional and that interpretation is subjective. The above is itself a very brief survey of the vast scholarship on the meaning of the word *arsenokoites* and gives only two, opposing, views. *Pilling* alludes to the difficulty of translation but provides no indication of the diversity and complexity of this scholarly debate. Readers may be left wondering what all the fuss is about, unless they are already invested in this debate, either as biblical scholars or as queer people whose lives are the subject of discussion.

Cultural meanings in scripture

The next section looks at the contexts in which the biblical texts were written and received. The contrasting views of David Runcorn and Keith Sinclair, which they present in their appended essays, are briefly summarized. The debate turns on the question of whether homosexual orientation and faithful, monogamous homosexual relationships were known to the writers of the Hebrew Bible and to authors in late antiquity, such as Paul. David Runcorn asks, 'Is *this* really *that*? In other words, when a text speaks of same-sex behaviour, is the phenomenon that is being described or condemned the same phenomenon that concerns the Church, today?'[80] The nineteenth and early twentieth centuries 'pathologized' homosexuality, so that what had been regarded as a behaviour came to be seen as a disorder; to be perverted or inverted[81] was to deviate from the accepted heterosexual norm.[82] Many scholars of the pre-modern world see same-sex activity as simply a kind of sexual conduct, more popular at some times and in some places than at others but having nothing to say about 'orientation'.[83] David Runcorn advocates a variant of this position, and one that is particularly popular among Christian apologists,[84] the view that same-sex partnerships in antiquity were inexorably abusive, in that the power in such relationships was always asymmetrical, for the active partner unmanned and degraded the passive. These, claims Runcorn, 'are a long way from the faithful and enduring same-sex relationships which are the subject of the Church's present consideration'.[85] Keith Sinclair takes a contrary view, arguing that same-sex relationships of equality and fidelity were known and recognized in the world of late antiquity and could have been familiar to Paul. However, as the report acknowledges, the existence and visibility of such relationships in the cities of the Graeco-Roman Empire would not tell us what was in Paul's mind as he wrote.[86] Moreover, *Pilling* argues that some scholars see cultural understandings of homosexuality as irrelevant since the scriptural texts treat all same-sex encounters as contrary to God's will. This is the position taken by Robert Gagnon in *The Bible and Homosexual Practice*. He sees the biblical texts as antipathetic to all same-sex activity, whether consensual or abusive, because it 'constitutes an inexcusable rebellion against the intentional design of the created order'.[87] Such relationships are to be rejected, he believes, because of their lack of gender complementarity.[88]

Male and female in the Genesis narratives

Here the *Pilling Report* views the creation narrative – in a mere seven paragraphs – maintaining that the two stories that tell of God's creation of humankind are not incompatible, but 'both categorize humanity as male and female [and] emphasize different aspects of God's truth'.[89] There is no mention of the historical or cultural origins and contexts of these narratives, yet *Pilling* reads them in a way in which the provisionality of earlier judgements about what texts might be saying is abandoned. The authors claim that 'Genesis 1 emphasizes the way in which male and female, together, reflect the image of God and implies the equality of male and female before God'.[90] They immediately undermine this emphasis on male/female equality by claiming that Genesis 2 'introduces an implication of priority for the male'.[91] Does 'priority' here indicate merely temporal antecedence, or is the implication one of precedence or superiority; or, indeed, are the two notions of primacy held together in the Working Party's understanding of 'priority'? Strangely, since this statement is left without further clarification or analysis, readers may be left wondering what the writers felt were the implications of male priority for the anthropological theology of human sexuality. The final paragraph again switches from the tentative to the certain, when it states: 'we can say with confidence that the created nature of humanity as male and female is built into that natural order.'[92]

'Scripture and Theology'

The second section in the *Pilling Report* that deals with scripture (in Part 3 of the report, 'Reflecting on the Evidence') returns to the need for provisionality in biblical interpretation. The previous section is, it is argued, 'an object lesson in the limitations of textual scholarship when it comes to questions of practical ethics ... Christians do not simply read Scripture as an academic exercise.'[93] 'Academic exercise' is contrasted with spiritual and prayerful reading as though the two were mutually exclusive and as if textual criticism were unable to contribute to ethical debate. Scholars who undertake textual criticism that is also avowedly polemical (such as Robert Gagnon and Dale Martin) might be disheartened by the view that their work could not change hearts and minds.

But *Pilling*'s provisionality, its 'focus on process',[94] is something of an illusion here. Although the authors state 'in the face of conflicting scholarship, as well as conflicting beliefs, we believe that the Church should be cautious about attempting to pronounce definitively on the implications of Scripture for homosexual people', they elsewhere adhere to existing teaching.[95] The section on 'The current teaching of the Church of England' on human sexuality[96] outlines the position as expressed in the 'Higton' motion at the 1987 General Synod, *Issues in Human Sexuality* in 1991 and the Lambeth 1.10 statement in 1998, together with later teaching on marriage and homosexuality. All agree that sexual intercourse belongs in marriage, which is a lifelong union between a man and a woman, and that homosexual genital acts fall short of this ideal. Some reservations about the continuing validity of the 'Higton' motion are expressed but in 'Reflecting on the Evidence', the report iterates: 'at the level of declared doctrine, we are agreed that there is not sufficient consensus to change the Church's teaching on human sexuality.'[97]

Despite the Working Party's avowed agnosticism about the biblical witness and their appeal to the lack of consensus among biblical scholars and commentators, the authors seem to conclude that some texts, especially those of the 'creation narrative' in Genesis 1 and 2, are simply foundational in the way in which complementarian commentary reads them. Regarding scripture, *Pilling* has seemed to model an epistemology that embraces the interim nature of interpretation and points towards the possibilities of uncertainty and failure, yet here it has been replaced, rather abruptly, with a statement that, without accord, there can be no change in the Church's teaching on 'human sexuality'. The Working Party has asserted an authority somewhat at odds with its earlier reservations about the clarity of the biblical narratives on 'human sexuality'. In any selection of scholarship on Christian scriptures there is, in the exercise of choice, a construction (or, at least, a favouring) of a particular hermeneutic. What I believe is missing here is the recognition of the contingency of hermeneutics such that some readings are 'unmarked', whereas others are presented as 'distinctive'. This is not to deny the necessary marginality of some hermeneutics – such as those coming from queer studies – that have no place in the supposedly neutral territory of the centre. In privileging particular readings and in presenting the work of male, white, Western biblical scholars as the unmarked norm, the authors bestow canonicity on the hermeneutical lenses that are selected to focus on chosen traditions. In the process, lament, dissent, anger and failure, as redemptive acts and as potential resolutions, are elided in the striving for a productive model of canonicity. Nor do the writers ever question the use and selection of such hermeneutical lenses, their hegemonic epistemologies, their normative narratives that blur cultural mores with perceived biblical prescripts, or their unacknowledged inhabiting of constructions of power and authority that view particular categories and conventions as unmarked and therefore never interrogated. In the process some voices and views are rendered as liminal and as objects of enquiry and problems to be resolved. The failure to recognize that their authority and the canonicity that they perform are themselves contingent does not admit the possibility of disrupting the epistemic hegemony that figures the unmarked as normative and even as divinely ordained.

I might have expected the authors of *Pilling* to be more comfortable with discourses on scripture than with science and society. Yet they appear confused, adopting an ostensible tentativeness that declines to foreclose on certain scriptural interpretations while being clear in other areas about what the Bible teaches. This suggests an apparent even-handedness accorded to the considerations of what science and culture might have to say about homosexuality, which is really concealing a sleight of hand since some voices and perspectives are privileged. And still, in *Pilling*'s brief treatments of scripture, there is the hope that, even if consensus cannot be reached, some kind of accord or harmony will ensue from further deliberations, discussions and conversations. The neoliberal project of achievement through more effort is a clear goal of this report and its intended afterlife. As I have suggested, *Pilling*'s authors do admit that achieving a consensus might not ever be possible, but they code this failure as defeat. I believe that an alternative telos (though it is *an* end not *the* end) is possible through embracing the art of unbecoming, undoing, unbeing, non-striving; inhabiting a site of abjection and negativity, and yet at the same time embracing the childish and the silly. These reports never engage with scripture playfully or imaginatively. Meanings might not be foreclosed, but epistemologies are.

The following two chapters critically examine the afterlife of *Pilling*: the Shared Conversations and the unofficial channels that discussed the report and its aftermath. I will consider whether these spaces are more porous, more receptive to liminal and unauthorized voices, or if they are still following the rules observed by the official reports. Have these spaces been able to produce and circulate what Foucault calls 'subjugated knowledges'? Can they be 'antidisciplinary'?[98] Or are they producing simulacra of quasi-academic discourses?

Notes

1 J. Halberstam, *The Queer Art of Failure* (Durham, NC: Duke University Press, 2011), 3.

2 The Archbishops' Council, *Report of the House of Bishops Working Group on Human Sexuality* (London: Church House Publishing, November 2013).

3 *Pilling*, 74.

4 *Pilling*, 101.

5 'The Church has, at many points in its history, sought to call people to embrace a world view that is deeply at odds with the prevailing culture', *Pilling*, 45.

6 J. Halberstam, *The Queer Art of Failure*, 3.

7 From the Archbishop of Canterbury's Presidential Address to General Synod, 5 July 2013, *Pilling*, 10.

8 The 'official' view, that is; many members of most denominations have expressed support for same-sex marriage. Indeed, the United Reformed Church voted on 9 July 2016 to allow its churches to opt in to perform same-sex weddings, http://urc.org.uk/marriage-of-same-sex-couples.html (accessed 15.2.24).

9 Individuals and groups who gave evidence are named in Appendix 2, but not specified here.

10 *Pilling*, 'Introduction', 5.

11 *Pilling*, 'Introduction', 6.

12 The Working Group comments that, although this report focuses on same-sex relationships, the experiences of those with transgender and intersex conditions also raise important theological and pastoral issues. These had been last addressed in the House of Bishops' Report *Some Issues in Human Sexuality*, 2003 (as was bisexuality, which *Pilling* touches on only briefly), *Pilling*, 'Introduction', 9. The term 'transgendered', which implies that the trans person lacks agency, is regarded as derogatory by many trans people. The GLAAD Media Reference Guide 11th edition, says that the term should be avoided, https://www.glaad.org/reference/trans-terms (accessed 15.2.24).

13 *Pilling*, 'Introduction', 8.

14 *Pilling*, 'Introduction', 7, emphasis added.

15 In 2013, Justin Welby, at his enthronement as Archbishop of Canterbury, remarked that '[y]ou see gay relationships that are just stunning in the quality of the relationship', a statement that implies that for the Church, gay relationships are held to a different standard from straight ones, Mark Duell (*Daily Mail*, 21 March 2013), https://www.dailymail.co.uk/news/article-2297062/New-Archbishop-praises-gay-couples-having-loving-relationships-stunning-quality.html (accessed 15.2.24).

16 *Pilling*, 'Introduction', 8.

17 *Pilling*, 8, 149.

18 *Pilling*, 8.

19 *Pilling*, 150.

20 *Pilling*, 11, see also para 376, 108: 'Opposition to same sex marriage has largely focused on the detriment to the social understanding of marriage which may follow from conflating heterosexual and same sex relationships within a single legal and social institution.'

21 For example, John Milbank, in the Westminster Faith Debates, founded and organized by Linda Woodhead and Charles Clarke, http://faithdebates.org.uk/debates/2013-debates/religion-and-personal-life/do-christians-oppose-gay-marriage/ (accessed 15.2.24).

22 *Pilling*, 11.

23 Alasdair Crockett and David Voas, 'A Divergence of Views: Attitude Change and the Religious Crisis of Homosexuality', *Sociological Research Online*, 8, no. 4, 2003, http://www.socresonline.org.uk/8/4/crockett.htm. This research is also cited in the 'Sexuality and social trends' section of *Pilling* (accessed 15.2.24).

24 The then Bishop of Manchester, Stanley Booth-Clibborn, spoke in the House of Lords in favour of an ameliorating amendment: 'I should regret it if this Bill were to go through with this clause unamended. If it were to do so, I think it should certainly be confined to schools because otherwise there would be a real danger that some organizations which do good work in helping those with homosexual orientation, psychologically and in other ways, would be very much impeded', https://www.legislation.gov.uk/ukpga/1988/9/section/28/enacted (accessed 15.2.24).

25 It was, in part, a response to the liberalizing policies of the Greater London Council, the Inner London Education Authority and the Gay Liberation Front; these may be seen as deliberately provocative or unexceptionably progressive.

26 Cf. the comments on intersex below the Psephizo blog 'Debating Transgender', 7 June 2017, https://www.psephizo.com/sexuality-2/debating-transgender/ (accessed 15.2.24).

27 *Pilling*, 48, citing The Office of National Statistics Integrated Household Survey, 28 September 2012, http://www.ons.gov.uk/ons/dcp171778_280451.pdf (accessed 15.2.24).

28 *Pilling*, 49, citing YouGov survey on attitudes towards same-sex marriage in church, March 2021, http://www.brin.ac.uk/sources/3164/ (accessed 15.2.24).

29 The question asked was: 'Do you think the Church of England is right or wrong to defend marriage as an institution for just heterosexual couples?' Options: Right/Wrong/Don't know.

30 Westminster Faith Debates commissioned YouGov poll, January 2013, cdn.yougov.com/cumulus_uploads/document/mm7go89rhi/YouGov-University of Lancaster-Survey-Results-Faith-Matters-130130.pdf (accessed 15.2.24).

31 Question: 'Do you think same-sex couples should or should not be allowed to get married?' Options: Should/Should not/Don't know.

32 *Pilling*, 49–50, citing, Ben Clements, 'Anglicans and Attitudes towards Gay Marriage', British Religion in Numbers, 14 September 2012, http://www.brin.ac.uk/anglicans-and-attitudes-towards-gay-marriage/ (accessed 15.2.24).

33 *Pilling*, 51–53, citing Alasdair Crockett and David Voas, 'A Divergence of Views: Attitude Change and the Religious Crisis of Homosexuality', *Sociological Research Online*, 8, no. 4, 2003, https://www.socresonline.org.uk/8/4/crockett.html (accessed 15.2.24).

34 From 13 December 2019, civil partnerships (devised solely for same-sex couples in the Civil Partnership Act of 2004) were extended to include heterosexual couples, https://commonslibrary.parliament.uk/research-briefings/cbp-8609/ (accessed 15.2.24).

35 Madeleine Davies, 'The proportion of self-identified Anglicans who agree that same-sex marriage is "right" has exceeded 50 per cent for the first time, a new YouGov poll ... suggests', *Church Times*, 1 March 2022, https://www.churchtimes.co.uk/articles/2022/4-march/news/uk/yougov-poll-more-than-half-of-anglicans-believe-same-sex-marriage-to-be-right (accessed 15.2.24).

36 *Pilling*, 98.

37 All references from *Pilling*, 100–101.

38 For example, *Pilling*, 45.

39 The Faith and Order Commission, 'Communion and Disagreement', *General Synod* (GS Misc 1139, June 2016), https://www.churchofengland.org/sites/default/files/2017-10/communion_and_disagreement_faoc_report_gs_misc_1139.pdf (accessed 15.2.24).

40 J. Halberstam, *The Queer Art of Failure*, 89

41 J. Halberstam, *The Queer Art of Failure*, 88.

42 General Synod Board for Social Responsibility, *Homosexual Relationships: A Contribution to Discussion* (London: Church Information Office, 1979), 14.

43 *Pilling*, 'Arguments about Science', 60ff.

44 The term 'homosexual', used as a noun, is offensive to many LGB people, since it carries a perceived homophobic freight.

45 Michel Foucault, *The History of Sexuality: 1 The Will to Knowledge* (London: Penguin, 1998), 43.

46 Philip Groves, ed., *The Anglican Communion and Homosexuality: A Resource to Enable Listening and Dialogue* (London: SPCK, 2008).

47 The Core Issues Trust, 'Statement of Belief', https://core-issues.org/about-us/ (accessed 19.4.24).

48 Incorrectly called Sybil in the report. Sibyls is a nationwide group for Christian transgender, non-binary and intersex people, partners and allies: 'Sibyls offer companionship along your journey, and supports advocacy work with churches and faith groups on behalf of trans people', https://sibyls.co.uk/ (accessed 15.2.24).

49 This statement indicates that Core Issues Trust is also conflating sexuality and gender issues in implying that being gay means being confused about one's gender identity.

50 The Core Issues Trust, 'Statement on Prejudice', https://www.core-issues.org/statement-on-prejudice (link no longer available).

51 The Royal College of Psychiatrists, 'Statement on Sexual Orientation', https://www.rcpsych.ac.uk/pdf/PS02_2014.pdf (accessed 15.2.24).

52 *Pilling*, 61.

53 David de Pomerai and Glynn Harrison, 'The Witness of Science', in Philip Groves, ed., *The Anglican Communion and Homosexuality*, 267–332.

54 David de Pomerai and Glynn Harrison, 'The Witness of Science'.

55 '[T]here is evidence that some individuals can achieve significant changes in

patterns of unwanted SSA [same sex attraction] ... a larger proportion may achieve satisfaction in bringing their unwanted SSA into line with their values, even if this implies long-term commitment to cognitive and behaviour disciplines (including sexual abstinence) in the face of a persisting mix of sexual attractions.' Glynn Harrison, 'The Witness of Science'.

56 Cf. the *Living Out* organization, http://www.livingout.org/ (accessed 15.2.24); although same-sex attraction is increasingly used as a synonym for gay by trans non-affirming groups such as the LGB Alliance, https://lgballiance.org.uk/ (accessed 15.2.24).

57 Pilling, 97.

58 Pilling, 66

59 J. Halberstam, *The Queer Art of Failure*, 2.

60 Karen Bray, *Grave Attending: A Political Theology for the Unredeemed* (New York: Fordham University Press, 2020), 141. The Martha and Mary narrative appears in the Gospel of Luke (10.38–42). Jesus visits Martha's home where her sister Mary sits listening at Jesus' feet while Martha makes all the preparations. Perhaps naturally, Martha is distracted and asks Jesus if he doesn't care that Mary has left all the work to her. Jesus tells Martha that Mary has chosen the better way. The narrative does not record Martha's reaction to Jesus' admonition.

61 The Thirty-Nine Articles of Religion: 'VI. Of the Sufficiency of the holy Scriptures for salvation. Holy Scripture containeth all things necessary to salvation: so that whatsoever is not read therein, nor may be proved thereby, is not to be required of any man, that it should be believed as an article of the Faith, or be thought requisite or necessary to salvation. In the name of the holy Scripture we do understand those Canonical Books of the Old and New Testament, of whose authority was never any doubt in the Church.' The Thirty-Nine Articles of Religion are part of the fifteenth-century Book of Common Prayer and are witness to the doctrine of the Church of England in the Elizabethan age; they were intended to provide a via media between Calvinism and Roman Catholicism. Priests are still required to assent to the Thirty-Nine Articles but, since 1975, they affirm their loyalty to 'this inheritance of faith', which suggests a recognition of the Articles as an historic formulary rather than a complete acceptance of the doctrines found therein.

62 As I have already set out above, this argument is developed in conversation with J. Halberstam, *The Queer Art of Failure*, and others.

63 The Archbishops' Council, *Some Issues in Human Sexuality: A Guide to the Debate* (London: Church House Publishing, 2003). It is, as I write, twenty years old.

64 Keith Sinclair, 'The *Pilling* Report: Bishop of Birkenhead's Dissenting Statement', *Virtue Online: The Voice of Global Orthodox Anglicanism*, 28 November 2013, http://www.virtueonline.org/pilling-report-bishop-birkenheads-dissenting-statement (accessed 15.2.24).

65 David Pocklington, 'Shared Conversations on Sexuality, Scripture and Mission', *Law and Religion UK*, 30 June 2014, outlines of which were agreed by the House of Bishops in May 2014, https://lawandreligionuk.com/2014/06/30/, on GS Misc 1083 (accessed 15.2.24).

66 Pilling, 105–106, 149.

67 The authors also cite Deryn Guest, *When Deborah Met Jael: Lesbian Biblical Hermeneutics* (London: SCM Press, 2005), and Patrick S. Cheng, *Radical Love: An Introduction to Queer Theology* (New York: Seabury Press, 2011), as examples of a 'distinctive hermeneutic'.

68 Phil Groves, John Holder and Paula Gooder, 'The Witness of Scripture'; Robert

A. J. Gagnon and Dan O. Via, *Homosexuality and the Bible: Two Views* (Philadelphia, PA: Fortress Press, 2003).

69 This view is, presumably, that of Bishop Keith Sinclair, the author of the dissenting statement and of one of the appendices on 'Scripture and same sex relationships'. That the Bishop has a disproportionate space to present his views is one of the ways in which the 'balance' of the report is skewed in favour of a non-affirming viewpoint. *Pilling*, 70.

70 See the final chapter's treatment of the creeping managerialism in the Church.

71 *Pilling*, 70.

72 Cf. Dale Martin, *Sex and the Single Savior: Gender and Sexuality in Biblical Interpretation* (Louisville, KY: Westminster John Knox Press, 2006); James V. Brownson, *Bible, Gender, Sexuality: Reframing the Church's Debate on Same-Sex Relationships* (Grand Rapids, MI: Eerdmans, 2013).

73 Sodomite is itself a problematic translation. It sounds archaic and it is also debated whether the sin of Sodom is lack of hospitality or attempted same-sex rape. Cf. Mark D. Jordan, *The Invention of Sodomy in Christian Theology* (Chicago, IL: University of Chicago Press, 1997).

74 *Pilling*, 71–72.

75 See Robin Scroggs, *The New Testament and Homosexuality: Contextual Background for the Contemporary Debate* (Philadelphia, PA: Fortress Press, 1983), 83, 85–86, 106–108, for the argument that the term is a translation of the Levitical *mishkav zakur* – lying with a male/a male bedder, and thus refers to the Levitical prohibitions.

76 The LLX (or the Septuagint) is the first extant Greek translation of the Hebrew Bible; so termed because it was supposedly translated by seventy scholars who, miraculously, came up with identical versions.

77 Robert A. J. Gagnon, *The Bible and Homosexual Practice: Text and Hermeneutics* (Nashville, TN: Abingdon Press, 2001), 312–332.

78 Dale Martin, *Sex and the Single Savior*, 39.

79 Dale Martin, *Sex and the Single Savior*, 43, emphasis original.

80 *Pilling*, 72, emphasis original.

81 See Michel Foucault, *The History of Sexuality 1: The Will to Knowledge*, 42–43: 'This new persecution of the peripheral sexualities entailed an *incorporation of perversions* and a new *specification of individuals*. As defined by the ancient civil or canonical codes, sodomy was a category of forbidden acts; their perpetrator was nothing more than the juridical subject of them. The nineteenth century homosexual became a personage, a past, a case history, and a childhood … Homosexuality appeared as one of the forms of sexuality when it was transposed from the practice of sodomy onto a kind of interior androgyny, a hermaphroditism of the soul. The sodomite had been a temporary aberration; the homosexual was now a species.' Emphasis original. Richard von Krafft-Ebing and Havelock Ellis preferred the term 'inversion', as did the lesbian novelist Radclyffe Hall who used it in her novel *The Well of Loneliness* (London: Jonathan Cape, 1928). It is, of course, a more neutral word than 'perversion', which suggests turning away from that which is normal or natural.

82 The term 'heterosexual' has the same history as 'homosexual', coming to us from the 1869 German pamphlet and into English from the translation of Krafft-Ebing. But it has an unexpected connotation in its early use; in Merriam-Webster's *New International Dictionary* it was defined as a 'morbid sexual passion for one of the opposite sex'.

83 This is the view taken by Kenneth J. Dover, *Greek Homosexuality* (Cambridge,

MA: Harvard University Press, 1989) (but note the anachronistic use of the term here); and by Thomas Laqueur, *Making Sex: Body and Gender from the Greeks to Freud* (Cambridge, MA: Harvard University Press, 1992). By some contemporary commentators same-sex activity was regarded as 'normal', even noble, while others judged it deviant or anomalous; see Dover, Laqueur, and Bernadette J. Brooten, *Love Between Women: Early Christian Responses to Female Homoeroticism* (Chicago, IL: University of Chicago Press, 1997).

84 See Robin Scroggs, *The New Testament and Homosexuality*.
85 *Pilling*, 72.
86 *Pilling*, 72.
87 Robert A. J. Gagnon, *The Bible and Homosexual Practice*, 37.
88 Gagnon, *The Bible and Homosexual Practice*, 360.
89 *Pilling*, 73.
90 *Pilling*, 73.
91 *Pilling*, 73.
92 *Pilling*, 74.
93 *Pilling*, 91.
94 *Pilling*, 92.
95 *Pilling*, 91.
96 *Pilling*, 28–36.
97 *Pilling*, 101.
98 Cf. J. Halberstam, *The Queer Art of Failure*, 11–12.

2

The Authorized Afterlife of the *Pilling Report*

Facilitated conversations would need to reflect the structures of the Church in which the parish, the deanery, the diocese and the national Church are each salient in different ways. We believe that dioceses would have a central role in promoting and shaping the process in ways that work with the grain of local contexts, but that a degree of national-level commitment from the House of Bishops would be needed to ensure that the Church as a whole could benefit from the process.[1]

Introduction

In this and the following chapter I interrogate the processes that *Pilling* initiated. Here I focus on the Shared Conversations in the dioceses and at General Synod and at the later debates following the launch of the *Prayers of Love and Faith* in January 2023. My intention is to explore whether, outside the boundaries of an institutional report, discussion and reflection were more permeable to dissenting, lamenting and liminal voices. These include not only voices from the margins – the poor and powerless in ecclesiological terms – but also those who might have acquired academic or institutional authority, but who, nevertheless, felt constrained in this debate, by undisclosed orientations and/or allegiances. I ask whether these are spaces where queer voices may be heard, and if there is the potential for queer dissent in discussions authorized by ecclesial authorities.

The quotation from *Pilling* that introduces this chapter suggests, however, that the authorities were intent on controlling the process and outcome of the Conversations: they were to be managed by the institutional Church and episcopally authorized. The authors of *Pilling* trusted that what they proposed was about listening attentively and with mutual respect for difference, and yet the design of the Conversations and their inherent submission to episcopal and ecclesial constructions of authority meant that the process was vulnerable to inherited constructions of power and privilege and was unlikely to allow space for the queering of theological, ethical and scriptural norms. Although failure to reach a consensus and thus to achieve unity through mutual listening was anticipated in the design of the Conversations, they were constructed on the neoliberal assumptions of progress and productivity that pervade a church that is (at least in part) a social construct of the Global North. These assumptions uphold cisheternormativity as the unmarked category that renders all other identities non-normative and thus abject, aberrant and liminal. This orientation towards progress and success refuses to comprehend failure as a possible telos. Using J. Halberstam's *The Queer Art of Failure*[2] as a foil to hegemonic notions of solutionism, I suggest that the potential failure of these processes to provide a harmonic solution has not been apprehended by their ecclesial designers. And processes that are not open to failure – even as a 'queer art' – are inhospitable to those queer voices that may disrupt and challenge their norms. The objective of 'mutual listening across differences'[3] and the regard for the 'relational' rather than the 'institutional' create an impression of openness and porosity – the possibility, perhaps, of a true agnosticism about the processes of conversations and debate and a willingness to enter liminal and uncertain spaces, which may offer no resolution or offer a very queer one. My question is whether the processes that *Pilling* itself initiated could ever become a site for queering the hermeneutical and teleological assumptions of a report produced by the neoliberal institution that is an established Church.

In *Sex, or the Unbearable*,[4] Lauren Berlant and Lee Edelman engage in a dialogue – an unusual literary genre for an academic work – about what it means to live with negativity and its transformational possibilities. In my final chapter I engage with Berlant's attempts to reconcile differences as 'benign variation', thus offering the possibility of the transformation of the norms 'supporting abjection, aggression and domination'.[5] Here I want to reflect a little on the introduction to their dialogical method that analyses conversation as a literary genre. They write that this

> experiment ... proceeds from the belief that dialogue may permit a powerful approach to negativity, since dialogue has some of the risk and excitement we confront in the intimate encounter. Not for nothing does the OED list 'communication' and 'conversation' as the primary meanings of *intercourse* ... throughout this book we try to attend not only to what we can readily agree upon but also to what remains opaque or unpersuasive about the other's ideas, what threatens to block or stymie us. Resistance, misconstruction, frustration, anxiety, becom-

ing defensive, feeling misunderstood: we see these as central to our engagement with each other and to our ways of confronting the challenge of negativity and encounter. Far from construing such responses as failures in the coherence or economy of our dialogues, we consider them indispensable to our efforts to think relationally.[6]

Although they are writing about dialogue as a literary genre, Berlant and Edelman's thoughts on conversation's intimacy, capacity for defensiveness and misunderstanding, and relinquishing of control could have been adopted as the guidelines for the Shared Conversations. Some of this is reflected in the hope of *Pilling*'s authors that the Conversations would be relational and would respect difference;[7] their aim was to facilitate 'good disagreement'.[8] What is never made quite clear about this process, however, is whether the art of disagreeing well is itself a telos and what could follow if disagreement became unpleasant and divisive. Could the failure to harmoniously disagree become a space for a 'queer art' to emerge in a liminal space where hegemonic epistemologies and authoritarian constructions of normality and canonicity falter and become attenuated?

First, I want to ask whether the Conversations permitted 'a powerful approach to negativity' and succeeded in 'thinking relationally'.[9] Some participants found the mutual listening very difficult, despite the skill of the facilitators, and others felt that differences in theology and scriptural readings were not explored in any great depth, but often elided. In the framing of the conversations, with the Bishops first, followed by participants in the dioceses, and then members of General Synod, I will explore how a framework of legitimating authority was constructed to support discussions on the topics of sexuality and of disagreement. The Bishops and members of General Synod are already invested with the authority and power of the institutional Church[10] and those selected to take part in the Regional Conversations were mostly chosen by the diocesan bishops or by someone holding the bishops' authority. It does not follow that the conversations did not reflect the varying shades of opinion to be found in the Church of England – they may have done – but they were very unlikely to include liminal voices or those from an ecclesiological precariat.

The Shared Conversations

The 'three circles' of the Shared Conversations addressed the question: 'Given the significant changes in our culture in relation to human sexuality, how should the Church respond?'[11] The first circle was undertaken by the College of Bishops in September 2014, almost a year after the publication of the report.[12] As with all of the Shared Conversations the Bishops met *in camera* and according to the St Michael's House protocols, developed by Coventry Cathedral's reconciliation ministry.[13] The meeting was, therefore, confidential, and the official press release spoke more about the objectives of the meeting than the content, apart from a generic observation that the 'college shared the different responses being expressed in the life of the Church and the deeply held convictions and experiences that inform them'.[14]

The Regional Shared Conversations

The responsibility for the Regional Conversations was placed on the diocesan bishops who established the processes and brought the 'experience and findings' back to the House or the College of Bishops.[15] The resource materials produced echoed this, suggesting that, although the conversations themselves had no authority, their reflections and conclusions would guide formal discussions by both the Bishops and General Synod.[16] This openness in the design of conversations that were not intended to foreclose on variant readings of scripture and tradition was not acceptable to all commentators on the process. Martin Davie, one of the 'staff team' behind *Pilling*, criticized the resources provided for the Shared Conversations for a number of reasons, among them being the failure to acknowledge that the majority conclusions of the authors of the report are 'controversial' and are not shared by many in the Church of England and that no mention is made of authoritative statements of belief on sexuality, such as the 'Higton' motion passed by General Synod in 1987, *Issues in Human Sexuality*, and Lambeth 1.10, as well as the Book of Common Prayer Marriage Service, Canon B30 and the Thirty-Nine Articles.[17]

Participants were advised to read the two *Pilling* appendices on differing (evangelical) readings of scripture, as well as the essays commissioned from Dr Ian Paul and Professor Loveday Alexander and published in the accompanying *Grace and Disagreement* booklet.[18] They were also advised that *Pilling* did not argue that the gospel itself is 'unclear', but rather that biblical scholars do not agree on scriptural interpretation. This lack of consensus is a result of the fallibility of human endeavour, rather than from an inherent property of scripture itself; biblical texts must not be read as ambiguous. This allows for the possibility of the Church's having baptized hermeneutical flaws that have stemmed from the cultures and the contexts in which they arose. Martin Davie, however, contended that hermeneutical errors are the result of human disobedience. Writing for the Church of England Evangelical Council (CEEC), he claimed that non-normative hermeneutics are produced not through revised, innovative and culturally sensitive readings, but because people have become rebellious:

> The reason a gap has opened up between the Church of England and the belief and behaviour of many people in this country is not because the Church's teaching about sexuality has been shown to be wrong, but because increasing numbers of people have forgotten about God or are unwilling to live lives that are obedient to what God says.[19]

Davie's objections to the process were endorsed by the evangelical group Reform, which directed its members not to take part in the Regional Shared Conversations nor in the conversations at General Synod. In certain of the Regional Conversations, Reform's absence was symbolized by empty chairs which some participants felt gave the organization an unwarranted 'voice' in the process. I will reflect further on this later in this chapter.

Blog Responses to the Shared Conversations

I found 20 blogs online written by participants in the Regional Conversations.[20] Some were published under the aegis of Thinking Anglicans or the Evangelical Group on General Synod (EGGS), so the reader can deduce with which ecclesiological 'tribe' the writers identify.[21] Contributors who read and contribute to Thinking Anglicans are mostly 'liberal', whereas members of EGGS are evangelical, and they tend towards the 'conservative' end of evangelicalism. Most of these blogs were written by people, clergy and lay, who have an investment in the process, either because they are themselves LGBTIQ+ or same-sex attracted, or because they have lobbied for the Church of England to revise or retain its teachings on homosexuality and marriage. So, what I am exploring here is most probably not even a representative sample from the possibly not very representative participants in the Shared Conversations process. These blogs cannot be used as a foil to the 'unofficial' reactions discussed in the next chapter, partly because there is a blurring between official and unofficial responses, but also because the 'authorized' blogs are, like the latter, a snapshot of views at particular times and in specific spaces. However, like the 'unofficial' blog responses to *Pilling*, they do reveal something of the process's constructions and the expectations of participants. The first is the overarching question posed by the resources: 'Given the significant changes in our culture in relation to human sexuality, how should the Church respond?'[22] In response to this question, Andrew Symes, the executive secretary of Anglican Mainstream,[23] wrote:

> We got into the main issue through a sharing of ideas on our tables on [this] topic ... Different opinions started to surface here, on whether the increased liberalization of the past 60 years has been good for the society and the church or not ... We were asked to locate ourselves on a spectrum as to our theological and ethical position with regard to homosexual practice. In my group I was one of two on the 'traditional' side, with seven identifying as 'affirming'.[24]

Ed Shaw, from the South West Conversations, lamented that the framing question was 'never really answered or properly explored',[25] which created a frustrating situation for the participants, especially for those who held strong views on either 'side'. Shaw contended that the opportunity to hear people's positions on particular issues and the personal stories behind them was thwarted by both the programme and the way in which the conversations were managed.[26] Another participant in these conversations, Erika Baker, had a rather different perspective. She wrote that the facilitators were outstanding, that everyone was heard with no one dominating conversations and that

> [a]lthough I often felt profoundly challenged I never felt unsafe, and as my awareness of others as genuinely loving and Christian people grew, I found myself in ever more intimate and emotional conversations with the kind of people I had previously only sparred with online.[27]

Perhaps their distinct experiences of this Conversation owes something to differing expectations. Baker writes that 'deep biblical debate was explicitly not the purpose of the conversations',[28] while Shaw lamented this, writing that if he could redesign the process he would 'include a proper amount of time to focus on the scriptures'.[29] Andrew Symes blogged at some length on the problem, as he saw it, that Christians don't now 'share the same worldview based on faith as defined by the Scriptures'.[30] Symes says that he

> gave a 3 minute overview of the Bible's teaching on marriage from Genesis 1 and 2 through to Revelation 21, including the positive affirmations of marriage in Proverbs and Song of Songs, the Gospels and epistles, and the warnings against sexual deviations or 'sexual immorality' in

Old and New Testaments ... I listened respectfully to what to my mind were woefully poor and erroneous understandings of the Bible and Christian tradition.[31]

Leaving aside Symes' assumption that the Bible teaches univocally of the good of monogamous, mixed-sex marriage and unambiguously of sexual deviation, I note that Symes constructs his understanding as unassailable, while variant understandings are seen as 'woefully poor' and 'erroneous', held by those who have 'widely varying levels of theological education and basic bible knowledge'.[32] He also deploys the hermeneutic of opening scripture and engaging with specific passages which suggests that if the Bible is 'opened' in a certain manner it will be perspicuous when read through the correct lens and that specific passages will deliver the 'biblical Gospel'. Fairly common too in the 'traditionalist' narrative is the suggestion that those who hold a different view on scripture and the tradition do so because of a failure to recognize the fallenness of their readings:

> I listened in vain for the theme of repentance from sin and salvation in Christ. There were accounts of moving from brokenness and low self esteem (attributed, in some cases, to the church's teaching on sin) to self justification and a feeling of being accepted by God in a self-determined identity ... I heard knowledgeable insights from secular psychology and/ or human rights forming the basis of thinking about sexuality which sat in dismissive judgement on the Bible as historically interpreted.[33]

Symes seems to suggest here that the opportunity of responding to and reflecting upon the framing question was lost in what he calls the participants' 'different constructions of reality'.[34] If these are to persist, he observes that 'evangelical networks [will] continue their fruitful focus on teaching and mission, maintaining only minimal contact with the institutional structures, and none at all with the wider church'.[35] John Dunnett, who was then chair of EGGS, recorded his disappointment in a blog about the Chelmsford and London Conversations, stating 'that we do not appear to be travelling this journey on the basis of substantial scriptural engagement'.[36] He too lamented that in none of the sessions did participants 'open up our Bibles and ask: "What does it say?"', and that the discussion was focused on experience and self-reflection 'rather than attempting to put ourselves "under" Scripture'.[37] His disappointment was due partly to an expectation that the Conversations would allow profound reflection on the interpretation and application of scripture, as, according to his understanding, *Pilling* had suggested. Another disappointed participant was Keith Sinclair, the former Bishop of Birkenhead, who wrote the dissenting statement included in the report as an appendix. Anxious that the outcome of these Conversations would be a loss of confidence in scripture as the 'supreme authority', Sinclair hoped that a 'patient reading of scripture' undertaken in parishes, dioceses and provinces might yet achieve consensus, though decades of church reports and biblical scholarship have not yet achieved such hermeneutical harmony.[38]

The East Midlands Conversations elicited the greatest number of blogs. Of these, two from EGGS also lamented the absence of scripture from the discussions. One, by Andrew Atwood, went so far as to suggest that every person was given space and listened to attentively, except God. He wrote of scripture that 'it has been known for centuries as the "holy" – bible because God himself authored it ... no doubt there are some parts of scripture that are unclear and difficult, but the significant body of scripture is in fact pretty straightforward'.[39] In an effort to understand the 'liberal perspective of the key scriptures in question', Atwood engaged with a gay man who had written a pamphlet to explain his own position. After a few exchanges the interlocutor asked if it was OK to stop talking about the Bible, to which Atwood's response was that: 'as a gay man it had perhaps been painful for him to keep looking at passages that weren't actually very ambiguous at all'.[40] Perhaps this highlights another difficulty in the Regional Conversations (despite what was generally acknowledged to be excellent facilitation): that of differing understandings of vulnerability and marginalization.

Andrew Symes and others from a 'traditionalist' position maintained that they were in a minority in the Conversations; apart from the comments on some blogs that the quota of young people or LGBTIQ+ people hadn't been met at some of the Regional Conversations there is no way of knowing how 'balanced' each of the Conversations was in terms of representative groupings. Ed Shaw, from the South West Conversations, felt that 'all the feedback I've heard so far suggests that it is those holding to the bible's traditional teaching that come back most battered and bruised'.[41] This is in sharp contrast to the gay and bi people who often reported that not only their views but also their lives were being scrutinized and critiqued. To return to the East Midlands Conversations, Jeremy Pemberton, a gay married priest, criticized the symbolism of two empty chairs giving a voice to people who would not take part in the process. He felt that there were enough 'articulate conservative evangelicals' present to oppose any change in the Church's traditional teaching based upon 'the plain teaching of Scripture'.[42] Pemberton left feeling distressed and angry that my salvation, my standing as a Christian, my vocation, my marriage, my ministry, my motives, my integrity, were all, sometimes explicitly, and sometimes implicitly, questioned or denied. It felt like the things I held most dear were trampled over by people who had no knowledge and little understanding or curiosity about me.[43]

This dismissal of one's personal 'holy ground' was also experienced by Ruth Wilde. She also took part in the East Midlands Conversations and wrote that she and other LGBTIQ+ people had to 'put up with some very offensive comments ... and some had their very salvation repeatedly called into question'.[44] Wilde and her one-time conversation partner identify each other in their blogs (according to the St Michael's House protocol, conversations may be reported but not attributed). Wilde wrote of one exchange in which she held that the Church's attitudes on same-sex relationships had caused mental and physical harm to people. A 'conservative evangelical' responded that in his church he had seen people damaged by same-sex relationships. This 'conservative evangelical' was John McGinley, then Vicar of Holy Trinity, Leicester and a New Wine Regional Leader, who also blogged on these Conversations and reported this exchange. He too was concerned by the two empty chairs and was pleased that he had attended because of the effect of 'these absences in weakening the orthodox representation' and left 'with great concern that the majority of the participants had lost any clear understanding of the Bible as authoritative in their lives'.[45] McGinley then recounts the conversations with Wilde:

> In a facilitated session one person said that the orthodox position was responsible for their friends' [sic] suicide. While I showed concern for their loss ... I rejected the direct link between holding an orthodox understanding of sexual relationships and their friends' [sic] decision ... I then shared how I felt that the celebration of same-sex relationships was deeply damaging to society through the confusion it brings to issues of identity, relationships, gender, sin, etc. and how it undermines the position of heterosexual marriage which is God's intended pattern for sexual relationships.

After this a complaint was made to one of the facilitators who, according to McGinley, expressed surprise that someone would hold the views he had shared with Wilde.[46] McGinley felt that sharing his views was part of the process, while Wilde expressed the hope that, with better facilitation, people wouldn't have to listen to such language and inferences in group work. It appears that some participants, especially those who were LGBTQ+ (I don't know of any intersex participants), felt that the Bible, or certain texts from scripture, were being weaponized, whereas those who subscribed to the 'plain meaning' were surprised that scripture wasn't 'opened' in the sessions so that its message was clear.

A rather different approach to scripture was proposed by David Nixon, another of the participants in the South West Conversations, and then vice-principal of the South West Ministry Training Course. In an article for *The Expository Times*, Nixon observed that since blogs have focused on process and reaction, 'there has been little attempt to make theological sense of the experience'.[47] Nixon described his own experience of the Conversations, writing that 'intellectually, what surprised me however was the almost complete absence of theology in most of our discussions, both small groups and plenaries'.[48] Further, he wrote that there seemed to be a reluctance to engage with theology because it was too academic and that there 'was a wide disparity between participants in their previous knowledge and experience in the area of sexualities'.[49] The discussion on the two essays on scriptural interpretation (by Ian Paul and Loveday Alexander) was brief, which echoes Erika Baker's observation – from the same Conversations – that many of the participants had felt that the resource material was too academic.[50] Nixon also suggested that the reluctance to engage might be due to divisive theological issues that, according to Elizabeth Stuart, writing in 2003, have resulted in the two sides 'wrestling each other to exhaustion'.[51] Nixon argued that, in this process,

> biblical theology risks being seen as the whole of theology ... if the arguments about sexualities are framed solely in terms of Scripture, whole other related areas are omitted, for example the way power is exercised in the Church; there is little engagement with other disciplines, especially the human sciences, which in this area have had a great deal to say in the last thirty years.[52]

Although writing from a different theological perspective, Nixon agrees with Andrew Atwood that this approach neglects the presence of God, while making, perhaps, an idol of process. Reflecting on the notion of embodied conversation, Nixon saw the participants expressing themselves not just with words, but in tones, facial expressions, postures, and as members of the Body of Christ, bearing the wounds of our divisions and at the same time accepting Christ's invitation to put our hands into his wounds. He adds that sharing a level of intimacy with strangers for the benefit of the Church did feel like 'a kind of ecclesial speed dating' and that, despite this embodiment, there was 'no real conversation about what our bodies did in a sexual sense'.⁵³ Here, Nixon suggests, was an opportunity for a Bible study, one focused on the Song of Songs. This is, I suspect, a rather different hermeneutical approach from that of Andrew Symes who used the Song as a positive affirmation of marriage in a three-minute overview of the metanarrative of scripture.⁵⁴ Perhaps this also represents a significant difference in participants in the Conversations: between those who brought an embodied experience to the process and those who experienced 'the cerebral pain of cognitive disagreement'.⁵⁵

Although the Regional Conversations were framed as having no particular outcome, more of the 'traditionalist' bloggers perceived an agenda towards the goal of 'good disagreement', which some felt to be ecclesially impossible if both 'sides' were deemed to be of equal value. Nevertheless, many participants tended to focus on the scriptural hermeneutic as *the* fundamental hermeneutic for these Conversations and lamented the lack of biblical study as a focus of the experience. This is very different from the *Pilling Report* itself, where scripture is not deployed as the primary hermeneutical lens, and it is somewhat at odds with the framing question suggested by the designers of the Shared Conversations. The lens of science is mentioned only, I believe, in David Nixon's article, and then very briefly.⁵⁶ There is, perhaps, a subtext about social and cultural change in some of the arguments from scripture, but it appears as an intimation that because the Gospel doesn't change nor should 'traditional' church teaching accommodate itself to the zeitgeist. Once again, most of the participants reviewed here – whether liberal or conservative – appear to believe in a process that will, ultimately, deliver solutions. Some hoped that the General Synod Conversations would be more decisive. I will turn next to these.

The Shared Conversations at General Synod, July 2016

The third round of Shared Conversations took place in July 2016 after General Synod was prorogued.⁵⁷ They differed from the Regional Shared Conversations in that presentations were added to the small-groups discussions: on scripture, on changing culture, and on walking forward together. These Conversations were also held under St Michael's House protocols and there is very little 'authorized' discussion about them. Ian Paul blogged about them, and this blog and the debate it provoked are discussed in the following chapter on the 'unauthorized' responses to *Pilling*. Anglican Ink, a US organization, posted a statement from 37 General Synod members criticizing the Shared Conversations, and particularly their neglect of scriptural engagement:

> We ... wish to express our lack of confidence in the process of the Shared Conversations. Whatever their stated purposes, the outcome has not led to a greater confidence that the Church will be guided by the authoritative voice of the Scriptures, and its decisive shaping of traditional Anglican teaching, in any forthcoming discussions.[58]

The only other 'official' account of the Conversations that I can find was written by David Bennett, one of the four who made presentations. From Ian Paul's blog, we learn that two of these contributors were members of an organization that believes it is important to work within the Church's current teaching, whereas the others belong to groups that prioritize the creation of safe space.[59] Paul does not, in line with the St Michael's House protocols, name these organizations, but in Bennett's own blog he writes that he is a member of the Living Out team and links to his testimony on their website.[60] Describing the experience of giving his presentation to Synod as a heavenly battle taking place in a realm beyond this one, and speaking as a member of the Lord's army, Bennett said:

> Today I stand in front of you representing 1000s of people like myself who aren't making a fuss about their sexuality – who are living costly lives of discipleship with their same-sex attractions. I want to implore you today in the sight of Jesus Christ to consider that blessing same-sex relationships will have very negative consequences on people like myself. Such a decision not only denies the clear teaching of scripture and the tradition of the Church for thousands of years but it denies the truth of Jesus' voice in our lives and impairs the vital marker of true evangelism: holiness. If the Church blesses same-sex couples that sends a clear message that holy celibacy as a response to grace and the teaching of scripture is pointless. It says that we are simply wasting our sacrificial celibacy and costly discipleship like the woman who poured the alabaster jar on Jesus' feet.[61]

This is a very particular account of the negative impact of inclusivity on church and society with Bennett comparing the anointing at Bethany – an act of transgressive love – to the wasting of 'sacrificial celibacy'.

It appears that Synod listened only to those who view such relationships as a problem or 'issue' of some kind. It is noteworthy – and perhaps a sign of the implicit conservatism of the process – that there were no voices supporting the unequivocal affirmation of same-sex marriages and partnerships, nor were there contributions from Christians who have experienced the 'goods' of these unions. The only voices critical of the structure of the debates and dubious about their outcomes came from those who refused to take part, those who were, in Halberstam's words, 'stalling the business of the dominant'.[62] Here, Halberstam is referring to those practices – styled by James C. Scott as 'weapons of the weak' – that are quietly subversive resistances to 'the dominant order'.[63] Yet, rather than being a tactic of the weak, those stalling here had the privilege of being invitees and the power of refusing the invitation.

Marriage and Same Sex Relationships after the *Shared Conversations* and the 'Take Note' Debate at General Synod, February 2017

In January 2017 the House of Bishops published GS 2055, which was the fruit of episcopal reflection following the three rounds of Shared Conversations.[64] At the outset the Bishops admitted that they 'know that this report may prove challenging or difficult reading' and it was, indeed, criticized by those on both sides of the sexuality debate. At their residential meeting in September 2016, the College of Bishops undertook a facilitated process to discover the range of their views and to find a 'centre of gravity' of principles and ideas. Unsurprisingly, no position in the College commanded unanimous support. Nevertheless, some consensus did emerge: first, there was little support for changing the Church's teaching on marriage, as expressed in Canon B30;[65] and second, there was 'a strong sense that existing resources, guidance and *tone* needed to be revisited'.[66] The favoured, though not unanimous, option was framed thus:

> Interpreting the existing law and guidance to permit *maximum freedom* within it, without changes to the law or to the doctrine of the Church.[67]

The outworking of this 'consensus' would be the establishment of a *fresh tone* and culture of welcome and support for lesbian and gay people and for those who experience same-sex attraction[68] and the provision of 'a substantial new Teaching Document' to replace *Marriage: A Teaching Document from the House of Bishops* (1999) and *Issues in Human Sexuality* (1991). The House also agreed to bring a 'Take Note' debate to the February Synod. In the section 'Guidance for clergy' the report draws attention to the declaration that clergy would 'use only the forms of service which are authorized or allowed by canon', and that it would not be right to produce an 'authorized public liturgy' for those entering a civil partnership, although clergy may pray informally with same-sex couples.[69] Authorized forms of liturgy guard against legal challenge but are the result of a 'complex legal obstacle course'; services can be 'commended' without synodical approval, although they are open to challenge since the clergy may not use forms that depart from the doctrine of the Church.[70] A Service of Prayer and Dedication after a Civil Marriage, commended in 1985, is one such form.[71] However, at this point, the House and College of Bishops chose not to recommend either authorized or commended liturgies for this purpose.

The last section of the report was on the consultation with General Synod in February 2017. This took the form of discussion in groups on 'case studies based on real pastoral situations',[72] similar to those used at the meetings of the House and College of Bishops, followed by a 'Take Note' debate in which voting to take note would not commit Synod members to acceptance of anything contained within it. As became evident in the 'Take Note' debate, a report that attempted to reconcile two perhaps incompatible positions on sexuality was not welcomed by many of those on either side of the debate. The line between official and unofficial responses to the report and the Synod debate is somewhat blurred. Some responses appeared in the form of blogs, a grey area in the authorized/unauthorized canon, but since many opinion pieces are now published in the form of blogs, I am going to take note of two of them here as 'official' commentaries on the report, especially since they were written either by members of Synod or by public theologians.

The first is by Martin Davie, who also wrote critically about the resources for the Regional Shared Conversations.[73] Davie gives a summary of the report's contents and then turns to how his readers should respond. The report's support of the Church's doctrine of marriage, its assertion that this will not change, and the proposal of a new teaching document should be welcomed. He also welcomes the emphasis on clarity regarding what clergy may offer in terms of ministry for same-sex couples and how ordinands and clergy may be questioned on their sexual conduct. Davie then turns to what he perceives as the report's weaknesses, the major one being that, although the bishops affirm the current teaching and doctrine of the Church of England, they do not give evidence of why they do so. For Davie, 'tentative ways forward' and the belief that 'those with whom we theologically disagree "still have something to teach us about the Kingdom of God"'[74] are, without demonstration, empty rhetoric. Davie also picks up on those potentially inclusive phrases, 'maximum freedom', 'a generous freedom for pastoral practice', and a 'fresh tone of welcome and support', fearing that they will push the boundaries on pastoral practice and lead to the affirmation of what is sinful. Furthermore, a recognition that unmarried heterosexual relationships and same-sex unions can embody 'crucial social virtues of mutuality and fidelity'[75] does not, Davie contends, mean that they are not sinful.[76]

THE AUTHORIZED AFTERLIFE OF THE *PILLING REPORT*

Miranda Threlfall-Holmes, a priest and member of General Synod, published a much shorter blog than Davie's, also criticizing the Bishops' report, but from a rather different perspective.[77] She begins by focusing on the word 'tone' and likened it, emotionally and ecclesiologically, to the 'interminable debates' on the ordination of women in which women were seen as an inconvenience, a problem and a difficulty. There is, she writes, a hand-wringing note on how painful and difficult this has been for the bishops, and notes that the report's recommendations are not to do anything but 'with a few hopeful noises about changing the tone and being a bit more permissive'.[78] She contends that you cannot change tone without altering the underlying assumptions, doctrines and rules; people can still be negative about LGBTIQ+ people in church because they can point to existing teaching and doctrine. Threlfall-Holmes also offers a number of suggestions to the House, focusing on marriage and sexuality generally rather than on the 'issue' of homosexuality. Maintaining that sex outside marriage should no longer be seen as sinful and that both historical and 'biblical' marriage are contingent, she argues that marriage does not create something new but celebrates what already exists. Threlfall-Holmes' blog, perhaps because it was written as a very personal reflection, albeit by a member of Synod, is much more expressive and direct than the quasi-academic tone of Davie's piece (note that I am not using quasi here in a pejorative sense, but to describe writing that is formal and, supposedly, dispassionate). In reality Davie's blog is no more disinterested than Threlfall-Holmes'; his arguments, as I have shown, in my critique of the resource material he wrote for the Regional Shared Conversations, are marshalled to persuade his readers of what 'orthodoxy' commands. This, too, is confessional writing, and its tone, like that of Threlfall-Holmes' blog, indicates that sexuality has become a touchstone for disputes about loyalty, orthodoxy and ecclesiology. Davie is explicit that scriptural readings with which he does not agree are wrong, not through interpretative differences, but because those holding them are indifferent to or disobedient to God's word. Thus, what seems at first glance to resemble academic discourse is much closer to polemic. The Bishops' report provoked what Andrew Goddard, writing for *Fulcrum*,[79] described as 'vehement reactions', not least because the Archbishops sent it to the Anglican Consultative Council [80] before it was debated at Synod as if the 'Take Note' motion was a mere formality, as, indeed they probably thought it would be. Despite this sanguine assurance, the House of Bishops clearly suspected that some measures in the report would not please either side, as Graham James, then Bishop of Norwich, indicated in the accompanying press release, saying, 'we hope that the tone and register of this report will help to commend it, though we recognize it will be challenging reading for some'.[81] It was certainly challenging reading for 12 retired bishops, who on 11 February 2017 published a letter, criticizing the report:

> Our perception is that while the pain of LGBT people is spoken about in your report, we do not hear its authentic voice ... The result of that focus on the issue of a change in the law is that your call for change of tone and culture, while absolutely right, does not carry conviction.[82]

The Lesbian and Gay Christian Movement (LGCM; now part of OneBodyOneFaith) also wrote a letter to its supporters on 31 January 2017 asking them to write to General Synod representatives requesting that they should vote not to take note of the report and that they 'should not take part in group work designed to gain approval of the document'.[83] The letter and the attached memo are sharply critical, declaring that for those who took part in the Shared Conversations in good faith 'this was a very significant betrayal of trust'.[84] In the event, an estimated 50–100 Synod representatives declined to take part in the case study groups and set up their own unofficial discussion group which was visited by the Archbishop of Canterbury. On 14 February 2017, Jeremy Pemberton, then chair of LGCM, wrote about the case studies that were to be discussed at Synod; the studies themselves were published on the LGCM website.[85] Pemberton wrote that the case studies were 'deeply unsatisfactory', problematizing LGBTIQ+ people and implying that if they were not there the difficult situations wouldn't exist. Furthermore, he argued, these are not stories about LGBTIQ+ people themselves but studies in 'congregational spiritual immaturity ... and serious and unpleasant parochial homophobia'. There is not one case study among the five that presents a gay person in a welcoming and affirming church presiding, preaching, singing, praying, providing hospitality or arranging flowers. Gay people are framed as the root of friction and discord, not as the fruit of supportive church life. It was not only the liberal wing of the Church, however, that was disparaging about the report. Susie Leafe, a General Synod member and (then) director of the conservative evangelical group Reform, was reported as saying: 'I can see them having problems getting it through. I haven't heard anyone saying positive things about the report. The main problem is that there are people from all sides of the debate who for very different reasons think the content of the report is deplorable.'[86]

On the afternoon of 15 February 2017, the 'Take Note' debate took place lasting just over two hours.[87] Many members were called to speak in the debate and several clergy and laity called on Synod not to 'take note' of the motion.[88] Susie Leafe, agreeing with the affirming evangelical, Jayne Ozanne, contended that more clarity was needed on contested beliefs before 'taking note' of this report and voted against taking note.[89] Sam Allberry, a same-sex attracted Christian who has chosen celibacy, spoke of his Church becoming an unsafe place, and that by Church he meant not his own congregation but Synod, declaring: 'I now feel that I am being bullied at Synod for being same-sex attracted and faithful to the teaching of Jesus on marriage.'[90] With the benefit of hindsight, it is a not unreasonable assumption that the tenor of the debate, and Synod members absenting themselves from the case studies, caused the bishops some unease. The Archbishop of Canterbury, Justin Welby, perhaps mindful that case studies presented people as 'issues' to be resolved, said in his speech, 'no one is a problem, there are no problems in this room that are people'.[91] The keynote was Welby's call for 'a radical new inclusion, a radical new Christian inclusion in the Church, founded ... in a proper twenty-first century understanding of being human and being sexual'.[92] He promised a teaching document,[93] put together by the whole Church, by every single part, not excluding anyone, and that, 'we will seek to do better, we could hardly fail to do so in the light of what has been said this afternoon', and urged Synod to 'take note' of the report.[94] Synod did not 'take note': the majority voted in favour, but the report failed to obtain a majority in the House of Clergy. Because the motion failed in this House, it failed in all three Houses (Laity and Bishops as well).[95]

The core of Justin Welby's speech was included in a letter from the Archbishops published the following day.[96] They announced that they would be formulating proposals for 'a large scale teaching document around the subject of human sexuality'. This teaching document must, they wrote, ultimately come from the Bishops, but since 'all episcopal ministry must be exercised with all the people of God, lay and ordained ... our proposals will ensure a wide-ranging and fully inclusive approach'.[97] One immediate reaction, among conservatives and liberals alike, was to view these words with a hermeneutic of suspicion. Conservatives distrusted the phrase 'radical inclusion', even though the Archbishops had qualified this with the word 'Christian'; it was suggestive of the 'maximum freedom' that some clearly thought was the thin edge of a pastorally inclusive wedge.[98] Some liberals were more cautiously welcoming:

> OneBodyOneFaith reminds the Archbishops that the homophobia long present in the Church of England has skewed its population and that this needs to be taken into account in Diocesan consultations, in the development of pastoral practices, and in formulating the wide ranging and inclusive new teaching document on human sexuality ... The

process needs to allow each participant to speak without fear for their own safety or fear of recrimination.[99]

The theological reflections of the Bishops remained behind firmly closed doors. Although this is intended to protect both collegiality and those who may be vulnerable in these discourses, in practice it continues to invest authority in those who build the frameworks of these resources, protecting them from scrutiny by 'outsiders'. The institutions that speak of 'radical inclusion' have the privilege of inviting those chosen to be included, radically or otherwise. And invitation or welcome always comes from those in power to those who are (relatively) powerless. Sometimes those on both sides of the debate have refused the invitation to take part in this process. On occasion, as when empty chairs were used to symbolize the absence of a particular group at the Regional Conversations, this has been seen as an unbecoming power play, but by making themselves deliberately voiceless, groups may practise the dumb insolence of resistance to the hegemonic narrative. This is a kind of failure, but one weaponized to critique dominant forms of power and to open up the possibility of subversive alternatives. One weapon available to the voiceless is not to demand that their voices be heard but to amplify their silence. It could be argued that queer people who are not allowed to participate fully in the life of the Church have far less agency and unquestioned privilege and therefore could be seen as utilizing silence and absence as a critique and a resistance to the epistemic hegemony of the process. However, it is unlikely that those who chose not to participate in the Shared Conversations are entirely devoid of agency; they do not belong to a 'subaltern class'.[100]

Failure as a 'Queer Art' in the Shared Conversations

For both 'orthodox' and 'revisionist' Christians, the Shared Conversations can be figured as failure. The former decried their lack of engagement with the 'clear teaching of scripture' and the 'unchanging message of the Gospel', while the latter were disappointed that a change in the teaching and doctrine of the Church was not even being spoken of as a possibility. Reading the 'authorized' responses to the debate, even the goal of 'good disagreement' seems to have failed since the interested parties have not agreed that compromise is possible nor that each 'side' (or several 'sides') may hold their views and beliefs in good faith and remain united in difference. To return to Berlant and Edelman's optimism about conversation as 'intimate encounter' that might be able to respond 'to the provocations of otherness',[101] it is apparent from reading the blogs that reflect upon the experience of the Shared Conversations that, although for some participants these were an 'intimate encounter', most did not seem to have experienced the transformative potential of misunderstanding, difference and negativity. The 'giving up of control' that conversation elicits, according to Berlant and Edelman, seems in reflection on the Shared Conversations to have been replaced by 'the defensive dramatization of differences';[102] perhaps because those taking part were afraid either of relinquishing their authority or of revealing their vulnerabilities.

In the aftermath of the Conversations, the debate at General Synod and the decision by the Bishops to create a teaching document in response to the failure to 'take note', the potentialities of failure were left unexplored. Returning to Halberstam's conception of failure as a 'queer art', the Church, in pursuing a solution to the 'issues' or 'problems' of homosexuality, overlooks the imagining of failure as a kind of resolution: a recognition that, as in other areas of ecclesiology, there may be *no* liturgical, doctrinal or theological harmony at hand. Failure might be a queer undoing of the epistemic norms on which church reports, synods, and teaching documents are founded, an acknowledgement that privilege queers the pitch for those whom the norms render voiceless and/or invisible. The dissenting, lamenting and liminal voices, which the introduction to this chapter notes were absent from *Pilling* itself, have not been heard in the official responses to the report. Not only are there no openly queer voices in this 'authorized' debate (though some who are potentially queer have been muted or have chosen silence), but also there is, in this process, no queering of the institution itself – its models of authority and those epistemic norms that it takes for granted as unmarked and neutral. Only David Nixon's essay in *The Expository Times* briefly que(e)ries the process itself and the constructions of authority that underlie it. Bloggers on the Shared Conversations criticized the process, but usually from the perspectives of content and facilitation, rather than reflecting on the 'inviolate' structures of which they are a part. Perhaps the queerest voices here have come from those who refused to take part in the Shared Conversations or in the debates on the 'cases' presented at General Synod in February 2017. They are those who have refused to cooperate in this process and have thus shunned the myth of progress (albeit, possibly, involuntarily), perhaps recognizing, as Halberstam writes, 'failure as a way of refusing to acquiesce to dominant logics of power and discipline and as a form of critique'.[103] Yet, these are also voices of privilege who can weaponize silence or refusal because they have been accorded legitimacy by the institution.

General Synod, 2023

> It should be possible to disagree and inhabit a generous theological, ecclesial and pastoral space that holds the Church together in different interpretations of the answers to these questions [from the Pastoral Guidance group].[104]

In the event, the promised teaching document never materialized. *Living in Love and Faith* is the fruit of extensive discussion and consultation and provides a resource for the Church, but it is not a magisterial pronouncement nor teaching guidance on the theologies of sexualities. Instead, after the publication of *LLF* and conversations among the Bishops, they published, in January 2023, draft texts of *Prayers of Love and Faith*: resources to be used as prayers of thanksgiving and dedication, and prayers asking for God's blessing, with same-sex couples living in faithful, covenanted relationships.[105] These draft prayers were discussed at the February General Synod and I will explore how the success of the motion to accept, refine and commend these prayers may, bizarrely, be a model of the 'queer art of failure' through the recognition that welcome and generosity are not dependent upon theological and scriptural consensus. This is, once again, a snapshot from a process; debate and guidance are, inevitably, moving on, but, as with *Pilling* and the Shared Conversations, my purpose is to deconstruct the process and to explore what a result might be if it ceased pursuing consensus and success and accepted the provisionality and joy of failure.

Alongside these texts the Bishops also issued another report – *Living in Love and Faith: A response from the Bishops of the Church of England about identity, sexuality, relationships and marriage*, which opens with a pastoral letter from the Bishops and includes an *Apology*

> for the ways in which the Church of England has treated LGBTIQ+ people – both those who worship in our churches and those who do not. For the times we have rejected or excluded you, and those who you love, we are deeply sorry. The occasions on which you have received a hostile and homophobic response in our churches are shameful and for this we repent.[106]

The Pastoral Letter assured its readers that the *Prayers of Love and Faith* (*PLF*) would not alter the Church of England's doctrine of marriage – a guarantee that failed to reassure some who oppose the introduction of these prayers – and announced the development of Pastoral Guidance which would replace *Issues in Human Sexuality*, the 1991 Bishops'

Report which had become a shibboleth in the selection of candidates for ordination.[107] The section 'About Prayers of Love and Faith' expanded upon the kinds of relationships that may be 'joyfully affirmed'; the nature of blessing – as something given to *people* rather than things, actions or ways of life'; and introduces a distinction between Holy Matrimony and civil marriage.[108] This last seems novel since the Church of England has recognized civil marriage doctrinally as marriage since its introduction in 1836.[109] But the Bishops argued that the extension of civil marriage to same-sex couples in 2013 'exposed' two hitherto unrecognized understandings of marriage: one that is gender neutral and Holy Matrimony (as defined in Canon B30) which is between a man and a woman.[110] This distinction between civil marriage and Holy Matrimony, which had, purportedly, lain unnoticed until the 2013 Act, stirred up something of a hornets' nest. The guidance from the Church of England's Legal Office at Church House, which offers counsel on the legality in Canon Law of the proposed *PLF*, argued that nowhere in the draft prayers is same-sex civil marriage construed as Holy Matrimony. Furthermore, the guidance undergirds the contention in the Bishops' response to *Living in Love and Faith* that the Marriage (Same Sex Couples) Act of 2013[111] introduced a fundamental difference between what is capable of constituting a marriage for the purposes of the general law and of ecclesiastical law.'[112] A buzz of concerned opposition arose in response to the Legal Note. *A Comment on GS Misc 1339*, issued by six members of General Synod, argued that the claims made in the Legal Note were problematic and that they might expose clergy to the risk of litigation if they relied upon this guidance when using the prayers.[113] The two primary concerns of the *Comment* are that the Legal Note 'may overstate' the distinction between marriage in general law and in ecclesiastical law, and 'may understate' the ways in which the prayers indicate a departure from the doctrine of the Church of England. The solution the authors suggest is that, instead of commending the prayers for use under Canon B5 which would be contentious, General Synod 'may consider' resolving whether the prayers and pastoral guidance are congruent with church doctrine under Canon B2. The latter route, which would result in the prayers being authorized as liturgy rather than commended for use, would require a two-thirds majority in General Synod. Commendation, as I noted earlier in this chapter, confers no specific legal status.[114]

Agreeing with the judgement given in the original Legal Note that there are distinctions, HH Peter Collier writing for *Law and Religion UK* argues that State intervention in marriage, such as the Clandestine Marriages Act, 1753, and the Marriage Act of 1863, which introduced civil marriages, have already made a distinction between civil marriage conducted by the State and Holy Matrimony.[115] The Bishop of Exeter, Henry Phillpotts, called the 1863 Act 'a disgrace to British legislation' and his twenty-first-century successor Michael Langrish argued in the House of Lords that in the passing of the 2013 Act 'we will have legislated into being two very different realities, but confusingly bearing the same name'. There is a provision, not widely known it appears, but dating from the 1836 Act, that allows for those who have already contracted a civil marriage to celebrate their marriage in church.[116] On these grounds, it could be argued that there is, indeed, a distinction between civil marriage and Holy Matrimony, even though the Church accepts civil marriages as de facto marriages without requiring a further ceremony in church.

General Synod met in London on 6–9 February 2023. The main debate on the *Prayers*, which lasted over eight hours, was scheduled for the afternoon of 8 February but continued on the morning of 9 February. A recording of the two sections is available on YouTube.[117] The motion for debate proposed by the Bishop of London, Sarah Mullally, was:

> That this Synod, recognizing the commitment to learning and deep listening to God and to each other of the Living in Love and Faith process, and desiring with God's help to journey together while acknowledging the different deeply held convictions within the Church:
>
> (a) lament and repent of the failure of the Church to be welcoming to LGBTQI+ people and the harm that LGBTQI+ people have experienced and continue to experience in the life of the Church;
> (b) recommit to our shared witness to God's love for and acceptance of every person by continuing to embed the Pastoral Principles in our life together locally and nationally;
> (c) commend the continued learning together enabled by the Living in Love and Faith process and resources in relation to identity, sexuality, relationships and marriage;
> (d) welcome the decision of the House of Bishops to replace Issues in Human Sexuality with new pastoral guidance;
> (e) welcome the response from the College of Bishops and look forward to the House of Bishops further refining, commending and issuing the Prayers of Love and Faith described in GS 2289 and its Annexes;
> (f) invite the House of Bishops to monitor the Church's use of and response to the Prayers of Love and Faith, once they have been commended and published, and to report back to Synod in five years' time.

The bulk of the debate comprised amendments to the main motion. Some of these were broadly supportive of the motion, others queried the precise wording of various clauses. The only Amendment (67) which passed was proposed by Andrew Cornes who argued that Jesus was both radically inclusive and radically conservative and that the word *porneia* (usually translated as fornication) would in its context have been seen as including homosexual sex. He concluded by stating that 'we cannot bless a relationship which, in its sexual aspect, Jesus calls sinful'.[118] What passed then became item (g) which was appended to the original motion. It reads:

(g) endorse the decision of the College and House of Bishops not to propose any change to the doctrine of marriage, and their intention that the final version of the Prayers of Love and Faith should not be contrary to or indicative of a departure from the doctrine of the Church of England.

This amendment was voted on and passed in all three Houses, though the vote was closest in the House of Laity. Earlier in the debate, Stephen Hofmeyr had raised a Point of Order asking if taking a vote on every amendment by Houses meant that the Bishops had, in effect, the right of veto. This was followed by applause in the chamber, but the voting figures show that all three Houses almost always voted the same way. On the four amendments (53, 56, 60, 62) when the House of Laity voted in favour and the other two Houses voted against, the amendment would still have been lost even if the vote had been of the whole Synod. The main motion, as amended by Item 67, was passed by a vote in all three Houses.[119] The debate, which naturally included many fervent speeches, was chaired with aplomb by Geoffrey Tattersall. It was a model of good-tempered engagement: the idealized discourse of a 'civilized' society, conjured by the values of the Global North. The very construct of the debating chamber where opposing voices are pitted one against another is predicated on success and failure: motions and amendments are won or lost. Losing or failure is seen as a bad thing in what is essentially an adversarial system. For those who have seen their options fail, the sense that something is thereby *lost* makes a generous ecclesial space more inhospitable perhaps, and they are more inclined to argue for a settlement in which the space is occupied differently.

Civility can hide deep divisions. Though many were pleased at the outcome, some – from both sides of the debate – remained deeply dissatisfied with a solution that was seen as either too much or not enough. Jayne Ozanne, a campaigner for LGBTIQ+ rights that include the introduction of equal marriage in the Church, abstained on the motion and a number of voices continued to call for the use of Canon B2 to authorize prayers that are seen as contentious, rather than using the commendation route of Canon B5 which does not require a two-thirds majority in all Houses. There are strong voices, too, which call for some kind of 'settlement' which would allow those who oppose the introduction of such prayers to walk separately. Key among these is the Church of England Evangelical Council (CEEC) which advocated for 'good protest':

> It is clear that the strength of feeling among parties with differing convictions indicates that we have to find a better way forward. In the event of the current proposals being pursued, CEEC will continue to advocate a settlement, without theological compromise, based on a permanent structural rearrangement resulting in visible differentiation.[120]

These 'good protests', which CEEC members were urged to adopt, included reviewing financial commitments to the dioceses and withdrawing from some participation in diocesan structures and events that may have signalled acquiescence to the development of the *PLF*. The shape of such a settlement was to be without 'theological compromise' and 'will have to be of a different order to the concept of extended episcopal oversight and the five guiding principles, because the current proposals involve a primary salvation issue: they are not adiaphora'.[121] The question of whether sexuality is a first-order salvation issue is contested within the Church, though conservative evangelicals and some catholics fervently believe that it is.[122]

Following the February debate three Working Groups of Bishops 'assisted by a group of advisers drawn from across the Church, both lay and ordained,' were set up to draft new Pastoral Guidance to replace the 1991 *Issues in Human Sexuality*; to further refine the texts of the *Prayers of Love and Faith*; and to provide Pastoral Reassurance for clergy to ensure freedom of conscience.[123] It is unclear what happened next for neither the Pastoral Guidance nor the amended prayers were ready for the July 2023 Synod. A paper providing an update to General Synod (GS 2303) reported back on the work of the groups, noting that although each contained members of the LGBTIQ+ 'community', representation of lay members was low.[124] There is a link on the LLF website to the composition of the groups.[125] Of particular note was the news that the House and College of Bishops were now considering the use of Canon B4.2 (rather than Canon B5) as a route for the introduction of the *PLF* since approval by the Archbishops might provide more legal protection for those ministers who chose to use the prayers.[126]

Cock-up or Conspiracy?

On 10 July 2023 General Synod heard an update on the Living in Love and Faith process. There were presentations from Philip Mounstephen and Sarah Mullally, a panel discussion from members of the Steering Group (which coordinated the work of the Implementation Groups), and a session of questions from Synod members.[127] Announcing that theological, scriptural and ecclesiological consensus is not the desired telos, Bishop Sarah suggested a potential agnosticism developing among the Bishops:

> There may be times when we need to suspend judgement in order to suspend hostilities. We may need to reimagine what it means to be fellow seekers of God's truth in God's Church. To reimagine what disagreement and uncertainty is in the Church – what it signifies and what God is calling us to.[128]

This was a moment when the Church appeared to be approaching uncertainty and failure as a tenable outcome; a reimagination of conversations as dissonance, the willing inhabiting of an unsafe space.

The update was again facilitated by Geoffrey Tattersall who, in conclusion, thanked Synod for a 'lovely tone' for questions and answers. Since it was not official business it was not livestreamed and there was no response from Synod to enquiries on why this was or when, and if, it might be available. The recording appeared on YouTube two days later. There was no suggestion that the proceedings had been deliberately withheld from the public, but it was, perhaps, a little inept of Synod not to realize that this item of business might be of more interest to the 'ordinary churchgoer' than most. Despite the 'lovely tone' there were questions that expressed discontent, even frustration, with the process. Both Ian Paul and Jayne Ozanne – coming from opposing sides of the debate – voiced their disappointment and irritation over the conduct of the planning and of the debates. Paul lamented the 'massive trust deficit' which he noted as coming from all sides and which resulted from a power play by the Bishops in continuing to meet in secret and to bypass the Synod through commendation by the Archbishops.[129] Ozanne expressed herself 'quite tired' of discussions that had being going on for far longer than the five years of the LLF process and which still resulted in a panel of eight straight people talking about LGBT lives.[130] This weariness was echoed by the Bishop of Dover, Rose Hudson-Wilkin, who found the debate 'painful listening'. All our children and grandchildren are having sex, most couples coming to get married are having sex, she declared, a bold speech to a chamber that is usually staid.[131] A little later in the questions session Miranda Threlfall-Holmes spoke of the joy of sex exemplified in scripture in the Song of Songs. In another intrepid question, she asked if the sex she had with her husband before marriage was entirely sinful, while the sex she had with him after was entirely holy. With this virtue ethics approach to the PLF process Threlfall-Holmes hoped that the forthcoming Pastoral Guidance would provide guiding principles rather than lists of rules.[132] Unsurprisingly both women received pushback. Stephen Hofmeyr, following Hudson-Wilkin, observed that his 37-year-old triplets would not agree with her that everyone was having sex and Richard Denno accused Threlfall-Holmes of false teaching, asserting that her views are outside mainstream Christian thought.

One theme that recurred from the February debate was the purported lack of theological reflection and biblical exegesis underpinning both the prayers and the work on pastoral principles. Ian Paul had urged Bishop Sarah to demonstrate that the theological work had been done and to 'show your workings out',[133] and here several voices begged the Bishops to produce an agreed, scriptural foundation to support the theology that lies behind the *PLF*.[134] Helen King, who has been involved in LLF as an historian, responded cordially, but with a hint of exasperation, that the *LLF* resources are extensive, that they had included both a theological and a biblical group, and that claiming 'we need more work does look horribly like delaying tactics'.[135] Two letters – one issued before the July Synod met, and one afterwards – revealed the division between those who resisted the process and those who supported it. The first letter, marked 'Private and Confidential', signed by conservatives from both catholic and evangelical wings of the Church of England,[136] opposed the proposed routes of Canon B5 or Canon B4.2, calling them 'unlawful, unconstitutional and illegitimate'. The writers argued that the process needs more time for 'due consideration' and that this 'can be done fast or it can be done well'.[137] The second letter, in response to this, was written as 'a Public Letter on behalf of Inclusive Organizations'.[138] The writers understood the recommendation to adopt Canon B2 as 'the growing campaign by some leaders and bishops in the Church of England to delay and obstruct the progress of the Living in Love & Faith journey'. They argued that this resistance arises from and was evident in the advice given by some conservative groups (such as the Church of England Evangelical Council) not to engage with the LLF process or resources. This refusal has meant that, without any experience of the process, some individuals and churches viewed the draft proposals as rushed, while those who have been involved saw them as 'the fruit of decades of debate and six years of intense work'.

Where Do We Go From Here?

It was not at all clear from the July presentation what the next steps were to be and the uncertainty about the processes continued in blog responses.[139] I have written much about power, authority and privilege – whether unacknowledged or overt – being in the hands of the House of Bishops and those whom the bishops choose to create agendas, write reports, draft guidelines and commission prayers. For some members of Synod, the bishops working secretly, or at least opaquely, undermined confidence in the process. Yet, as the signatories to the 'inclusive letter' cited above observed, many initiatives, such as the publication of *Issues in Human Sexuality*, the acceptance of civilly partnered clergy only if they promised sexual abstinence, and the decision not to ordain or license those in same-sex marriages, were all decisions of the House of Bishops. It is, therefore, 'quite legitimate for the House to revisit them according to its own processes'. I would add that, although all these initiatives could be regarded as controversial, none was criticized at the time by the conservative wing of the Church for being an illegitimate use of power.

I want to argue here that, although I have reservations about the Bishops' transparency, they were, in this instance, acting on behalf of Synod and in accordance with the Living in Love and Faith processes. This does not mean that LLF was unimpeachable. Far from it. As I demonstrated in the Introduction, the composition of groups and the exercises of authority were flawed in terms of representation and unacknowledged power. But the process did produce a huge suite of resources from various theological perspectives and a realization, perhaps, that consensus was neither achievable nor desirable. Hence the desire of the Bishops 'to inhabit a generous theological, ecclesial and pastoral space'.[140] There is here a tentative hope that this is a liminal space where the failure to agree or harmonize is recognized as an ecclesial possibility. Furthermore, some of the LLF processes, though not exactly from the bottom up, since the 'bottom' was never the designer of these initiatives, did, at least, consult the grassroots and appear to have listened to these voices. Churchgoers who took part in the *LLF* course were invited to give feedback and many did so through an online questionnaire. As David Runcorn observed:

> Around 6400 responded through the questionnaire – a highly significant level of response (for comparison, professional polling companies normally use a base of 1000 people to accurately represent the views of thousands or millions, or up to 2500 when seeking further accuracy).[141]

The results, published in September 2022, showed that most respondents wanted the Church to offer same-sex marriage, or blessings for same-sex partnerships; that they wanted churches to be more welcoming; and that the Church should hold together, encompassing a diversity of views.[142] The respondents also looked to the Bishops to give 'clear, bold leadership'. In line with the churchgoing demographic most respondents were heterosexual, married and over 45. It is significant that this cohort, usually regarded as socially conservative, were clearly in favour of welcome and inclusion. There was also a desire for that 'generous theological, ecclesial and pastoral' space which would enable those with different views to hold together.[143] Eleven days after David Runcorn published this welcoming piece, Andrew Goddard responded with a blog disagreeing with his interpretation of the LLF process.[144]

The thousands of words produced by the LLF process and proceeding from these two debates in Synod – and proliferating as I write – can be added to the streams of words engendered by *Pilling* and the Shared Conversations. Some of this is theological and anthropological reflection which may enhance the Church's understanding of its doctrines on marriage and sexuality. But much is theological and ecclesial positioning, the desire to draw boundaries and to signal to one's tribe where these boundaries lie. One of the difficulties with boundary markers is that they obstruct the sharing of generous ecclesial space. Furthermore, the very act of putting down a doctrinal marker inhibits the exploration of failure as a liberative move: the undoing of hegemonic constructs of theological progress and success in the recognition of uncertainty and diversity. Christians speak often of self-sacrifice, but the selves we are least willing to surrender are those invested in the concept of 'proper knowledge' and the convention of a discourse that will lead either to consensus or to the victory of the successful interpretation.

The Synod vote in February was, nevertheless, decisive; 57 per cent voted in favour of the amended motion and it is this decision by Synod which compelled the Bishops to continue the work on the prayers and on guidance. Indeed, Synod may be said to have instigated this process through their refusal to 'Take Note' in February 2017 of the Bishops' report that prompted the Archbishop of Canterbury to promise work towards 'a radical new Christian inclusion in the Church'.[145] Both Synod and the consultation following LLF have urged the Bishops to undertake this work and, although it can hardly claim to be the labour of marginalized voices, it is a response, albeit partial and provisional, to those voices own experiences of pain, exclusion and damage. It is significant that the Bishops now want to 'joyfully affirm' those in committed same-sex relationships.

The recognition of this generous space as a place of uncertainty and contention is tentatively hopeful. It has the potential to be an interim where failure is, if not welcomed, at least accepted as a pre-eschatological 'art', the skill of holding the irreconcilable and the uncertain in an unresolved, maybe unresolvable, state. This supple approach to the theology of marriage and sexuality could then inform a church polity where failure could be seen as the art of the conditional, the provisional, the unfulfilled 'not yet'. I have amplified some of the voices involved in this process in this chapter; they were invited to speak and so their responses are, in some sense, 'official'. In the following chapter on some 'unauthorized' responses to *Pilling*, I will critically reflect on how – and if – the unchosen and the unelected, or even the deliberately dumb,[146] had access to the discourse on this process, and I will ask whether these voices in any way queered either the debate or the institutional processes that generated it.

Notes

1 The Archbishops' Council, *Report of the House of Bishops Working Group on Human Sexuality* (London: Church House Publishing, 2013), 105.
2 J. Halberstam, *The Queer Art of Failure* (Durham, NC: Duke University Press, 2011).
3 *Pilling*, 105.
4 Lauren Berlant and Lee Edelman, *Sex, or the Unbearable* (Durham, NC: Duke University Press, 2014).
5 Lauren Berlant and Lee Edelman, *Sex, or the Unbearable*, 64.
6 Lauren Berlant and Lee Edelman, *Sex, or the Unbearable*, ix-x, emphasis original.
7 *Pilling*, 104–105.
8 'This report on Communion and Disagreement was written by the Faith and Order Commission to support the process of shared conversations in the Church of England, including the participation of Synod members in July 2016, and the discussion and discernment that will continue beyond it.' William Nye, *General Synod (GS Misc 1139). Communion and Disagreement: A Report from the Faith and Order Commission* (Church of England, June 2016), https://www.churchofengland.org/sites/default/files/2017-10/communion_and_disagreement_faoc_report_gs_misc_1139.pdf (accessed 15.2.24).
9 Lauren Berlant and Lee Edelman, *Sex, or the Unbearable*, ix–x.
10 The House of Bishops and the Houses of Clergy and Laity at General Synod form the 'government' of the Church of England; see 'Introduction', n. 12.
11 The Church of England, 'Shared Conversations Archive', https://www.churchofengland.org/about/leadership-and-governance/general-synod/bishops/shared-conversations-archive#na (accessed 15.2.24).
12 This was before the consecration of women to the episcopate in the Church of England; however, some senior women attended the Conversations.
13 These three protocols seek to create a safe and inclusive space; to promote active listening and sensitivity to the views of others, respecting their agency; and to

share knowledge and understanding gained but without attribution to specific participants. The Church of England, 'Shared Conversations Archive'.

14 Peter Owen, 'College of Bishops – Shared Conversations', Thinking Anglicans, 17 September 2014, https://www.thinkinganglicans.org.uk/6729-2/ (accessed 15.2.24). The press release seems to have disappeared from the Church of England website.

15 *Pilling*, 106.

16 'Grace and Disagreement 1 – thinking through the process', 4, in The Church of England, 'Shared Conversations Archive', https://www.churchofengland.org/about/leadership-and-governance/general-synod/bishops/shared-conversations-archive#na (accessed 15.2.24).

17 Martin Davie, 'Grace and Disagreement, Shared Conversations on Scripture, Mission and Human Sexuality' (London: CEEC, 2015), http://www.ceec.info/grace-and-disagreement-martin-davie.html (link no longer available). See also the discussion on p. 110.

18 Martin Davie, 'Grace and Disagreement 2'.

19 Martin Davie, 'Grace and Disagreement'.

20 Some have since disappeared from the internet.

21 Simon Kershaw, 'About Thinking Anglicans', 9 August 2003: 'Thinking Anglicans is a website for thoughtful contributions to the proclamation of the gospel message. Here writers reflect on what it means to be a Christian, particularly in Britain today. Thinking Anglicans will actively report news, events and documents that affect church people, and will comment on them from a liberal Christian perspective', https://www.thinkinganglicans.org.uk/65-2 (accessed 15.2.24). Evangelical Group of the General Synod (EGGS): 'The object of EGGS is to promote the witness of Evangelicals in the life, policy and work of the Synods of the Church of England ... Membership is open to any member of the General Synod who assent to the EGGS Basis of Faith', http://www.eggscofe.org.uk/about.html (accessed 15.2.24).

22 The Church of England, 'Shared Conversations archive', https://www.churchofengland.org/about/leadership-and-governance/general-synod/bishops/shared-conversations-archive (accessed 15.2.24).

23 'Anglican Mainstream began in 2004 as part of a united international response of Anglicans from different backgrounds (Reformed, Charismatic and Catholic) to re-state and support traditional understandings of marriage, the family and human sexuality in the face of erosion of these values in church and society', https://anglican-mainstream.org/anglican-mainstream-who-we-are/ (accessed 15.2.24).

24 Andrew Symes, 'Shared Conversations: A snapshot of the C of E, and a pointer to the future?', Anglican Mainstream, 8 March 2016, https://anglicanmainstream.org/shared-conversations-a-snapshot-of-the-c-of-e-and-a-pointer-to-the-future/ (accessed 15.2.24).

25 Ed Shaw, 'Shared Conversations' (EGGS) n.d., http://www.eggscofe.org.uk/uploads/5/5/6/3/5563632/ed_shaw_shared_conversations_eggs_article_v2.pdf (accessed 15.2.24).

26 Ed Shaw, 'Shared Conversations'.

27 Erika Baker, 'The Shared Conversations: A Personal Reflection', *LGBTI Anglican Coalition*, 3 May 2015, https://www.lgbtianglican.org.uk/2015/05/02/accounts-of-conversations-in-sw/ (accessed 15.2.24).

28 Erika Baker, 'Shared Conversations'.

29 Ed Shaw, 'Shared Conversations'.

30 Andrew Symes, 'Shared Conversations'.

31 Andrew Symes, 'Shared Conversations'.

32 Andrew Symes, 'Shared Conversations'.

33 Andrew Symes, 'Shared Conversations'.
34 Andrew Symes, 'Shared Conversations'.
35 Andrew Symes, 'Shared Conversations'.
36 John Dunnett, 'Shared Conversations – January 2016 – A Personal Reflection'. Previously online at https://www.eggscofe.org.uk/.
37 John Dunnett, 'Shared Conversations – January 2016 – A Personal Reflection'.
38 Keith Sinclair, 'A Conversation Hardly Begun: Reflections on the Shared Conversations, September 2015', EGGS, http://www.eggscofe.org.uk/uploads/5/5/6/3/5563632/shared_conversations_-_a_conversation_hardly_begun_-_keith_sinclair.pdf (accessed 15.2.24).
39 Andrew Atwood, 'Shared Conversations', previously online at https://www.eggscofe.org.uk.
40 Andrew Atwood, 'Shared Conversations'.
41 Ed Shaw, 'Shared Conversations'.
42 Jeremy Pemberton, 'Shared Conversations – Talking in Circles', *From the Choir Stalls*, 14 May 2015, https://jeremypemberton.wordpress.com/2015/05/14/shared-conversations-talking-in-circles/ (accessed 15.2.24).
43 Jeremy Pemberton, 'Shared Conversations – Talking in Circles'.
44 Ruth Wilde, 'Shared Conversations', 11–13 May 2015. https://www.lgbtianglican.org.uk/2015/05/15/east-midlands-conversations/ (accessed 15.2.24).
45 John McGinley said, 'I returned with great concern that the majority of the participants had lost any clear understanding of the Bible as authoritative in their lives ... This confirmed that we are already two churches, one which sees the Bible as a helpful collection of writings from which to draw inspiration but which can be used to say whatever we want it to, or simply be ignored. The other seeks to submit to Scripture as we interpret it and apply it to our lives and trust in its goodness as God's word to us, even when it is painful and challenging', cited in Ian Paul, 'What is at Stake for the Church and Same-Sex Marriage?', *Fulcrum*, 9 July 2015, https://www.fulcrum-anglican.org.uk/articles/what-is-at-stake-for-the-church-and-same-sex-marriage (accessed 15.2.24).
46 Ian Paul, 'What is at Stake for the Church and Same-Sex Marriage?' Paul expresses concern that 'this lack of safety' has encroached into the 'Shared Conversations'.
47 David Nixon, 'Ecclesial Speed Dating? A Theological Reflection on One Shared Conversation', *The Expository Times*, 127, no. 8, 2016, 390–393, 391–393, https://journals.sagepub.com/doi/abs/10.1177/0014524615592804 (accessed 15.2.24).
48 David Nixon, 'Ecclesial Speed Dating?'
49 David Nixon, 'Ecclesial Speed Dating?'
50 David Nixon, 'Ecclesial Speed Dating?'; and Erika Baker, 'The Shared Conversations'.
51 Elizabeth Stuart, *Gay and Lesbian Theologies: Repetitions with Critical Difference* (Aldershot: Ashgate, 2003).
52 David Nixon, 'Ecclesial Speed Dating?', 391.
53 David Nixon, 'Ecclesial Speed Dating?', 392.
54 Andrew Symes, 'Shared Conversations'.
55 David Nixon, 'Ecclesial Speed Dating?', 393.
56 David Nixon, 'Ecclesial Speed Dating?', 392
57 The programme is available at https://www.churchofengland.org/sites/default/files/2017-12/participants_programme-july2016.pdf (accessed 15.2.24).
58 George Conger, 'General Synod Shared Sex Conversations Place Unity Above Truth, Critics Claim', *Anglican Ink*, 20 July 2016, http://anglican.ink/2016/07/20/

general-synod-shared-sex-conversations-place-unity-above-truth-critics-charge/ (accessed 15.2.24).

59 Ian Paul, 'Synod's Shared Conversations', Psephizo, 13 July 2016, https://www.psephizo.com/sexuality-2/synods-shared-conversations/ (accessed 15.2.24).

60 David Bennett, 'David', *Living Out,* 29 October 2020, https://www.livingout.org/stories/david (accessed 15.2.24).

61 David Bennett, 'The Bishops' Decision: My Reflection on General Synod and Participating in Shared Conversations', *Daily Roll – Reflections*, 29 January 2017, https://illuminaet.wordpress.com/2017/01/27/the-bishops-decision-my-reflection-on-general-synod-and-participating-in-shared-conversations/ (accessed 15.2.24).

62 J. Halberstam, *The Queer Art of Failure*, 88.

63 J. Halberstam, *The Queer Art of Failure*, 88.

64 The House of Bishops, 'Marriage and Same-Sex Relationships after the Shared Conversations' (Church House, GS 2055, November 2016), http://www.tgdr.co.uk/documents/229P-GS2055.pdf (accessed 15.2.24).

65 Church of England, Canon B 30 Of Holy Matrimony: 'The Church of England affirms, according to the Lord's teaching, that marriage is in its nature a union permanent and lifelong, for better for worse, till death do them part, of one man with one woman, to the exclusion of all others on either side, for the procreation and nurture of children, for the hallowing and right direction of the natural instincts and affections, and for the mutual society, help and comfort which the one ought to have of the other, both in prosperity and adversity', https://www.churchofengland.org/about/leadership-and-governance/legal-services/canons-church-england/section-b (accessed 15.2.24).

66 The House of Bishops, 'Marriage and Same-Sex Relationships after the Shared Conversations', emphasis added.

67 The House of Bishops, 'Marriage and Same-Sex Relationships after the Shared Conversations', emphasis added.

68 The expression same-sex attracted is primarily used by those who understand themselves as having a homosexual orientation but seek not to identify themselves as gay, and who undertake the discipline of sexual abstinence in response to what they see as the traditional teaching of the Church. Like earlier reports, this one encompasses only lesbian and gay 'identities'; there is no reflection on bi, trans or intersex people.

69 The House of Bishops, 'Marriage and Same-Sex Relationships after the Shared Conversations'.

70 The House of Bishops, 'Marriage and Same-Sex Relationships after the Shared Conversations'.

71 The House of Bishops, 'Marriage and Same-Sex Relationships after the Shared Conversations'.

72 The House of Bishops, 'Marriage and Same-Sex Relationships after the Shared Conversations'.

73 Martin Davie, 'A response to GS 2055: "Marriage and Same Sex Relationships after the Shared Conversations"', Reflections of an Anglican Theologian, 1 February 2017, https://mbarrattdavie.wordpress.com/2017/02/01/a-response-to-gs-2055-marriage-and-same-sex-relationships-after-the-shared-conversations/ (accessed 15.2.24).

74 Martin Davie, 'A response to GS 2055'.

75 Martin Davie, 'A response to GS 2055'.

76 In September 2015 a Lay Reader, Jeremy Timm, had his licence withdrawn after converting his civil partnership to marriage, *BBC News*, 29 September 2015, https://www.bbc.co.uk/news/uk-england-humber-34307063 (accessed 15.2.24).

77 Miranda Threlfall-Holmes, 'Sex and the Bishops', 29 January 2017, http://mirandathrelfallholmes.blogspot.com/2017/01/sex-and-bishops.html (accessed 15.2.24).

78 Miranda Threlfall-Holmes, 'Sex and the Bishops'.

79 *Fulcrum* describes itself as 'a network of evangelical Anglicans, seeking to renew the centre of the evangelical tradition and the centre of Anglicanism, acting as a point of balance within the Church of England', https://www.fulcrum-anglican.org.uk/about/ (accessed 15.2.24).

80 'The role of the Anglican Consultative Council (ACC) is to facilitate the co-operative work of the churches of the Anglican Communion, exchange information between the provinces and churches, and help to co-ordinate common action', https://www.anglicancommunion.org/structures/instruments-of-communion/acc.aspx (accessed 15.2.24).

81 Peter Owen, 'Marriage and Same-Sex Relationships After the Shared Conversations – A Report from the House of Bishops: General Synod Press Conference, 27 January 2017: Statement by the Bishop of Norwich', Thinking Anglicans, 27 January 2017, https://www.thinkinganglicans.org.uk/7440-2/ (accessed 15.2.24).

82 Callum May, 'Church of England "not listening" to Gay Christians say Retired Church of England Bishops', *BBC News*, 12 February 2017, https://www.bbc.co.uk/news/uk-38940915 (accessed 15.2.24).

83 'LGCM calls on members of General Synod not to "take note"', http://www.onebodyonefaith.org.uk/news/not-take-note/ (link no longer available).

84 'LGCM calls on members of General Synod not to "take note"'.

85 Jeremy Pemberton, 'Church of England Synod – GS2055 Case Studies', http://www.onebodyonefaith.org.uk/news/church-of-england-synod-gs2055-case-studies/ (accessed 15.2.24).

86 Patrick Sawyer and Olivia Rudgard, 'Anglicans Braced for New Clashes Over Gay Marriage in Church', *The Telegraph*, 11 February 2017, https://www.telegraph.co.uk/news/2017/02/11/anglicans-braced-new-clashes-gay-marriage-church/ (accessed 15.2.24).

87 'General Synod – Take Note Debate on GS2055', 15 February 2017, (YouTube), Graham James speaks at 6.20, https://www.youtube.com/watch?v=Oyj5xfSCzMY. (accessed 15.2.24).

88 They included Simon Butler, Andrew Foreshew-Cain, Giles Goddard, Jayne Ozanne, Lucy Gorman and Andrew Nunn, all prominent in LGBTIQ+ campaigns.

89 Zachary Guiliano, 'No Winners', The Living Church: Serving the One Body of Christ, 15 February 2017, https://livingchurch.org/2017/02/15/no-winners/ (accessed 15.2.24). 'General Synod – Take Note Debate on GS2055', 15 February 2017, (YouTube), Leafe speaks at 42.24, https://www.youtube.com/watch?v=Oyj5xfSCzMY (accessed 15.2.24).

90 'General Synod – Take Note Debate on GS2055', 15 February 2017 (YouTube), Allberry speaks at 1.07.27, https://www.youtube.com/watch?v=Oyj5xfSCzMY. (accessed 15.2.24).

91 'Church of England Votes Against Same Sex Marriage Report', *BBC News*, https://www.bbc.co.uk/news/uk-38982013 (accessed 15.2.24).

92 'General Synod – Take Note Debate on GS2055', 15 February 2017 (YouTube), Welby speaks at 1.59.17, https://www.youtube.com/watch?v=Oyj5xfSCzMY (accessed 15.2.24).

93 The resulting *Living in Love and Faith* resources do not constitute a 'teaching document', but that's another story.

94 'General Synod – Take Note Debate on GS2055', 15 February 2017 (YouTube), Welby speaks at 1.59.17, https://www.youtube.com/watch?v=Oyj5xfSCzMY (accessed 15.2.24).

95 Peter Owen, 'Debate on the Bishops' report – take note motion defeated', Thinking Anglicans, 15 February 2017, https://www.thinkinganglicans.org.uk/7469-2 (accessed 15.2.24).

96 'Letter from the Archbishops of Canterbury and York following General Synod, 16 February 2017', https://www.churchofengland.org/more/media-centre/news/letter-archbishops-canterbury-and-york-following-general-synod (accessed 15.2.24).

97 *Living in Love and Faith: Christian Teaching and Learning about Identity, Sexuality, Relationships and Marriage*, https://www.churchofengland.org/resources/living-love-and-faith (accessed 15.2.24).

98 Ian Paul, 'On Synod, Sexuality, and not Taking Note', Psephizo, 16 February 2017, https://www.psephizo.com/sexuality-2/on-synod-sexuality-and-not-taking-note/ (accessed 15.2.24).

99 Tracey Byrne, cited in 'Press Release, Archbishops: Bold Proposal for Radical Inclusion', *LGBTI Mission*, 19 February 2017, https://lgbtimission.org.uk/2017/02/19/press-release-archbishops-bold-proposal-for-radical-inclusion/ (accessed 15.2.24).

100 See J. Halberstam, *The Queer Art of Failure*, 88–89.

101 Lauren Berlant and Lee Edelman, *Sex, or the Unbearable*, ix.

102 Lauren Berlant and Lee Edelman, *Sex, or the Unbearable*, x, 64.

103 J. Halberstam, *The Queer Art of Failure*, 88.

104 General Synod, 'Update to General Synod of the Implementation Work for Living in Love and Faith' (GS 2303), 4, https://www.churchofengland.org/sites/default/files/2023-06/gs-2303-living-in-love-and-faith-update.pdf (accessed 15.2.24).

105 Church of England, *Prayers of Love and Faith*, https://www.churchofengland.org/sites/default/files/2023-01///final-draft-prayers-of-love-and-faith.pdf (accessed 15.2.24).

106 The Church of England, *Living in Love and Faith: A Response from the Bishops of the Church of England about Identity, Sexuality, Relationships and Marriage*, 3, https://www.churchofengland.org/sites/default/files/2023-01/final-bishops-response-to-llf-20-jan-23.pdf (accessed 15.2.24).

107 Church of England, 'Bishops' Advisory Panel on Selection for Training for Ordained Ministry', https://www.google.com/url?sa=t&rct=j&q=&esrc=s&source=web&cd=&ved=2ahUKEwjrt-CKxe2BAxVaivoHHWzWAMIQFnoECBoQAQ&url=https%3A%2F%2Fwww.churchofengland.org%2Fmedia%2F6249&usg=AOvVaw3CbrbZxbPfujqNOjMvaUXk&opi=89978449 (accessed 15.2.24).

108 *Living in Love and Faith*, 6–7.

109 The Act for Marriages in England 1836 introduced civil marriage as well as allowing other religious premises, such as Roman Catholic churches, to be registered legally in their own buildings.

110 *Living in Love and Faith*, 7.

111 Marriage (Same Sex Couples) Act 2013, https://www.legislation.gov.uk/ukpga/2013/30/contents/enacted/data.htm (accessed 15.2.24).

112 General Synod, *Prayers of Love and Faith: A Note from the Legal Office*, GS Misc 1339, 2.

113 *A Comment on GS Misc 1339*. Of the authors five are barristers and one is a retired solicitor. They have consulted widely, they write, with experts in the field of family and ecclesiastical law and beyond.

114 For those interested in the options available under various Canons and the author's views on the advantages of Canon B2, Andrew Goddard has written three articles published on the Psephizo blog and on his own website, Andrew Goddard, https://www.psephizo.com/sexuality-2/prayers-process-and-powers-b2-or-

not-b2-that-is-the-question-part-1/, https://www.theologyethics.com/179-2/ (accessed 15.2.24).

115 HH Peter Collier KC, 'Marriage and/or Holy Matrimony', *Law and Religion UK*, 28 June 2023, https://lawandreligionuk.com/2023/07/06/marriage-and-or-holy-matrimony/ (accessed 15.2.24).

116 'that … 1856 statute that barred any religious ceremony in a civil wedding did make provision for an additional subsequent religious ceremony. The same s.12 that barred religion in the register office provided that after a couple have been married in a civil ceremony, they could produce their wedding certificate to the minister of their church and ask the minister of their church to celebrate the marriage service of their church in church? [*sic*] That is still the position in s.46 of the Marriage Act 1949 which repeats that same provision.' HH Peter Collier KC, 'Marriage and/or Holy Matrimony', *Law and Religion UK*, https://lawandreligionuk.com/2023/07/06/marriage-and-or-holy-matrimony/ (accessed 15.2.24).

117 General Synod, 8 and 9 February 2023, https://www.youtube.com/watch?v=n_gcI5hYyc4 (accessed 15.2.24); https://www.youtube.com/watch?v=A3mSp969mJY (accessed 15.2.24).

118 General Synod, February 2023, https://www.youtube.com/watch?v=A3mSp969mJY, 1.21.14 (accessed 15.2.24).

119 House of Bishops: For 36, Against 4, Abstentions 2. House of Clergy: For 111, Against 85, Abstentions 3. House of Laity: For 103, Against 92, Abstentions 5.

120 From a suite of resources on the CEEC website setting out their views of the problems with the February Synod decisions and on what a settlement might entail, https://ceec.info/keepingfaith/ (accessed 15.2.24).

121 https://ceec.info/wp-content/uploads/2023/03/What-do-we-need-ver-21-march-2023.pdf (accessed 15.2.24).

122 For an extensive summary of why sexuality has become a first-order issue for evangelical members of the CofE, see Mark Vasey Saunders, *Defusing the Sexuality Debate: The Anglican Evangelical Culture War* (London: SCM Press, 2023).

123 The Church of England, 'Bishops Agree Key Areas for Further Work Implementing Living in Love and Faith', 1 May 2023, https://www.churchofengland.org/media-and-news/press-releases/bishops-agree-key-areas-further-work-implementing-living-love-and (accessed 15.2.24).

124 The General Synod of the Church of England, *Update to General Synod of the Implementation Work for Living in Love and Faith*, The Archbishops' Council 2023, https://www.churchofengland.org/sites/default/files/2023-06/gs-2303-living-in-love-and-faith-update.pdf (accessed 15.2.24).

125 Church of England, 'Update from Living in Love and Faith Implementation Working Groups', 2 May 2023, https://www.churchofengland.org/media-and-news/press-releases/update-living-love-and-faith-implementation-working-groups (accessed 15.2.24).

126 Canon B4.2. The Archbishops may approve forms of service for use in any cathedral or church or elsewhere in the provinces of Canterbury and York on occasions for which no provision is made in the Book of Common Prayer, or by the General Synod under Canon B 2, or by the Convocations under this Canon, being forms of service which in both words and order are in their opinion reverent and seemly and are neither contrary to, nor indicative of any departure from, the doctrine of the Church of England in any essential matter.

127 General Synod, 12 July 2023, https://www.youtube.com/watch?v=CamIXZ_gL4o&t=4121s (accessed 15.2.24).

128 Cited in 'Oh, Mr Porter', *Anglican Futures*, 14 September 2023, https://www.

anglicanfutures.org/post/oh-mr-porter (accessed 15.2.24). A blog on David Porter, The Archbishop of Canterbury's Strategy Advisor as Eminence Grise to the Shared Conversations and Living in Love and Faith process.

129 Ian Paul, https://www.youtube.com/watch?v=CamIXZ_gL40&t=4121s, 1.08 (accessed 15.2.24).

130 Jayne Ozanne, https://www.youtube.com/watch?v=CamIXZ_gL40&t=4121s, 1.08. 1.30.49 (accessed 15.2.24).

131 Rose Hudson-Wilkin, https://www.youtube.com/watch?v=CamIXZ_gL40&t=4121s, 1.08. 2.05 (accessed 15.2.24).

132 Miranda Threlfall Holmes, https://www.youtube.com/watch?v=CamIXZ_gL40&t=4121s, 1.08. 2.39 (accessed 15.2.24).

133 Ian Paul, https://www.youtube.com/watch?v=CamIXZ_gL40&t=4121s, 1.08 (accessed 15.2.24).

134 Cf. John Laverton, https://www.youtube.com/watch?v=CamIXZ_gL40&t=4121s, 1.08.2.27 (accessed 15.2.24).

135 Helen King, https://www.youtube.com/watch?v=CamIXZ_gL40&t=4121s, 1.08.2.47 (accessed 15.2.24).

136 Though the Chairman of the Prayer Book Society explained later that he was signing in a personal capacity and not on behalf of the Society.

137 Cited in Thinking Anglicans, https://www.thinkinganglicans.org.uk/wp-content/uploads/2023/07/Letter.pdf (accessed 15.2.24).

138 *Inclusive Evangelicals*, https://www.inclusiveevangelicals.com/post/public-letter-on-llf-process (accessed 15.2.24).

139 Cf. Helen King's blog, Shared Conversations, https://shared-conversations.com/ (accessed 15.2.24).

140 General Synod, 'Update to General Synod of the Implementation Work for Living in Love and Faith' (GS 2303), 4, https://www.churchofengland.org/sites/default/files/2023-06/gs-2303-living-in-love-and-faith-update.pdf (accessed 15.2.24).

141 David Runcorn, 'General Synod, LLF and the mind of the church', *Inclusive Evangelicals*, 24 July 2023, https://www.inclusiveevangelicals.com/post/general-synod-llf-and-the-mind-of-the-church (accessed 15.2.24).

142 'Living in Love and Faith Consultation results now published', *Equal: The Campaign for Equal Marriage in the Church of England*, 3 September 2022, https://cofe-equal-marriage.org.uk/llf-consultation-results-published/ (accessed 15.2.24).

143 Nic Tall, 'Living in Love and Faith: What the Church of England Really Thinks', *Equal: The Campaign for Equal Marriage in the Church of England*, 3 September 2022, https://cofe-equal-marriage.org.uk/llf-what-the-c-of-e-really-thinks/ (accessed 15.2.24).

144 Andrew Goddard, 'General Synod, LLF and the mind of the church: What is the evidence?', 4 August 2023, https://www.psephizo.com/sexuality-2/general-synod-llf-and-the-mind-of-the-church-what-is-the-evidence/ (accessed 15.2.24).

145 The Archbishop of Canterbury, Justin Welby, 15 February 2017, https://www.archbishopofcanterbury.org/statement-archbishop-canterbury-following-todays-general-synod (accessed 15.2.24).

146 I am aware that by using the word 'dumb' I may be criticized for employing ableist language. I choose it here to denote what James C. Scott called 'the weapons of the weak', as resistance to authority/authoritarianism. James C. Scott, *Weapons of the Weak: Everyday Forms of Peasant Resistance* (New Haven, CT: Yale University Press, 1987), 29.

3

The Unauthorized Afterlife of the *Pilling Report*

When, like Kathryn Tanner, we pay attention to the nature of theology as a cultural practice, we do not simply apply a sociological theory or anthropological method to a theological end. Rather, such interdisciplinarity actually changes how the processes of theological knowledge production work; it introduces new practices and norms, for example, new starting points and pathways, new goods and goals. When we speak of 'carnal theology,' then, we are talking as much about something shaped by bodily practices associated with ethnographic fieldwork as it is by the somewhat disembodied practices of textual analysis, typically prioritized in academic theological writing.[1]

Introduction

The discussion of the biblical record, on both sides of the dispute over the licitness of gay/queer sexually active relationships for Christians, has reached a stalemate. Arguing about the meaning and relevance of proof texts, or contesting the meanings of sex and sexuality and the concept of normativity in the metanarrative of scripture, has resulted in an impasse in which neither side is willing to concede ideological ground to the other and in which both tend to view their position as an ecclesiological imperative. As Linn Marie Tonstad writes:

> Both sides in Christian debates over sexuality often take similarly bankrupt forms. Opponents of the full participation of queer persons commonly resort to proof texting – tearing texts out of place, space, context, and history to deploy them as weapons, shutting down debate ... These debates produce exhaustion and boredom and have done little to advance thinking about sexuality or to deepen theological reflection.[2]

In the authorized conversations and reflections on homosexuality it was clear that entrenched positions endure despite the goals of disagreeing well and that neither (nor, indeed, any) 'side' was contemplating experiencing the liminal spaces of Holy Saturday, as articulated by Karen Bray, as a site of doubt and provisionality, as a queer resource for this theological bankruptcy.[3] Failure, it appears, is regarded as breakdown or defeat rather than as a potential resolution to 'the disembodied practices of textual analysis'.[4] Certainly, these 'disembodied practices' have been privileged in this discourse over the experiential and the discursive, which Wigg-Stevenson speaks of as 'carnal theology'.[5]

In the previous chapter I reviewed the 'authorized' afterlives of the *Pilling Report*; in this chapter I interrogate what I will call the 'unauthorized' afterlife of the report, the non-institutional responses by individuals and groups in the virtual world. I will do this by focusing on discussions on a particular blog – in itself a snapshot of unofficial reactions – and asking whether blogs are more porous or democratic spaces that are able to accommodate the voices of the marginalized and those with little formal authority or power in the Church. Are these voices a 'queer archive' that can enact 'carnal theology'? Or are they still speaking from an ecclesially minded, educated elite, albeit a self-selected one, serving to perpetuate neoliberal notions of progress and productivity and valorizing solutionism? My survey of the response to some of the *Pilling* discussions will show that there is space for unofficial voices in the virtual world, but that they almost invariably employ 'the disembodied practices of textual analysis', as if the price of admission to the debate is playing by the habitual ecclesial and quasi-academic rules.

My aim is to take these snapshots of internet commentary at critical points in *Pilling*'s afterlife – after the publication of the report in November 2013, after the Shared Conversations (April 2015–March 2016), and after the 'Take Note' debate at Synod in February 2017 – and to look at these through the hermeneutical lenses of the report itself. I will ask if we know whether these are the concerns of the 'ordinary' churchgoer, or simply those of people who take an interest in these debates, either because they are themselves LGBTIQ+ or because they believe that changes in church teaching will irrevocably change the Church of England, for good or ill.

Despite some of the 'new media' platforms being decades old, there is very little research on digital ethnography, in the sense of the digital being the thing researched rather than the method by which some other ethnographic subject is studied. Sarah Pink et al., writing in *Digital Ethnography: Principles and Practice*, seem to blur the line between the digital as method and the digital as subject/object:

In digital ethnography, we are often in mediated contacts with participants rather than in direct presence ... we might be in conversation with people throughout their everyday lives. We might be watching what people do by digitally tracking them, or asking them to invite us into their social media practices. Listening may involve reading, or it might involve sensing and communicating in other ways. Ethnographic writing might be replaced by video, photography or blogging.[6]

Studies on queering digital ethnographic research, on observing how it might be non- or anti-normative, or how it might disrupt the hegemonic authority of conventional print media, appear to be elusive. There are queer studies of digital media, but these are specifically about queer identity and the experience of 'coming out' on social media, and not on the way social media discourse itself may have the potential to que(e)ry and to disrupt the dominion exercised by institutions such as the Church and the Academy.[7] This chapter, then, is an essay in digital ethnography, an attempt to study participants engaging in discussions on *Pilling* and sexuality on blogs and to ask whether these media invite a rupturing of hegemonic and authorized discourse or whether they replicate the processes of the sanctioned publications and conversations that *Pilling* initiated.

The Psephizo blog, with the strapline 'scholarship. serving. ministry', was launched in 2011 and is hosted and mainly written by Ian Paul. Paul is an independent theologian and biblical scholar who describes the purpose of his blog thus:

My aim is (in the main) to post my own, original research, observations and reflections, often relating to study, teaching or ministry I am engaged in.

My blog is called *Psephizo*, using the Greek verb meaning 'to calculate', 'work out' or 'reckon'. The word only occurs twice in the New Testament, once in Luke 14.28 in his version of Jesus' warning to reckon the cost of discipleship before embarking on it, and in Rev 13.18 ... perhaps the most notorious verse in the Bible! It is related to the word *psephos* meaning 'pebble', which would have been used to do such calculations, and also occurs only in Luke and Revelation.[8]

Ian Paul is interested mainly in ecclesiology, doctrine and biblical hermeneutics; his blogs on sexuality and the Church always attract the most comments. Here, I have to declare an interest since I have engaged in debate on Psephizo, sometimes to pursue an interesting hermeneutical argument and at others to engage with those with whom I disagree. In *Ethnographic Theology*, Natalie Wigg-Stevenson argues that those of us using cultural theory and ethnographic methods to engage lived Christian practice should, as we participate in this theological cartography, theorize carefully the relationship between ourselves and our fields of study. Lack of such reflexive self-awareness leads us to employ methods that are laden with unarticulated and unrecognized assumptions.[9]

Thus, I cannot pretend to be a dispassionate observer of these debates: no one who engages with them is, and, through engaging, the participant helps to alter and shape the contours and parameters of the debate itself. Who knows whether, without that particular observation or digression, the discussions might have taken a different turn? There is a particular risk in being a part of the research discussions one is analysing, of 'the "blurring of boundaries" between researcher & participant ... your own social media activity ... may be part of the dataset you are researching, which is potentially problematic'.[10] Onlookers have their own presuppositions about the matters being debated, even if minds might occasionally be changed by powerful argument or convincing evidence. Anecdotally, this seems very unlikely: social media engagement appears to polarize discussion and petrify opinion. 'Virtue signalling' (the indications to one's own tribe that one has orthodox or 'right on' views and beliefs) is one of the hazards of social media, although criticism of these gestures is deployed mostly by the self-identified right against those perceived as being on the left. All shades of opinion virtue signal and it is often no more than indicating to one's own tribe the existence of those holding similar – and thus 'virtuous' – views. This is an attempt to point towards a consensus, a majority or a significant minority of people who hold these 'commendable' views: a reassuring recognition of others who share the same worldview and a building of alliances.

Since blogs are such an amorphous, and ephemeral, mass of opinion, debate and controversy, I have chosen to focus on three suggestive moments in the post-*Pilling* debate and the resulting interactions on the chosen social media platforms. These are: the publication of the *Pilling Report*; the 'Shared Conversations' among General Synod members in July 2016; and the 'Take Note' debate at General Synod in February 2017. These appear to have been publicly significant events in the life of the report and its afterlife and so they may be taken to represent periods during which social media commentary might be at its most active and revealing. They have not been chosen to be representative of the debate nor as typical of the ways in which *Pilling* and its afterlife have been interrogated on social media: they are simply snapshots of the discussion at particular moments.

The *Pilling Report*

Psephizo

'*The* Pilling Report: *divisive and damaging?*'

Following the *Pilling Report*'s publication on 28 November 2013, Ian Paul published two blog posts: 'The *Pilling Report*: divisive and damaging?' (2 December 2013), and 'The Bible, *Pilling* and Changing One's Mind' (7 February 2014). In his first blog post, published five days after the publication of the report itself, Paul comments that

> a measure of its success is that (from what I can glean of the blogosphere) people on both sides are equally offended ... On one side, there is the desire for a more serious engagement with Scripture and biblical theology, which many felt was in fact present in *Some Issues in Human Sexuality* in 2003 – how little we have travelled in 10 years! On the other, there is a desire for either the experience of the 'LGBT' community, or at the very least sociological and psychological understandings of sexuality, to shape the discussion. The Church of England (at least in recent years) has characteristically wanted to occupy the middle ground – but in this discussion, there simply is no ground in the middle to occupy! I suspect this is why, from both 'sides' of the debate, it feels like 'Make your mind up' time.[11]

Focusing here on the ecclesial perspective rather than the scriptural, the social or the scientific, Paul argues that the report contains a contradiction or a tension in that while it claims that 'the recommendations do not propose any change in the Church's teaching on sexual conduct', *Pilling* also proposes the allowance of services to 'mark' same-sex civil partnerships using locally developed liturgies.[12] Paul argues that the introduction of 'unofficial blessings' for same-sex partnerships would divide the local from the national and the Church of England from other denominations, and that a change in pastoral discipline ineluctably effects a change in doctrine. It need not, he concludes, because the Bishops should put their collective feet down:

> the House of Bishops can rescue this situation relatively easily. *Pilling* is *not* proposing a change in Church policy or doctrine. They should accept this. *Pilling is* proposing 'facilitated discussions' to deepen our understanding of the issue. Personally, I doubt that these will make any progress at all – but I'm all for increased mutual understanding,

even if it is understanding of how much we disagree, so I don't think the HoB could reject this. But in order to create any credibility at all for these discussions, the bishops need to agree to *and implement* an absolute moratorium on *any* liturgical change, however local and however 'pastorally accommodating'. The only alternative, as others have pointed out, would be a slow and painful death by a thousand (pastoral, local, liturgical) cuts.[13]

Ian Paul also notes Keith Sinclair's dissenting statement appended to the report that sets out the argument from a 'traditional' understanding of biblical teaching on sexuality and he writes that he will return to the biblical engagement of the report and of the appendices by two evangelicals, Keith Sinclair and David Runcorn. Paul comments that dissenting statements are 'normal practice' in Anglican reports.[14] That is not true of reports on sexuality: only one, the *Gloucester Report*, appends 'Critical Observations'. These were made by the Board for Social Responsibility, who commissioned the report, and are not the censure of a lone dissenting voice, like Keith Sinclair's. Following Paul's blog post, there are 58 'thoughts' (comments) posted by 13 commentators that are fairly equally divided, so far as one can tell from their comments, into affirming and non-affirming 'camps'. Compared with some later blog posts on Psephizo on sexuality and the Church of England, this is a modest response.[15] Some commentators used their full names, others a first name only or a pseudonym, such as 'etseq'. Much of the debate was between Ian Paul himself and Simon Butler, both of them on General Synod and the Archbishops' Council (and fellow students at theological college): it centred on the tension between doctrine/discipline and liturgy that Paul focused on in his blog. Simon Butler argued in opposition to what Ian Paul sees as an intractable conflict:

> Ian, the liturgical question is not primarily one that I think poses major problems for Evangelicals, in that our theology of blessing does not primarily emerge from the authorization of the Church but from the nature of God. So if I pray 'Almighty God, bless you Adam and Steve …' that is not authorized liturgy. If, however, I pray 'Lord, we pray that you would bless Adam and Steve …' I've not broken the rules and yet a pastoral response has been offered. And it's what I'll continue to do. I was simply responding to your point about 'no liturgical change' in a rather impatient way.[16]

To which, Ian Paul responded:

Thanks for the clarification. I guess I would put the integrity of practice in relation to the Church's teaching higher up on the scale than the question of 'not breaking the rules.' I do think that following the letter of the law in relation to what we say we believe, while breaching it quite knowingly in spirit is what has got us into this mess, and continuing to do so will make it harder, not easier to resolve it (if resolution of any kind is in fact possible).[17]

Ian Paul and Simon Butler also touched upon the biblical hermeneutical lens in a reference to a blog post also published on 2 December 2013 by a retired bishop, David Gillett.[18] Butler commended the blog post's pastoral and missional stance on same-sex relationships. Paul responded:

I did ask David about the reasons for his change, and I hope he won't mind me mentioning this. At first he said it was about 'trajectory' but the trajectory from OT to NT is hardly liberalizing. Then it was about the 'inclusion' principle. From whom do we get this? From Jesus and Paul, who did not appear to think that this principle led to a revision on this issue. Again, this will all be old hat to you – but the fact that there are leaders in the Church advocating change without having integrated pastoral experience with theological thinking is truly concerning to me. This lack of integration is writ large across the *Pilling* report.[19]

It is clear that this was an exchange between two people who are entirely au fait with the *Pilling Report* and the Church of England's various treatments of the 'issues' in 'human sexuality'; people who are, moreover, part of the church 'establishment'.[20] Other 'voices' in the comments section raise the issue of biblical hermeneutics – the question of whether scripture proscribes same-sex relationships – and, as is customary in these debates, there are three distinct (though sometimes nuanced) positions: scripture proscribes all same-sex relationships; or scripture proscribes only those same-sex relationships that were cultic or exploitative; or 'scriptural authors very clearly didn't like gay sex, but this tells us nothing about God's opinion on the subject'.[21] Although it is not always clear who these people are or what their 'theological qualifications' might be, 'Lorenzo', for example, cites Theodosius, Justinian and Chrysostom, they do not appear to be the voices of those who are often described as 'ordinary Christians' or the 'ordinary person in the pew', still less of those who are on the margins of hegemonic, middle-class, educated, cisheteronormative Christianity; although one commentator, 'Stephen', does disclose that he is gay and on the cusp of being post-Church. The voices here are those of an educated and interested elite; both those who would argue for a change in the Church's teaching – or, at least, in its pastoral practice – and those who would maintain the status quo, the 'traditional' and 'biblical' teaching on sexuality and marriage.

'The Bible, Pilling *and Changing One's Mind'*

In order to determine whether this level of prior engagement with hermeneutical issues among the commentators is a characteristic of the Psephizo blog, I will turn, briefly, to the other blog post on *Pilling*. 'The Bible, *Pilling* and Changing One's Mind' (7 February 2014)[22] was a lengthy response to a reflection on the *Fulcrum* website by David Runcorn, the author of the 'including evangelical' appendix to *Pilling*.[23] As in the exchange with Simon Butler, this is a debate between two members of the same 'tribe', one a conservative and the other an open evangelical.[24] The lenses that the blog deploys reflect Runcorn's own: biblical hermeneutics, ethics and experience. In answer to David Runcorn's suggestion that we take notice of 'ordinary readers of scripture', Ian Paul wrote:

> I think there is an important hermeneutical principle here, and I have learned much by simply asking others what they see in a text. Just as the Reformation took a stand against the mediation of truth through the priesthood, we too need to question power plays involved in the mediation of the truth of Scripture by authority figures. But we cannot discern the truth by simply aggregating the views of readers. If that were so, Jesus would have said 'Facebook will set you free.'
>
> There has, in fact, been quite a lot of research done on both ordinary theology and ordinary hermeneutics, that is, the way that members of congregations in churches actually read and make sense of the Bible. Some of the conclusions are quite startling. Jeff Astley, in his Grove booklet P 110 *Taking Ordinary Theology Seriously*, discovers that many ordinary Anglicans do not believe in the divinity of Christ ... neither do they believe that in any objective sense Jesus death has 'saved' us. ...
>
> As a plea for serious respect of those we encounter, David is making an important pastoral statement here. But as an expression of the interaction between scripture and experience, this is really quite extraordinary. It suggests that we need to take a radical reader response approach to Scripture; its only meaning is the meaning I construct from it. This position actually silences Scripture; it prevents us hearing the Word of God as something that comes to us from beyond ourselves and beyond our experience.[25]

Here, Paul is articulating a particular conservative approach to biblical hermeneutics, one that disavows the perspective that all scriptural texts and their readings are the fruit of experience, and that 'orthodox' and 'traditional' interpretations are not eternal verities but subject to change and fashion over the centuries. If this position – that of attentively listening to other voices – 'actually silences Scripture', why is Paul writing his popular blog and inviting comments with only the lightest moderation? Is listening to 'other' voices 'aggregating' their views to achieve a synthetic consensus, or an attempt to hear the discrete and the particular by widening the conversation? If 'ordinary Christians' are denied a voice in the reading of scripture, because their understanding might be heterodox, then constructions of power and authority are being employed to mediate scriptural authority, creating a sort of Protestant magisterium. This may be a desirable outcome for some in the Church of England, who construct authority and obedience to it as correct thinking and belief, which they can then construe as 'orthodoxy', but it controverts *Pilling*'s declaration that the report was intended to facilitate a process of discussion and discernment.[26] Paul's dismissal of reader response interactions with the text is one epistemic approach. In contrast, in writing about her own ethnographical practice, Wigg-Stevenson states that her chief concern

> has been theological epistemology: how is theology produced – and how might it be produced and how ought it to be produced – when the organic overlap between everyday and academic forms of theological knowledge is made apparent and nurtured? ... While it is not *doctrinal* ... it is nevertheless still *theological*.[27]

There are twenty-seven 'thoughts' in response to 'The Bible, *Pilling* and Changing One's Mind' made by nine commentators, the majority of whom are non-affirming and critical of David Runcorn's *Fulcrum* piece.[28] The most extended discussion is between Ian Paul, James Byron and Peter Waddell on the concept of biblical inerrancy and some debate on what I shall term, following one of the commentators, 'trajectory hermeneutics': the premise that the Church can change its mind on sexuality as it has changed its mind on matters such as slavery, usury, divorce and women's ordination. One of the commentators, the conservative biblical scholar Robert Gagnon, who has written extensively on the Bible and homosexuality from a non-affirming perspective, criticizes *Fulcrum* for publishing 'such a theologically (and logically) unsound article'.[29] Another commentator, the Revd Peter Kane, demonstrates a comfortable familiarity with biblical and theological scholarship:

Having read the two appendices to the *Pilling Report*, I was rather concerned about the approach David Runcorn was taking in his contribution, in contrast to what I believe is a very sound and well-presented offering by Bishop Keith Sinclair ... I was intrigued by his raising of the slavery issue. When I spent a year at Wycliffe Hall, I undertook a lengthy piece of research on slavery in the Pauline writings, in which I argued that the nature of the Gospel is such that the early Christians were compelled to move in a direction that would eventually see the demise of slavery in Christian civilization. By a careful exegesis of the relevant texts, I attempted to demonstrate that, contrary to what might be the case on the surface, the Pauline approach is rather more 'radical' than one might at first imagine. One of my underlying motives for exploring the issue of slavery in the NT is precisely because of what in my opinion is a rather 'sloppy' thinking which goes like this: 'if the NT fails to condemn slavery and we now know this to be wrong, then why should we trust what the NT texts say about homosexual practice'.[30]

Magisterial comments like these suggest that, even if some of these commentators consider themselves to be 'normal', 'commonplace' or 'run of the mill' Christians, they are not among those who would be described in ecclesial discourse as 'ordinary Christians' or 'ordinary people in the pew'. It is hard to discern how educationally privileged many have been, but their reading, writing and easy familiarity with exegesis, theology and ethics suggest that they are confident in quasi-academic discourse and in being able to express their own principles and arguments through that medium. They have access to those who do hold authority in the Church of England and in academia, by virtue of their knowledge and their ability and desire to engage in erudite and privileged discourse. They are also aware that in the Church in general and, in this particular context, the Church of England, there is an ongoing debate on sexuality and, knowing that such a discussion is in process, they are able to access it. Access is both physical – owning or being able to use electronic equipment – and intellectual – being familiar with the discourse and the social media on which this might be discussed. Having, for example, access to the internet and a keen interest in sexual ethics will not allow participation in these discussions unless you know which groups and individuals are holding them and where they are being held.

The Shared Conversations at General Synod

These took place, after the conclusion of the Regional Shared Conversations, at General Synod in York, in July 2016. They were also undertaken in line with the St Michael's House protocols:

> The St Michael's House Protocols (which underpin the Shared Conversation) highlight the importance of creating a private space in which all feel welcome and respected and in which those taking part commit to becoming mutual and interdependent participants for the duration of the process. In order for this to be possible, it is essential that all participants are fully present – physically, mentally and emotionally – in the process. It is also important that only those who have committed to working within the guidelines ... are part of the Shared Conversation while it is taking place. As such, the Shared Conversation will be private sessions of synod, with no fringe meetings, media presence or live streaming. For the same reason, participants are asked to refrain from using any form of social media throughout the two days.[31]

Psephizo

Psephizo has one blog post on the Synod's Shared Conversations (with a number of others that discuss the process of the facilitated conversations generally). This was posted on 13 July 2016, the day following these conversations in Synod, and it provoked 463 'thoughts' from 48 commentators, some of them contributing only once, but others engaging in long discussion threads.[32] Again, I am one of the commentators, so I cannot be a dispassionate witness to the ensuing discussion. I also have the benefit of knowing some of the commentators and being aware of the backgrounds of some of the others. I thus have privileged access to information about the academic qualifications and other 'expertise' of many of the participants.

But, before turning to the comments threads, I will review the hermeneutical lenses that the synodical Conversations used, and at those on which Ian Paul chose to focus. In the afternoon of Sunday 10 July 2016 small groups shared personal faith journeys; on Monday there were presentations on scripture and sessions on studying scripture together, followed by two presentations on changing culture and small-group sessions discussing this; on the morning of Tuesday 12 July, there were two sessions on 'walking forward together'.[33] Paul praised the time spent in groups of three talking about personal faith journeys and how these related to views on sexuality, and the groups looking at scripture together. He is more ambivalent about the plenary sessions on the Monday afternoon: the first, which involved listening to the experiences of four 'same-sex attracted' young people, was 'deeply moving and challenging'; the second session exploring issues of changing culture was considered the best; the last session was 'far more problematic' since Paul found the presentations of the African and US church leaders, and the other two speakers advocating a 'live and let live' approach, unconvincing. But the worst plenary, for Paul, was the one that engaged the hermeneutic of the scriptural lens, about which he writes:

> I don't think it is an exaggeration to describe it as an absolute travesty of process. There were three speakers, one of whom supports the current teaching position of the Church, the other two arguing for change. The first person stayed within the brief, and spoke for seven to eight minutes; the second appeared to ignore the brief and spoke for 17 minutes, without intervention from the chair; the third spoke for 12 minutes ... Added to that, the first speaker, while eminently qualified in other ways, was not a biblical scholar, while the next one advocating change was. There was no voice from a Catholic perspective, engaging with the reception of Scripture within the tradition, and the 'orthodox' view was repeatedly labelled not as the Church's teaching, but as 'conservative'.
>
> Even worse than that was the content of the second and third presentations, and the way the format prevented proper interrogation of the claims made. It was claimed that the givenness of sexual orientation is the settled view of Western culture, when it is contested both within and outside the Church, is not supported by social-scientific research, and has been abandoned as a basis of argument in secular LGBT+ debate. It was claimed that all the texts in the NT referring to same-sex activity are in the context of *porneia*, 'bad sex', which was either commercial or abusive – which is a basic factual error ... But the format of the presentation precluded proper exploration of these authoritative claims. It felt to me like a serious power play, and I felt I had been subject to an abuse of expert power.[34]

Paul continues that there was no one to support the 'Church's current teaching position' and he wonders whether some of the 'conservative' members of Synod opted out of the process – of the Shared Conversations there – because the 'orthodox' speakers were not finalized until the previous week. However, he is even more critical of the facilitation in groups:

The fundamental problem here was the underlying approach – that there are no right answers, and no given positions, and so what is needed is a juxtaposition of different views so that mutual respect can emerge. This might be just right for a position of political conflict, where there is no 'objective' position which can act as a reference point. But how can this be right in a context where the Church itself already has a committed position, one that has the weight of history behind it, and a position which, in theory, all the clergy and the bishops have themselves signed up to believing, supporting and teaching.[35]

While Paul argues that small-group discussion is preferable to the win/lose binary of 'old-style Synod debate', he queries whether Synod – a group of 500 people elected not on the basis of their theological ability – is 'genuinely competent to debate and decide on this issue' and whether this might usurp the role of episcopal leadership. He concludes by contending that a change in the doctrine of marriage or further pastoral accommodation for same-sex couples will lead to a split in the Church and he warns that 'if those managing the process do not demonstrate a much better understanding of and engagement with those *who actually believe in what the bishops currently teach* then there will be trouble ahead'.[36] The readiness to ignore certain views takes us right to the heart of the concern with queer and liminal voices and where and how they are situated within this debate. Clearly, for Paul some of those who addressed Synod had more admissible voices than others, and some members of Synod, who are not theologically 'competent', have voices that should be less attended to. Discussion and decision should, he contends, be left to the House of Bishops, which is ironic given that Paul is now one of the vocal critics of the *Prayers of Love and Faith* suggested by the bishops themselves. A doubt on whether members of the House are trained or 'competent' theologians is frequently raised in the comments section of the Psephizo blog, now that the bishops are perceived by some as ominously 'liberal'.

A divide is being constructed here by Paul between those who are theologically 'competent' (and should, therefore, have a voice) and those who aren't. Furthermore, the question arises as to whose is the authoritative voice in this debate. Paul argues that this role belongs to those who would seek to defend current church teaching on marriage and sexuality and to those who would promote the belief in an 'objective position', and he gives short shrift to those voices that speak of other readings of scripture and tradition:

It was claimed that St Paul 'could not have known of stable same-sex relations' which is not supported by the historical facts. And it was claimed that same-sex relationships were the 'eschatological fulfilment of Christian marriage' since they involved loving commitment without procreation. It was not even acknowledged that many in the chamber would find that a deeply offensive assertion, quite apart from its implausibility.[37]

The authoritative voices, then, are those who are theologically qualified, but not those whose views Paul considers unhistorical or implausible, even though the two claims he rebuts in this quote are those of other scholars – an historian and a theologian.[38] Among the first comments on the thread, one addresses the question of whether Paul could have known of stable same-sex relations. Professor Helen King, author of an essay on Pausanias and Agathon, argues that mapping classical (i.e. Greek and Roman) same-sex relationships on to modern ones is problematic, and that taking the discussion in the Symposium – a text that predates Paul by nearly 400 years – as historical is uncertain.[39] The other partners in the conversation are Ian Paul himself, David Beadle, who has since gained a PhD in Hebrew Bible studies, Jonathan Tallon (a lecturer on the New Testament), and David Shepherd (an articulate and frequent commentator on Psephizo). Shepherd, however, interrupts this historical discussion, to turn the debate to biblical hermeneutics, the condemnation of same-sex activity in Paul's Letter to the Romans:

> Righteousness here is *dikaiosunes, the public settlement of a matter of dishonour (as between Menelaus and Antilochus in Ilead 23) For those who follow Him, Christ* [sic] *death and resurrection has expunged the dishonour caused by their offences against God ...*
> Notably in Romans, Paul uses the phrase *para phusin* (Rom. 11:24 'contrary to nature') to compare the influx of Gentile converts into the faith, which began as predominantly Jewish, with the technique of grafting a wild-olive bud into the branch of the cultivated olive tree ...
> Paul uses the same phrase to describe same-sex sexual activity ... The locus of Paul's denunciation of homosexual behaviour is its offence against what God has made self-evident through intrinsic physical characteristics. It's not about whether such relationships could exhibit long-term stability or mutuality.[40]

Given the familiarity with classical literature, and biblical exegesis and hermeneutics, that this comment illustrates, it is paradoxical that Shepherd begins by observing that, although 'the genteel parry-and-thrust of these arguments might well flatter the importance of intellectual scholarship, they are a diversion from the train of thought revealed in St. Paul's actual words'.⁴¹ This might not be a voice from the Academy, but it speaks academic discourse fluently. Helen King, Jonathan Tallon, David Beadle and Ian Paul himself respond with further discussion about the un/likelihood of Paul having known about stable same-sex relationships, what Paul might have meant by the phrase *para physin*,⁴² and whether Romans 1 condemns all humanity or all gentile humanity. Shepherd introduces Pseudo-Phocylides (first century BCE to first century CE) into the discussion, to demonstrate that a Jewish writer from this period denounces female same-sex sexual activity. Tallon disagrees, writing that Pseudo-Phocylides may be referring to forms of female–male sex. The object of this summary of the discussion on one of the presentations that Ian Paul reviews in his blog is to observe that most of the contributors are academics and the one whose educational background I do not know is familiar with the semantics of New Testament Greek and Jewish writers of late antiquity. These contributors are not on the margins of the wider debate, at least in educational terms. They, unlike some of the participants in the Regional Conversations, understand the characteristics of the debate and the language and concepts deployed in the synodical presentations, and they have extensive (or so it would seem) knowledge of text and context. Further contributors include a priest who is an honorary canon; another commentator with a PhD in biblical studies; another person with a doctorate in political philosophy and a diploma in biblical and theological studies; David Runcorn, the author of one of the appendices in *Pilling*; and another five members of General Synod, one of whom is Simon Butler, then Prolocutor of the House of Clergy for the Province of Canterbury, who writes:

> From an evangelical perspective, the elephant in the room is not the meaning of texts, or the rather uninteresting question of whether this is about the official teaching of the Church (which I don't think it is as we don't have any official teaching beyond Scripture, the BCP and the Canons and same sex marriage is not at stake in the near future I'm sure). We need to have the discussion about hermeneutics which is about how to interpret the texts and whether the idea of authority is the best lens through which to read them.⁴³

In fact the blog discussion is chiefly on biblical hermeneutics and on the exegesis of particular texts and phrases, such as *para physin*, with a fairly long digression on whether same-sex sex is 'unnatural' or harmful (in which I took part), a threnody on the lack of unity in the Church, a discussion on the aetiology of homosexuality, and some reflection on the purpose, 'content, aim and approach' of the Shared Conversations process. One of the final contributors is a retired academic, Dr Daniel Lamont, who commented on the process of the Shared Conversations:

> I sympathize with those who feel that the process has been manipulative and ultimately frustrating. To some extent the process is a reflection of the anti-intellectualism which has gripped English (I use the term advisedly) public life ...[44]

When I observed that some participants in the Regional Conversations had not read the background essays by Loveday Alexander and Ian Paul because they found them too 'academic', and that we were speaking from a position of privilege, he replied:

> There is a reluctance to press people to handle difficult material and I think that this in part lies behind the process used in the Shared Conversations. Similarly, I am uneasy about the word 'privilege' as it is used since so often a kind of guilt about this can lead to a 'dumbing down' or at worst being patronizing. My experience is that if approached in the right way, it is possible to make complex ideas accessible – teaching critical theory has taught me this. I do feel that if people are going to participate in such events as the Shared Conversations, they should be prepared to do some homework. By all accounts, Synod members were inundated with material to read in advance of the meeting.[45]

Hence I return here to the question of privilege and of voices that might be accounted authoritative. There are few, if any, voices in this commentary thread that do not come from a place of advantage: the Academy, priests and leaders in the Church, and the heart of the establishment of the established Church. Even among those whose backgrounds and church allegiances are less clear, there is no hesitation in participating in discussions that range from ecclesiology, through science to hermeneutics and exegesis. And for many commentors, the aim is to win the debate by rebutting the arguments of others. There seems to be little space for performing the 'art' of unknowing, undoing and unbeing. Although it is not overt, the impression from these discussions is that success in persuasion and conviction of certainty are the goals of most of the participants. Failure to convince by demonstrating the power of one's argument might be construed as shameful in this particular arena. An artless person who stumbled upon Psephizo without doing the 'homework' might not linger.

The 'Take Note' Debate

The 'Take Note' debate at General Synod the following February covered much of the same ground. As discussed in the previous chapter, 'a take note debate is a neutral motion which allows Synod to discuss the content and recommendations contained in a report without committing the Synod to the formal acceptance of any matter'.[46] However, this debate on the document *Marriage and Same Sex Relationships after the Shared Conversations: A Report from the House of Bishops* (GS 2055), published on 23 January 2017, was unlikely to prompt a 'neutral' debate.

Psephizo

In his Psephizo blog on the 'Take Note' debate, published the day after the debate itself, Ian Paul observed the following:

> The form of the debate was unusual; rather than proposing anything, the motion was simply to 'Take note' of the report, which essentially means acknowledging that it exists. In most contexts, this functions as an opportunity for general discussion, after which a substantive motion is offered which proposes action in the light of the report. Because of this, 'Take note' votes are usually uncontroversial; a Synod 'old hand' commented that, in 28 years of experience, the person had only known of 2 or 3 occasions where a 'Take note' motion had not been passed.[47]

Both conservatives and progressives opposed the Bishops' report, as noted earlier, though, of course, for rather different reasons. The blog focuses on the lenses through which both sides viewed the report and the debate and why they (especially the conservatives) found it unsatisfactory:

> I had the impression that two moments were key for [the conservatives]. The first was the speech of Paul Bayes, Bishop of Liverpool, who wanted to honour the 'anger, the fury' of campaigners (I am still trying to work out where in Scripture 'fury' towards your fellow believers is a commended virtue), and who was determined to make the most of 'maximum freedom' in his diocese.
> The second came in Archbishop Justin Welby's speech, the last to be taken, in which he emphasized the need for 'Christian inclusion'. I am not clear whether he intended the emphasis to be on 'Christian' or 'inclusion', but it was clearly a trigger phrase for Conservatives, who put it alongside Justin's other positive comments about gay relationships

as a signal that he cannot be trusted on this issue ... He concluded his short speech with: 'The way forward needs to be about love, joy and celebration of our humanity; of our creation in the image of God, of our belonging to Christ – all of us, without exception, without exclusion.'

If this means anything, I am not sure what it does mean. Including clergy defying the Church's teaching, and ignoring their bishop and their ordination vows? Including 'non-realists' who don't believe in the existence of God? Including all? Moving boundaries is one thing, but abolishing them is quite another. (And where is mention of kingdom, redemption, newness of life?) Once Justin had said this, the die was cast, and I suspect just enough Conservatives joined with liberals in voting not to take note for the motion to fall.[48]

None of the 152 'thoughts' that follow this blog post focus on scriptural hermeneutics. Many of the commentators lamented the impasse that the vote exposed, while others, such as Don Benson, saw the defeat as the 'saddest of days' marking the Church's turn away from 'orthodoxy':

I think the great benefit of yesterday's vote is that the Archbishop of Canterbury has finally come off the fence ... He's a liberal revisionist. Some of us will have suspected this from day one of his tenure ...

Yet there is freedom in truth. Orthodox members of the Church need no longer (indeed they cannot any longer) join in the game of pretence, which loyalty to their archbishop has forced them to do. I have the greatest of admiration for faithful Christians who have calmly and persistently fought off every specious argument, weathered the insults, sat through the 'Conversations', pointed out the woeful lack of church discipline, asked that theology be addressed honestly, written and spoken month after weary month, read the documents, analysed the data – only to be undermined at every turn by a church hierarchy that, quite simply, cannot be trusted. Well now there's no possibility of hoping that those at the top of the Church will, in the end, come good. And that, although hard to bear, is the end of an uncertainty that has held the Church in limbo for at least three years. 'Good disagreement' is dead, and there's honesty and genuine freedom in that ...

My own view is that there should be one last major effort by orthodox members of the Church to fight for its soul. The gloves are clearly off; the noise and anger from revisionists may sound like that of the prophets of Baal, but let us remember what the outcome was for them.[49]

This is a rhetorically powerful statement, which is why I have quoted it at some length, and it is representative of the conservative response to blogs such as this on Psephizo: a lament for a church that is seen as compromised, heterodox and apostate and a call to rally what may be figured as the 'righteous remnant' to contend for orthodoxy. Another commentator, Will Jones, repeatedly censured the clergy for their lack of obedience to episcopal authority, for example:

> the bishops were leading as they had been asked to do. The clergy, appallingly, undermined that leadership on a key issue at a key moment. What good exactly do you think can come of this? Certainly not any kind of unity, order or moving forward together. This is a mess.[50]

Canon Sue Booys, the chair of General Synod's Business Committee, replied to this,[51] so once again those reading and interacting with Psephizo are manifestly influential and well informed. Much of the debate, however, focuses once again on the aetiology of (male) homosexuality. This is a popular topic for some of the contributors to the Psephizo blogs on sexuality. We have met some of the participants in the previous Psephizo discussion; they include at least two PhDs, a canon and some whose credentials are unknown, but who, nevertheless, appear very familiar with the sources. As is usual on Psephizo most of the commentators are male and some of the comments quoted above give a flavour of the school debating society nature of the debate; itself an apparently middle-class enterprise.

Speaking with confidence; the ability to articulate thoughts and arguments, an understanding of the issues being raised, of biblical hermeneutics and apposite research; the emotional resilience not to be dismayed by often robust, even ill-mannered engagement – these are the hallmarks of participants in these blog conversations. Contributors are aware that the debates are taking place and where they are taking place and they must, for the most part, be confident and knowledgeable in order to enter these spaces and engage with those who seem to belong there because they are there so often and seem so at ease in this context, in assertion and riposte. Using Wigg-Stevenson's category of 'carnal theology', as an embodied practical theology in which all who engage are practitioners, it may be inferred that the theology espoused on the platforms considered here is consciously disembodied, rather than fleshly. Psephizo – both the blog and the comments threads – tends to valorize the cerebral: experience, especially bodily experience, is figured as being unreliable and deceptive; although experience is the lens through which the body and mind apprehend materiality, even textual materiality – both word and flesh. Despite the erudite nature of the commentators on these blogs there is an alternative narrative in that not all of the participants enjoy privilege and power in the ecclesial corridors of power. Being a priest, working for a diocese or taking part in the Shared Conversations does not of itself give people access to church authority or give them a voice that will be invited to speak or be heard during the processes of reflection upon *Pilling*. Even if such voices are canvassed, there is no assurance that what they are saying will be reflected in any official report by the House of Bishops. The ephemeral, contingent and provisional nature of social media means that it is a relatively safe space in which to experiment: to rehearse arguments and ideas, to converse spontaneously, and to be playful. But, again, being playful with theological or scriptural themes requires that contributors are informed, engaged and robust. These are not spaces designed for the inarticulate or the vulnerable.

The indications are that, in the blogs I have analysed in this chapter, there is little or no attempt to que(e)ry *Pilling*'s methodology or the processes of the Shared Conversations and Synod debates. Nor is there any challenge to the constructions of authority and inhabiting of privilege that these 'unauthorized' channels epitomize. There is criticism of both the process and its perceived outcomes from both sides, but really no interrogation of why the Church is doing this thing in this particular way, nor any suggestions on how the discussion might have been conducted or the processes conceived. No participant in these conversations even appears to que(e)ry this construct of discussion or to interrogate the models of progress and productivity that it assumes. There are no alternatives offered by these 'unauthorized' voices that would contest the epistemological legitimacy of these discursive norms and might offer hope of an engagement with Halberstam's 'queer art of failure' or Bray's theology of Holy Saturday as a liminal space that holds both hope and despair in tension and eschews facile and certain redemption.

Queer discourse aims to disrupt, to rupture, and to render 'indecent' the hegemonic heteronormativity and cispatriarchal constructs that the Global North (and, in this case, the Church of the Global North) take for granted as both natural and canonical. The discourse here takes for granted what I have called canonical hermeneutics, the belief that particular readings – often white, Western, male, class-bound readings – are correct and decent and eternal. It is not only the bloggers who are perpetuating these canonical approaches to interpretation and discussion, but also the participants (of whom I am one) who follow the 'rules' laid out by those who have been accorded authority and influence. We are all obeying the unwritten rules of that classed construct, the debating society, so that even where we disagree with each other, we do so on terms that are, perhaps, buttresses for the very structures that we criticize. It is as if these discourses, instead of being open to those who do not have voices in the official structures of the Church of England, remain safe spaces for contributors with vested interests and some influence, to affect those who do hold power. They may appear to be potentially porous, but my ethnographic research has suggested that they are accessible mostly to those who are aware of and comfortable with cerebral and sometimes antagonistic discourse. Of course, people without power, without influence, the inarticulate and the indifferent, might not wish to enter such spaces and, even if they did enter, they might not wish to trouble the normative discourse there. For there are, it seems, no disinterested contributors to these internet debates. No one joins in out of a desire simply to see what its contours are; we are all arguing our cases and pleading our causes. And so, because participants have subscribed, maybe unconsciously, to the rules, they play by those rules; there are often sarcasm and irony and *ad hominem* attacks, but they belong to the mores of the debating society, as revealed by the occasional injunction to 'play the ball not the man'. They are disembodied voices, not because they speak into a virtual world, but because they do not seek to embody 'carnal theology' by creating new practices and norms. Contributors to these blogs appear to feel more at home in reproducing the 'disembodied practices of textual analysis'.

There are few, if any, queer voices. Even those who are sexually queer or genderqueer speak from and into the hegemonic cisheteronormative discourse; they seem to accept its authority and its norms, rather than seeking to trouble them or to que(e)ry the dominion they hold in the Church and its ways of speaking and conversing. Perhaps there are queerer and queering voices on Twitter/X, YouTube and TikTok, that may challenge the hermeneutics of church reports and church conversations.[52] Where, in more mainstream discourse, might the disruptive, the indecent, the insecure, the inarticulate, the aberrant, the nonnormative, the denaturalized, the queer hermeneutic that might engage *Pilling* and its afterlife, be found and what might it say and do? I hope to answer some of those questions in the following chapter.

Notes

1 Natalie Wigg-Stevenson, *Ethnographic Theology: An Enquiry into the Production of Theological Knowledge* (London: Palgrave Macmillan, 2014), 117.

2 Linn Marie Tonstad, *God and Difference: The Trinity, Sexuality, and the Transformation of Finitude* (Abingdon: Routledge, 2017), 14.

3 Karen Bray, *Grave Attending: A Political Theology of the Unredeemed* (New York: Fordham University Press, 2020).

4 Natalie Wigg-Stevenson, *Ethnographic Theology*, 117.

5 Natalie Wigg-Stevenson, *Ethnographic Theology*, 117.

6 Sarah Pink et al., *Digital Ethnography: Principles and Practice* (Thousand Oaks, CA: Sage, 2006).

7 Julie Rak, 'The Digital Queer: Weblogs and Internet Identity', *Biography*, 28, no. 1, 2005, 166–182, https://muse.jhu.edu/article/183605/summary (accessed 15.2.24); Yvette Taylor, Emily Falconer and Ria Snowden, 'Queer Youth, Facebook and Faith: Facebook Methodologies and Online Identities', *New Media and Society*, 16, no. 7, 2014, 1138–1153, http://journals.sagepub.com/doi/abs/10.1177/1461444814544000 (accessed 15.2.24).

8 Ian Paul, 'Psephizo: about', https://www.psephizo.com/about/ (accessed 15.2.24).

9 Natalie Wigg-Stevenson, *Ethnographic Theology*, 19.

10 Leanne Townsend and Claire Wallace, *Social Media Research: A Guide to Ethics* (The University of Aberdeen, n.d.), 11, https://www.gla.ac.uk/media/Media_487729_smxx.pdf (accessed 15.2.24).

11 Ian Paul, 'The *Pilling Report*: Divisive and damaging?', Psephizo, 2 December 2013, https://www.psephizo.com/sexuality-2/the-pilling-report-divisive-and-damaging/ (accessed 15.2.24).

12 The Church of England, '*Pilling Report* Published', press release, 28 November 2013, https://www.churchofengland.org/news-and-media/news-and-statements/pilling-report-published (accessed 15.2.24).

13 Ian Paul, 'The *Pilling Report*: Divisive and damaging?', emphasis original.

14 Ian Paul, 'The *Pilling Report*: Divisive and damaging?'

15 Later blog posts on sexuality elicited over 500 and over 600 comments: Ian Paul, 'What does the Oxford Ad Clerum mean?', Psephizo, 7 November 2018, https://www.psephizo.com/sexuality-2/what-does-the-oxford-ad-clerum-mean/#comments (accessed 15.2.24); Ian Paul, 'Is the Bishops' policy on Civil Partnerships Sustainable?', Psephizo, 9 October 2018, https://www.psephizo.com/sexuality-2/is-the-bishops-policy-on-civil-partnerships-sustainable/#comments (accessed 15.2.24).

16 https://www.psephizo.com/sexuality-2/the-pilling-report-divisive-and-damaging/comment-page-1/#comment-190567 (accessed 15.2.24).

17 https://www.psephizo.com/sexuality-2/the-pilling-report-divisive-and-damaging/comment-page-1/#comment-190604 (accessed 15.2.24).

18 David Gillett, 'Bishop David's Afterwords: Musings and Reflections from Retirement in Norfolk', 2 December 2013, http://bishopdavidgillett.blogspot.com/2013/ (accessed 15.2.24).

19 https://www.psephizo.com/sexuality-2/the-pilling-report-divisive-and-damaging/comment-page-1/#comment-191176 (accessed 15.2.24). OT stands for the Old Testament and NT for the New Testament.

20 Ian Paul is on the Archbishops' Council; Simon Butler was then Prolocutor for the House of Clergy for Canterbury on General Synod and also on Archbishops' Council.

21 'Stephen', https://www.psephizo.com/sexuality-2/the-pilling-report-divisive-and-damaging/comment-page-2/#comment-216588 (accessed 15.2.24).

22 Ian Paul, 'The Bible, *Pilling* and Changing One's Mind', Psephizo, 7 February 2014, https://www.psephizo.com/biblical-studies/the-bible-pilling-and-changing-ones-mind/ (accessed 15.2.24).

23 David Runcorn, 'And how do I know when I am wrong? Evangelical faith and the Bible', *Fulcrum*, 28 January 2014, https://www.fulcrum-anglican.org.uk/articles/and-how-do-i-know-when-i-am-wrong-evangelical-faith-and-the-bible/ (accessed 15.2.24).

24 'Including evangelical' is the term Runcorn chooses in his appendix for the per-

spective which is also called 'open', inclusive, affirming and revisionist. Liberal tends to be used by and of people who do not describe themselves as evangelical.

25 Ian Paul, 'The Bible, *Pilling* and Changing One's Mind'.

26 As evidenced by the ensuing Shared Conversations and General Synod debates.

27 Natalie Wigg-Stevenson, *Ethnographic Theology*, 168, emphasis original.

28 David Runcorn, 'And how do I know when I am wrong?'

29 https://www.psephizo.com/biblical-studies/the-bible-pilling-and-changing-ones-mind/#comment-325565 (accessed 15.2.24).

30 Ian Paul, 'The Bible, *Pilling* and Changing One's Mind'.

31 'General Synod Shared Conversations – FAQS', 2017, https://www.churchofengland.org/sites/default/files/2017-12/160603_gs_members_faq-july2016.pdf (accessed 15.2.24).

32 Ian Paul, 'Synod's Shared Conversations', Psephizo, 13 July 2016, https://www.psephizo.com/sexuality-2/synods-shared-conversations/ (accessed 15.2.24).

33 Church of England, 'Shared Conversations Archive', https://www.churchofengland.org/about/leadership-and-governance/general-synod/bishops/shared-conversations-archive (accessed 15.2.24): 'The Shared Conversation for members of General Synod took place after General Synod had been prorogued in July 2016. A full programme was issued to all General Synod members'; the programme is no longer available online.

34 Ian Paul, 'Synod's Shared Conversations'.

35 Ian Paul, 'Synod's Shared Conversations'.

36 Ian Paul, 'Synod's Shared Conversations', emphasis original.

37 Ian Paul, 'Synod's Shared Conversations'.

38 Helen King, 'Pausanias and Agathon: a same-sex relationship?', *Shared Conversations: reflecting on sexuality and gender identity in the Church of England*, 4 July 2016, https://shared-conversations.com/2016/07/04/pausanias-and-agathon-a-same-sex-relationship/ (accessed 15.2.24); and Robert Song, *Covenant and Calling: Towards a Theology of Same-sex Relationships* (London: SCM Press, 2014).

39 Professor Helen King was at this time a professor of classics at the Open University.

40 https://www.psephizo.com/sexuality-2/synods-shared-conversations/comment-page-1/#comment-340690 (accessed 15.2.24). Italicized in the original text.

41 https://www.psephizo.com/sexuality-2/synods-shared-conversations/comment-page-1/#comment-340690 (accessed 15.2.24).

42 My preferred transliteration of παρὰ φύσιν.

43 https://www.psephizo.com/sexuality-2/synods-shared-conversations/comment-page-1/#comment-340509 (accessed 15.2.24). BCP is the Book of Common Prayer.

44 https://www.psephizo.com/sexuality-2/synods-shared-conversations/comment-page-2/#comment-340935 (accessed 15.2.24).

45 https://www.psephizo.com/sexuality-2/synods-shared-conversations/comment-page-2/#comment-341012 (accessed 15.2.24).

46 Peter Owen, 'Debate on the Bishops' report – take note motion defeated', Thinking Anglicans, 15 February 2017, https://www.thinkinganglicans.org.uk/7469-2/ (accessed 15.2.24).

47 Ian Paul, 'On Synod, Sexuality, and Not "Taking Note"', Psephizo, 16 February 2017, https://www.psephizo.com/sexuality-2/on-synod-sexuality-and-not-taking-note/ (accessed 15.2.24).

48 Ian Paul, 'On Synod, Sexuality, and Not "Taking Note"'.

49 https://www.psephizo.com/sexuality-2/on-synod-sexuality-and-not-taking-note/#comment-344021 (accessed 15.2.24).

50 https://www.psephizo.com/sexuality-2/on-synod-sexuality-and-not-taking-note/#comment-343992 (accessed 15.2.24).

51 https://www.psephizo.com/sexuality-2/on-synod-sexuality-and-not-taking-note/#comment-344006 (accessed 15.2.24).

52 These are a few random examples of queer faith stories from YouTube. Queer faith stories, 'Can you be religious and queer? | them' (YouTube) 3 May 2018, 6.55, https://www.youtube.com/watch?v=gnG3BSDfvhk (accessed 15.2.24).

4

Queering Hermeneutics

Introduction

In this chapter, I pursue alternative epistemologies, through biblical hermeneutics and transgressive theologies, which *Pilling* chose to disregard or to consign to the fringes of hegemonic ecclesial discourse. Halberstam, commenting on the neoliberal dismissal of alternative ways of being, observes:

> The dream of an alternate way of being is often confused with utopian thinking and then dismissed as naïve, simplistic, or a blatant misunderstanding of the nature of power in modernity. And yet the possibility of other forms of being, other forms of knowing, a world with different sites for justice and injustice, a mode of being where the emphasis falls less on money and work and competition and more on cooperation, trade, and sharing animates all kinds of knowledge projects and should not be dismissed as irrelevant or naïve.[1]

Here I ask if the *Pilling Report* privileges a particular construal of scripture in reading the so-called creation ordinances of the Genesis narratives as normative for a Christian understanding of the binary gendered nature of humankind, the proper ordering of sexuality, and the institution of marriage. Where it may be admitted, as *Pilling* itself does, that other biblical texts can be read through differing hermeneutical lenses, the Genesis accounts of creation and of the institution of marriage, as divine fiat, are presented as unexceptionable and immutable.[2] Although *Pilling* does not turn to biblical texts until Part 2 of the report, the writers there acknowledge that their inability to produce a 'single set of recommendations' stems from their debate 'on the meaning and authority of Scripture'.[3] There is, they find, a dichotomy between maintaining the eternal verities of scripture and the disagreements that arise owing to different readings of the texts:

The problem we are unable, collectively, to solve is between the belief that God's purposes revealed in Scripture are eternal, unchanging and consistent, and the plain fact that faithful, prayerful, Christians who aspire for their lives to be governed by Scripture, do not agree about the implications of the scriptural texts for same sex relationships. To point to the fact of disagreement in the Church is one thing, but to validate differing views or to endorse the idea that the Church's understanding of the meaning of Scripture might change seems, to some in the Church and on our Working Group, to be tantamount to denying that Scripture is authoritative to the Church and to open the door to relativistic readings of all scriptures.[4]

However normative, or otherwise, its prescriptions and proscriptions are considered, the Bible is the arbiter of the original divine plan. Thus, the writers of *Pilling*, although they have given precedence to other lenses in reflecting on sexuality, acknowledge that it is the authority of scripture that undergirds church teaching. They seem perplexed both by the existence of varying readings and by the thought that interpretation may change in the ongoing reception of these texts, so that what was once proscribed is now permitted and what was once permitted is now proscribed.[5] In their Introduction to the report, the writers do go on to say that their difficulty lies in discerning the mind of the Church on sexuality given that traditional readings and the work of the Spirit in the Church may seem to be at odds, just as differing opinions on sexuality, even among the members of the Working Group, appear to be becoming more entrenched. But in the earlier discussions of the biblical hermeneutics employed in the report, the 'traditional' reading of biblical texts is privileged by being presented as the default interpretation. Any other reading is seen as 'distinctive', which seems to imply that it is idiosyncratic, irregular, or marginal. *Some Issues in Human Sexuality* and the chapter 'The Witness of Scripture' in *The Anglican Communion and Homosexuality*[6] are presented as useful background reading although both were, at the time *Pilling* was published, several years old and neither engages in any depth with what might be called 'distinctive' hermeneutics.[7]

The one biblical hermeneutic that is presented in *Pilling* as incontrovertible is that of the Genesis accounts of the creation of two (binary) genders. They are read as foundational for Christian theological anthropology and the disparities between the two narratives are glossed over as having little theological importance: 'the question here is not about one or the other being "true"', since 'we can say with confidence that created nature of humanity as male and female is built into the natural order'.[8] Implicit in this harmonized reading of Genesis 1 and 2 is the belief that mixed sex/gender marriage is the partnership that God decreed 'at the beginning' as a creation ordinance and it is this understanding of the Genesis narratives together with Matthew 19.4–5 that the writers of *Pilling* see as overriding revisionist or contextualized interpretations of the same-sex activity proscribed in the clobber texts.

Not all scholars would argue that the Genesis narratives can be read unproblematically as foundational texts for the Christian understanding of the creation of human gender, sexuality and marriage. Hugh Pyper, for example, queries the notion of Genesis as *the* beginning, rather than as *a* beginning *in media res*, and Ken Stone proposes that the creation narratives are as much concerned with agriculture and food as they are with sexuality.[9] But voices that attempt to que(e)ry normative readings of the scriptural narrative (rather than presenting disruptive readings of specific, contingent, texts) are muted – whether consciously or inadvertently – by the authors of *Pilling*. That the creation accounts both describe and prescribe male/female marriage and that this is the context for procreation is rarely, if ever, interrogated, despite scant support for these pillars of a normative understanding of Christian marriage in the Genesis narratives. Nor does *Pilling* interrogate the concept or the tradition of Christian marriage, beyond a brief section that quotes the Book of Common Prayer marriage service, Canon B30, the Bishops' 2005 statement on civil partnerships, and the 2013 report *Men and Women in Marriage*.[10]

Genesis 1 commands that humanity should be fruitful and multiply but is silent on whether male and female need to be married in order to do so. In Genesis 2 the man and the woman become one flesh, but there is no mention of – perhaps no need for – procreation until chapter 4, after the expulsion from Eden when Adam 'knew' the now-named Eve and she conceived. The creation of Eve seems to be important because of her species, rather than her gender: she is 'bone of my bones and flesh of my flesh', unlike the cattle, the birds of the air and the animals of the field that God presents to Adam as prospective, but unsuitable, companions.[11] In this second narrative, procreation appears to be the result of the loss of potential immortality, a consequence of the Fall.[12] This cannot easily be aligned with the ordinance given in Genesis 1 that male and female shall 'fill the earth and subdue it'. And in both accounts the 'couple' are described as either male and female, or man and woman; the translation of the Hebrew word for woman, *ishah*, as wife, in Genesis 2.24–25 and 4.1 turns the autochthonous coupling into a 'marriage'. Even if the original couple portrayed in Genesis 2 and beyond is intended to represent an ideal of faithful, companionate, procreative mutuality, it is odd that it has taken over 2,500 years to attain (potentially) this ideal and that it is mainly available to couples in Western, industrialized and capitalist societies.[13] Christian theology has appropriated these texts by colonizing them to import normative, yet mutable, understandings of the goods of marriage into the tradition. Augustine's three goods – offspring, faithfulness and permanence – have become axiomatic for Christian theology, although contemporary Christian marriage (which is not itself univocal) has little resemblance to marriage(s) in late antiquity or to marriage(s) in the Yahwist's Judea.[14]

In what follows, I will attempt to queer *Pilling*'s account of God's good purposes in creation being read off from the Genesis narratives and understood not simply in terms of Christian orthodoxy but as a culturally transcendent, universal and normative depiction of sexuality and marriage. The concept of queering *Pilling*'s hermeneutic of the Genesis archetypes is not to present a singular subversive and alternative reading that will replace a straight archetype with a kinky one – and which would, in any case, only serve to reinscribe the inviolability of the hetero-patriarchal norm – but to explore readings that query the view that there is one overarching narrative within the provocative and multivocal biblical texts that remains constant for a Christian ethic of marriage and sexuality.

One of my conversation partners in this will be Robert Song, who was a member of the Working Party that produced the *Pilling Report*. His 2014 book, *Covenant and Calling: Towards a Theology of Same-Sex Relationships*, argues that both celibacy and (unprocreative) covenant partnerships are fruits of the new eschatological age in which the coming of Christ has relativized the sexual ethical norms of the Genesis edicts.[15] Ultimately, I find Song's argument unpersuasive, as I shall argue, but I choose to critically reflect upon it here because it is a model of how foundational theological narratives can be que(e)ried; albeit in a rather moderate manner. The second conversation partner is Lee Edelman, whose *No Future: Queer Theory and the Death Drive* queries procreative norms that attach ethical value to investment in the future and in 'the Child'.[16] Edelman presents a radically non-eschatological eschatology that is theologically gnostic in its disinvestment in the goods of procreation and future hope. Yet Edelman's denial of reproductive futurism finds echoes and patterns in biblical texts, particularly in the New Testament, which celebrate the barren and the eunuch, relativize traditional family and kinship ties, and speak of marriage as a one-flesh union or as a remedy for lust, but these texts are, largely, silent on the good of offspring. Jesus says that there will be no marriage in the resurrection life, presumably because there will be no mortality and, therefore, no need to reproduce. But the Gospels do not say that there will be no sex or sexuality in the new creation, despite a type of etiolated embodiment being the inference of most biblical scholars.[17] Edelman's queering of society's idolizing, or fetishizing, of the Child is curiously echoed in the New Testament narratives, with their offensive (to some modern sensibilities) anti-family strains. Church reports, like *Pilling*, which canonize heterosexuality and valorize marriage and procreation, have ignored these subversive strains within their own scriptures and traditions.

A third strand of enquiry will be to consider whether the non-procreative, non-conventional family/kinship choices of the Christian homosexual people who subscribe to an ethic of sexual abstinence, such as that prescribed by the organization Living Out, reflect the ascetic and anti-family strains of New Testament thought and practice.[18] Is the renunciation of sexual intimacy and conventional family structures – the decision to surrender 'the Child' – more apposite to the interim age of inaugurated eschatology than the extension of what has, traditionally, been an asymmetric institution – Christian marriage – to accommodate the covenantal relationships of same-sex couples?

Robert Song, *Covenant and Calling*

Professor Robert Song was an advisor to the Working Group that produced the *Pilling Report*. His book is an attempt to answer the question of whether the two vocations of celibacy and (potentially procreative) marriage are the only Christian callings, or whether a third may now be discerned. Song argues that

> sex BC is not the same as sex AD. Before Christ, marriage as a good of creation was inseparable from procreation; but after Christ, while marriage and procreation do not stop being goods, we are also directed to a future resurrection life in which marriage and procreation will be no more. The vocation of celibacy is the first sign of this resurrection life, witnessing as it does to a time when God will be known as the fulfilment of all our desires. The question is whether this 'time between the times' in which we live, between Christ's resurrection and his return in glory, also admits of another calling.[19]

Song begins with the normative assumption that Christian marriage is a creation ordinance and therefore an immutable, divine archetype, a conviction to which I will return. Secondly, he argues that celibacy – the call to sexual abstinence – is a fruit of the new creation. It is evident that asceticism was valorized by the Jesus of the Gospels and by Paul in his teaching on marriage, particularly since 'the appointed time has grown short' (1 Cor. 7.29). But abstinence and self-restraint are also found in pre-Christian Roman and Jewish cultures: in the desire for *enkrateia*, in the disciplines of the Essenes, and in Nazirite vows like those (probably) taken by John the Baptist.

Song's third vocation is that which he terms 'covenant partnership', a union that would be 'non-procreative' and may be the calling of either mixed-sex or same-sex couples. He writes: 'I argue ... that the fundamental division is not between heterosexual and homosexual relationships, but between procreative and non-procreative relationships.'[20] These 'non-procreative relationships' would be a mark of the end times, a sign of the breaking in of the new creation, relativizing, though not superseding, the original command to be fruitful and multiply. Since procreation is an unconditional good of the one-flesh male/female relationship in creation ordained as marriage, then same-sex relationships, which cannot be physically procreative, cannot be marriages within this definition. Song argues that such relationships cannot even be marriages analogically, because, although they may exhibit the other goods of marriage, procreation 'is a morally relevant difference'.[21] So, not only is the intention to procreate essential to the nature of marriage in creation, but it is also, according to Song, more intrinsic to the principle of marriage, as divine fiat, than the other two goods. However, since 'procreation has become redundant, theologically speaking, for those who are in Christ',[22] Song proposes a new eschatological witness in what he terms 'covenant partnerships', which would also be characterized by three goods: those of fidelity, permanence and fruitfulness, the last characterized by something other than physical offspring. Deliberate rather than contingent childlessness would signify that a mixed-sex relationship would be, ontologically, a 'covenant partnership' rather than a marriage.

This third vocation, which would be open to both mixed-sex and same-sex couples, is not, Song argues, a lesser vocation or inferior covenant relationship, in the way in which civil partnership has sometimes been construed as a separate water fountain for gay couples. Nevertheless, he admits that, since the Church has married purposefully childless couples since 1930, it is probable that mixed-sex couples who did not intend to procreate would opt for marriage rather than a civil partnership, deemed to be a 'covenant partnership'.[23] As Song acknowledges, the theological niceties of equal but different are unlikely to work in practice; it is difficult to imagine most heterosexual couples, who have had the privileges of religious or civil marriage ceremonies for over a century, whatever their age and intentions, being prepared to exchange these for a civil partnership. In any case couples might not wish to advertise their decision to remain childless in this manner and thus, perhaps, leaving their union open to prurient questioning and speculation.

Since Song's book was published, however, a campaign for extending civil partnerships to heterosexual couples, who may or may not have children, has been successful. These couples, and their supporters, argued for mixed-sex civil partnerships because they wanted the financial and legal protection that a civil partnership confers and believed that this should be available under equality legislation.[24] Writing before these changes and the impact they may have on the institution of marriage,[25] Song proposes that, for some heterosexual couples, civil partnership might be the more ethical choice. Song argues that, after the birth of Christ, covenant partnership might be the deeper and more embracing category, with procreative marriage now being the special case.[26] I have shown that this kind of que(e)rying of familiar biblical narratives is nowhere evident in the *Pilling Report*, nor in the authorized and unauthorized processes that followed the production of the report. As far as I am aware, the only response that queried the biblical theology being deployed in the *Pilling* process was, as I have observed, that of David Nixon in his reflection on one of the Regional Shared Conversations.[27]

The Church of England Doctrine of Marriage and *Covenant and Calling*

However appealing such a theological resolution might be for liberal Christians who wish to see same-sex marriages celebrated and contracted in church, it interrogates neither the institution of marriage itself, as a patriarchal construct, which might not accommodate graciously the devices and desires of same-sex partnerships, nor the creation norms that are supposed to underlie the very nature of marriage as an original good. Both the Book of Common Prayer and Canon B30 describe companionate marriage in which the emphasis is on mutuality, yet this obscures the constitution of secular law that has, until recently, reinforced the androcentric nature of marriage. Marriage belongs neither to the Church nor to the State; in Europe and Western Asia, it was a compact between a couple or a contract between two families, before either the civil State or the Christian Church claimed authority over the institution.[28] In the early Christian centuries many of the Church Fathers taught that ascesis was the higher calling and the first record of a marriage being invalid unless blessed by a priest occurs in the ninth century CE.[29] But the power of husbands and the proper submission of wives, enshrined in English law, canon and civil, were justified by appeals to the natural order discernible in scripture. As Song himself allows, the Christian tradition has known no other marriage than that between 'opposing' sexes, but this is, he argues, because the differentiation between the sexes in creation is not merely contingent, but intrinsic to the procreative purposes of marriage. The reasons why marriage should be sexually differentiated are, according to Song's argument:

1 'That marriage embodies a hierarchical relationship between the sexes',[30] which is evidenced by various texts, such as Eve's being taken from Adam's side, the teaching that wives should be subject to their husbands (Eph. 5), and the husband being head of his wife (1 Cor. 11).[31]
2 'That it embodies an intrinsic complementarity that is not hierarchic, at least in principle.'[32] This complementary nature is firstly biological; secondly it can be observed from the social sciences that 'the differences between men and women are so profound that the only kinds of sexual relationship that should be socially and legally recognized must be heterosexual'.[33] Thirdly, the traditional heterosexual family unit is the glue that holds society together.
3 'That marriage in creation is intrinsically procreative ... the significance of being created male and female in Genesis 1 is not that humankind thereby images the inner relationship of God, but that sexual differentiation is the necessary basis for human being to procreate.'[34]

This third reason is, for Song, the crowning purpose for heterosexual marriage being grounded in the differentiation of the sexes and in their ability to produce offspring. Song, cites, unironically, Augustine's reflection that if God had intended marriage for companionship, They would have created another man alongside Adam.[35] But here, Song is in danger of concluding that because humankind is mostly divided into two biological sexes that, mostly, reproduce sexually, then the telos of the sexual relationship between them, which we shall call marriage, is sexual reproduction. He writes: 'sexual differentiation is therefore justified within marriage, but it is only justified because marriage in creation is oriented to procreation. There are no other grounds that can provide the theological weight needed to *require* that marriage be sexually differentiated.'[36] And this, in turn, is in danger of collapsing into a circular argument of epistemological doubt about the primacy of the evolutionary chicken or the theological egg. Indeed, although procreation is one of the goods of marriage described in the marriage service and in Canon B30, it is not the only end, and those other purposes – sexual delight/remedy for lust and companionship, contra Augustine – are closer to the scriptural precepts of the writers of the Gospel of Matthew and of 1 Corinthians than they are to the Genesis ordinances.

Marriage has always, perhaps, been able to accommodate those relationships that in some senses queer its norms – the barren, the abstinent and the elderly, for example – while still remaining marriage. Song's answer to the quandary he poses himself is in his claim that the new eschatological age, testified to in the New Testament scriptures, has relativized the creation good of procreation and opened the way to non-procreative sexual relationships. But, while arguing that 'procreation is no longer eschatologically necessary',[37] Song does not acknowledge the full implications of Galatians 3.28 in which Paul's contention that in Christ there is no longer male *and* female undoes Genesis 1.27.[38] Many commentators construe 'in Christ' as a curiously spiritual state that has no traction on the divinely differentiated sexes and their separate roles within a godly hierarchy. But surely, in quoting Genesis 1, rather than stating that there will no longer be male *or* female, Paul is deliberately annulling the creation ordinance that humankind is male and female in the image of God, with the extraordinary claim that, for a new eschatological age, humankind is no longer male and female in (the image of) Christ.[39] He is not, however, suggesting that male and female are replaced by a new eschatological androgyne, for Paul is certain that our resurrection bodies will have continuity with our earthly bodies (1 Cor. 15.42ff).[40] Physical difference has not been erased but it no longer signifies, for Paul, the exemplary rootedness of human creation. This kind of scriptural reflection is absent both from *Pilling* and from the processes that followed, which, when the Bible was brought into play, seem to have weaponized it to confirm heteronormativity as divine fiat.[41] There was potential in the authorized and unauthorized responses to *Pilling* to reflect on scripture as a 'queer art'[42] – tentatively, as Song has done without troubling the heterosexual reading of the creation ordinances, or more radically, in an attempt to disrupt the hegemony of cisheteronormative readings of Genesis and of Matthew 19. It is possible to agree with Linn Marie Tonstad that 'Christian debates over sexuality often take similarly bankrupt forms',[43] and yet to try to reach beyond that stalemate to engage creatively with scripture in ways that enquire into its more bizarre accounts and that queer dominant, normative, often post-Reformation epistemologies.

Asceticism and Eunuchs for the Kingdom of God: Halvor Moxnes

The second strand in the New Testament texts is that of asceticism. Paul wishes that all were like himself, presumably celibate and abstinent, but he does not clarify whether ascesis is in itself a theological good or whether it is simply desirable because of living when 'the present form of this world is passing away', and care of a spouse distracts from care of the Lord (1 Cor. 7.31–35). The other significant teaching on asceticism in the canon is the gnomic eunuch saying in Matthew 19. In this passage, after shocking his disciples by proscribing divorce for any cause but *porneia*, and when they protest that in that case it is better not to marry, Matthew's Jesus replies:

> Not everyone can accept this teaching, but only those to whom it is given. ¹²For there are eunuchs who have been so from birth, and there are eunuchs who have been made eunuchs by others, and there are eunuchs who have made themselves eunuchs for the sake of the kingdom of heaven. Let anyone accept this who can.[44]

This enigmatic saying, particular to Matthew's Gospel, has been interpreted in various ways: primarily, up until the Reformation, as advocating virginity, abstinence and celibacy for the clergy and an ascetic, abstemious sexuality for the married laity.[45] In *Putting Jesus in His Place*, Halvor Moxnes argues that both the Church Fathers and modern commentators have ignored or suppressed the implication that 'eunuch' was an insult thrown at Jesus that he himself then appropriated to describe his and his followers' 'place'; a marginal condition in which their status and masculine identity were que(e)ried.[46] Ignoring the queerness of the term – its effeminacy, ambiguity and liminality – commentators such as Jerome in the early Church and Dale Allison today have, Moxnes argues, spiritualized the action of disciples making themselves eunuchs for the Kingdom.[47] In reality those who were made eunuchs were disadvantaged socially, although many held prominent and confidential positions as servants; an example is the Ethiopian eunuch who is a court official in Acts 8.27. Occupying both male and female space in the household, eunuchs were the objects of both trust and suspicion. They were useful in that they could not establish their own households, so that they were dependent on their masters, and some eunuchs were valued as sexual partners.[48] Reading the eunuch as a figure of chastity and continence is another misstep the Church has made in making Jesus' words in Matthew 19 an appeal to an ascetic Christian ideal. Eunuchs were not able to procreate, but some were capable of and celebrated for their sexual prowess. According to some sources, there were three types of eunuch in the Graeco-Roman Empire: *castrati* (those who had neither penis nor testicles), *spadones* (those lacking testicles), and *thlibiae* (those with crushed testicles).[49] Those who made themselves eunuchs, such as the *galli*, the self-castrated followers of the Cybele and Attis cults, were especially abominated. Contemporary observers were repelled by both the 'orientalism' of these cults and by the *galli*'s alleged unchastity, and also by that effeminacy and liminality that they shared with involuntary eunuchs. Jerome and Origen wrote to discourage self-castration, but their main intent in interpreting the eunuch saying figuratively was to emphasize the hyper-masculinity of abstinence and renunciation. Ascetics were thus constructed, not as effeminate or *semiviri*, but as possessors of the masculine virtue of *enkrateia*, figured as warriors and soldiers.[50] Thus, in the early centuries of Christianity, manly self-control was encouraged but self-castration which made the male into an ambiguous, feminized creature was suppressed. The Council of Nicaea forbade men who had castrated themselves from becoming or remaining priests, which suggests that the practice was not uncommon in the first centuries of Christianity.[51]

Moxnes argues that this virile construal of continence erases the 'queer space' that Jesus arrogates from the slander of those who criticized him and his followers for abandoning conventional male space and embracing ambiguity.[52] They were 'eunuchs' because, although male, they were no longer men, since to be a man was a status of honour, which could be achieved but could also be lost.[53] Rather than being seen as a positive ideal – the virile contest for celibacy – Moxnes sees Jesus as identifying with the slander and putting himself and his followers alongside other marginalized and ambiguous groups who are included in the Kingdom, such as tax collectors and prostitutes. He writes:

> Eunuchs were men who were permanently out of place, in a liminal position where there was no possibility of integration into the order of masculinity ... I suggest that the modern term that can best provide a lens for viewing the material and a category of interpretation is that of 'queer'. This is in contrast to suggestions that Jesus could be understood by means of categories like feminine or gay. These would be categories that once more attempted to view Jesus in terms of a fixed identity, as feminine in contrast to masculine, or gay in contrast to heterosexual. 'Queer', on the other hand, does not indicate another category. Rather, it signals a protest against fixed categories. As a protest or opposition to fixed categories of identity, it points out that all categories are historically and socially constructed, and that human experiences are forced into these categories. The use of the term 'eunuch' in antiquity illustrates this point. It defied categorization. It did not fit into the categories of either male or female. In modern terminology, it is sometimes spoken of as a 'third gender'. The term queer is often used in questions of gender and identity, but it can be used in much broader terms than sexuality. It concerns power, social roles, places in hierarchies, in short,

all aspects of identity. I suggest, therefore that 'queer' is the most useful term to apply when we try to make sense of Jesus' eunuch saying from a modern perspective.[54]

Jesus leaves the male household and enters this 'queer space', where those who are placed in the Kingdom, alongside the ambiguous eunuchs, include children, the barren and asexuals, who live like angels. Moxnes draws a distinction between what he figures as queer asceticism and the virile asceticism that the Church Fathers drew from these texts; he views Jesus as subverting cultural norms and establishing new identities, where the Fathers' support for sexual continence conformed to existing Graeco-Roman ideals of (male) self-mastery. In Matthew's Gospel, Jesus' welcome to children, who are being held back by the disciples, follows the logion on eunuchs. This action disturbed the 'natural' order, for children are being placed first in this reversal motif.[55] Moxnes, reading the *Gospel of Thomas* logia alongside Matthew,[56] argues that the child represents asceticism in that it is regarded as presexual or asexual and as an exemplar of chastity. On the other hand, as Moxnes himself recognizes, the *Gospel of Thomas* figures the idealized androgyne as more *andro* than *gyne*, though he does not interrogate the implications of this construal. In one logion, male and female are subsumed into one another, into one androgynous being: 'When you make the two into one ... and when you make male and female into a single one, so that the male will not be male nor the female be female' (22.5); yet later in *Thomas*, Jesus says to Peter: 'Look, I will guide her [Mary] to make her male, so that she too may become a living spirit resembling you males. For every female who makes herself male will enter the kingdom of Heaven' (114). The female is no longer an eschatologically androgynous figure but is saved by making herself not liminal and ambiguous but male. This suggests that for this Gospel, at least, neither the *imago dei* nor the inheritors of the eschatological Kingdom are truly androgynous, but are conceived of as masculine.

The barren woman also represents a reversal of status, for the ability to produce children was part of God's promise to Israel. From a position of shame, which she shares with the eunuch, the infertile woman is now called 'blessed': 'blessed are the barren and the wombs that never bore and the breasts that never gave suck' (Luke 23.29). This eschatological reversal is also found in 'late' Jewish apocalyptic and wisdom texts where the woman and the eunuchs are both promised blessings:

> For blessed is the barren woman who is undefiled, who has not entered into a sinful union; she will have fruit when God examines souls.

Blessed also is the eunuch whose hands have done no lawless deed, and who has not devised wicked things against the Lord; for special favour will be shown him for his faithfulness, and a place of great delight in the temple of the Lord (Wisdom 3.13–14).

For Moxnes, such reversals show not only what can be expected in the future but also that which might be becoming reality in the eschatological present. A question about marriage in the resurrection receives the response in Matthew and Mark that there will be no marriage in the resurrection life for they 'are like angels in heaven' (Mark 12.25). But in Luke those who are considered worthy of resurrection have already attained that status; they are living in the eschatological age:

Jesus said to them, 'Those who belong to this age marry and are given in marriage; but those who are considered worthy of a place in that age and in the resurrection from the dead neither marry nor are given in marriage. Indeed they cannot die any more, because they are like angels and are children of God, being children of the resurrection. (Luke 20.34–36)

Like most commentators on these passages, Moxnes assumes that not marrying correlates with sexual renunciation – and, thus, celibate asceticism – because 'they are like angels'. However, scripture suggests that angels were not always reckoned as asexual or chaste beings, as the Nephilim in Genesis 6 demonstrate.[57] Might the eschatological age abolish marriage, but not sexuality? That would also be countercultural, overturning the family and household identities of the 'present age' and including those in the Kingdom who, like eunuchs, children and barren women, did not conform to the shared social norms of either Jewish or Graeco-Roman polity. For a church that has come to celebrate marriage as *the* Christian vocation the idea that sexuality or sexual intimacy can be separated from marriage and that it can belong properly to the new eschatological age is too disturbing to discuss. Or, at least, it is not being discussed in any of the reports that have been issued by the Church of England. Song, who sees non-procreative covenant partnership as a sign of the eschatological age, does not reflect on what sexual relationships might look like in a context where partnership is relativized by being 'children of the resurrection'.

Marriage as Creation Ordinance Versus Queer Asceticism

As I have shown, neither the authors of the *Pilling Report*, nor Song in *Covenant and Calling*, que(e)ries the precept that marriage is an immutable creation ordinance rooted in the combined narratives of Genesis 1 and 2. Song does relativize the goods of marriage, arguing that, although procreation remains a protological good, non-procreative covenant partnerships (which can be sexual in expression) are the fruit of the new eschatological age inaugurated by the coming of Christ. Both acknowledge that celibacy is a distinctive calling for the Christian disciple (though abstinence was not unknown as a virtue in pagan late antiquity) without exploring the almost univocal tradition of the early Church that valorized virginity and sexual abstinence and that saw ascesis, not marriage, as the paramount Christian vocation. Both *Pilling* and Song also overlook the tradition of the early Jesus movement that relativized, if not rejected, the goods of family, household and procreation. Jesus and the disciples seem to have gathered around them a community of the liminal – those outside traditional households: barren women, eunuchs and children; as well as tax collectors and prostitutes. The Matthean pericope in which Jesus conflates the two Genesis passages and thus, it is argued by conservative scholars, defends the goods of male/female marriage, occurs in a debate about the licitness of divorce. In any case, the one-flesh union that cannot be sundered is proclaimed without any reference to the goods of procreation, also assumed as a divine fiat in the creation narratives, and it is followed by the eunuch saying that encompasses the non-procreative in the Kingdom. This pericope on marriage must also be nuanced by those logia that claim the Kingdom for the liminal, the ambiguous and the androgynous, as Halvor Moxnes has persuasively argued. Moxnes' 'queer space' reads the Kingdom as a 'place' that queers the norms of patriarchal households; it includes, for example, women who do not seem to be under the authority of husbands/men. But he does not, as we have seen, explore how the anti-family/household sayings also construct a community that queers (if not annuls) the creation ordinance of procreative marriage; 'where there is death, there is marriage', wrote John Chrysostom, in the fourth century.[58]

Marriage and Celibacy

Another way in which queer people feel marginalized by the Church of England, and thus by processes like *Pilling*, is that the hegemonic good of heterosexual marriage construed as the preeminent Christian calling also marginalizes those who choose celibacy (or abstinence) rather than seeking same-sex marriage or sexual relationships. There is some discussion of how this might que(e)ry the Church's connubial assumptions in *Pilling* and at the General Synod conversations, but the idea of asceticism subverting heterosexual and nuptial norms is largely unexplored.

One of the effects of the sixteenth-century reform that construes marriage, rather than celibacy, as *the* Christian calling, is that churches can become inhospitable places for the ascetic and the abstinent: those people who were once honoured have become an embarrassment for a tradition that idolizes the family. Many single, widowed and divorced people say that they feel unwelcome in churches where both worship and social activities are focused on couples and families.[59] Some gay Christians who adhere to the belief that scripture and tradition teach that there are only two godly vocations – heterosexual marriage or abstinent celibacy – maintain that they are marginalized, both in contemporary secular society and by churches that focus on the family as the locus of godly living.[60] A number of organizations and charities exist to support gay (or same-sex attracted) Christians to follow what they construe as biblical teaching on sexuality. The True Freedom Trust and Living Out are two of the better-known such organizations in the UK, with established web and social media presences. Although Living Out uses the word 'gay' under the welcome at the top of its home page, it, like the True Freedom Trust, prefers the term same-sex attracted (SSA) because, they claim, gay is an 'identity' that assumes certain behaviours and attitudes, and the Christian's true identity is in Christ. Living Out also avoids the term bisexual which suggests that bisexuality is still regarded as 'inevitably involv[ing] being unfaithful'.[61] However, one of the trustees, Sean Doherty, assures me that the absence of the term in the Living Out materials is because the Trust tends to steer clear of sexual identity and orientation language and that the language of same-sex attraction includes what might be described as bisexuality since being SSA doesn't exclude opposite- sex attraction. Doherty also recognizes the problem of the understanding of bisexuality in *Issues in Human Sexuality*, which implies that bisexual people are inherently unfaithful.[62] Eschewing reparative therapy, which aims to change sexual orientation (unlike some other ministries that offer counsel on 'unwanted same-sex attraction'),[63] Living Out seeks to call Christian disciples to the two vocations of male/female marriage or sexual continence.[64] Two of the contributors to Living Out, one a trustee, are in mixed-sex marriages, though Sean Doherty (the trustee) describes himself still as same-sex attracted, as well as being attracted to his wife, Gaby.[65] In contemporary, late capitalist, Western culture, this call to continence before and outside marriage may be regarded as curiously countercultural. Ed Shaw, another of the trustees and a celibate man who, in his own words, 'experiences same-sex attraction', claims that the Church, even in some of its evangelical expressions, is becoming more affirming of same-sex sexual relationships that are permanent, faithful and stable. Shaw sees that the plausibility issue in the Church is that

> what the Bible clearly teaches sounds so unreasonable to so many of us today ... A few, high-profile leaders in our churches have already broken ranks. The worrying silence of a number of other key leaders and churches should prepare us for more and more sudden departures from the biblical teaching that sex is for marriage, and that marriage is the lifelong union of a man and a woman.[66]

Shaw's *The Plausibility Problem* is an apologia, declaring that 'we just have to make what the Bible clearly commands plausible again',[67] and to make it reasonable, not to 'the predictable target – compromising liberals – but to those who belong to his [Shaw's] own evangelical tribe'.[68] The book is a call to evangelical Christians to avoid apostasy; it is unlikely to appeal to those 'compromising liberals' – those who are now, perhaps, the majority in the Church of England who are affirming of stable same-sex relationships.[69] Yet, in naming the missteps that he believes the Church has taken in conforming to the world, Shaw returns to the tradition of the charism of celibacy, a calling that, he feels, has been neglected especially in evangelical churches that have privileged marriage and the nuclear family and marginalized the single, unless they are young people being steered towards the goal of godly matrimony. Shaw, like Song, recognizes that procreation is less of a good in the New Testament than in the Hebrew Bible and that the Jesus movement's family are those who follow Jesus rather than his blood kin. Unlike Song, Shaw does not infer from this that in Christ there is a new charism – covenant partnership – but he does call upon churches to rediscover their calling of being family as the first Christian communities were arguing that we must 'wake up to the radical New Testament idea that church really is family – and that Mum, Dad and 2.4 children as the "only" family is just an unhealthy late-twentieth-century construct'.[70] Shaw sees churches as places where loneliness is banished by being part of an authentic community, and he writes that his own church family is moving towards this model. He also wishes to rehabilitate the tradition of celibacy, of lifelong singleness, as a plausible way of living, in which there is struggle and self-sacrifice but the hope of a future eschatological reward. Obedience to the 'traditional' teaching of the Church is the touchstone here: 'access is not for all: sinful attitudes and actions that you haven't repented of (like sex outside marriage) mean you won't get in'.[71]

Living Out and the gay conversion therapies and ministries described by Tanya Erzen in *Straight to Jesus* have created queer spaces for those who describe themselves as same-sex attracted or ex-gay in that, despite their circumvention of identity language, they acknowledge the existence and the reality of queer desire and queer lives.[72] Queer is a contested term and there will be, perhaps, queer theorists and gay and bi people who would not wish to share a queer space with those who seem to deny or eschew their own queerness. But queer queries the normative – even the normative identities, behaviours and traditions of (sometimes) oppressed minorities; otherwise there would be a hierarchy of queerness, with only those deemed properly queer admitted. As David Halperin's indeterminate (and now renowned) definition claims:

> Queer is by definition *whatever* is at odds with the normal, the legitimate, the dominant. *There is nothing in particular to which it necessarily refers.* It is an identity without an essence. 'Queer,' then, demarcates not a positivity but a positionality vis-à-vis the normative ... [and] describes a horizon of possibilities whose precise extent and heterogeneous scope cannot in principle be determined in advance.[73]

Yet, although *The Plausibility Problem* is, in some respects, a radical approach to the desire, both secular and religious, for the unconditional right to self-affirming and self-fulfilling identities predicated on living life in its fullness, Shaw makes his own missteps. The fear of not getting in (to Heaven) suggests a contractual theology, where salvation is seen not as a gift of grace, but as a reward for self-denying sexual continence. Another misstep is that, although Shaw speaks of recovering the gift of celibacy, for him and for other same-sex attracted people, it is not so much a gift or calling as a prerequisite. There is no acknowledgement that, in spite of the variety of sexual desires, orientations and identities, some people are called to celibacy and others are not. Thus, despite an appeal to the scriptural and Church traditions that privileged continence and community over marriage and family, Shaw does not attempt to undo 'traditional' readings of the Bible, in particular the Genesis narratives. There is no question that 'by the end of the second chapter [of Genesis], all the core biblical ethics are in place. We are clearly told that marriage is for a man and a woman, and that sex is for marriage. God's parameters for me with my same-sex attraction are unambiguous', and that '[Jesus] based his sexual ethics on the timeless truths of Genesis, despite all that had changed since then'.[74] Rather than finding and claiming a 'queer space' in which he and others who do not conform to the heterosexual 'norm' are admitted into the Kingdom, Shaw capitulates to a narrative that figures gay people as queerly other, who can inherit the Kingdom only by renouncing their queerness. He has not destabilized the paradigms but reinscribed them.

In reinscribing these paradigms Song and Shaw leave protological claims about the creation ordinances and the goods of Christian marriage unchallenged. They seek to interrogate the ways in which these divine archetypes have been construed rather than que(e)rying whether they are divine fiats and intended to be read thus in the current doctrine of the Church of England. The edifice upon which such readings are built – church doctrine and church authority – remains untroubled by their arguments, although these arguments are, perhaps, the queerest to have emerged from the *Pilling* process. The tendency of such a debate is almost invariably assimilationist and although in Butler's words a 'livable life'[75] might be preferable to the trauma of self-imposed exile from these norms, a debate of this type allows the institution to pursue the goals of success and harmony. The queer art of failure, which offers a 'dream of an alternative way of being'[76] (or many ways), is dismissed or unacknowledged or simply not dreamt of.

Lee Edelman, *No Future: Queer Theory and the Death Drive*

My last conversation partner in this chapter is Lee Edelman whose *No Future: Queer Theory and the Death Drive* proclaims a queer theory that nullifies order, security and futurity; a queer ethics that '[accepts] its figural status as resistance to the viability of the social while insisting on the inextricability of such resistance from every social structure'.[77] *No Future* is a fervent polemic against the 'Symbol' of the Child, a rejection of the good of reproductive futurity, and a paean to the death drive: 'the Child ... marks the fetishistic fixation of heteronormativity: an erotically charged investment in the rigid sameness of identity that is central to the compulsory narrative of reproductive futurism'.[78] Edelman que(e)ries the putative goods of heteronormative futurity that permeate even liberal outlooks: the sexual and social telos of the Child. Quoting the film *Children of Men*, Edelman notes the pronatalism of the narrator's lament that 'sex totally divorced from procreation has become almost meaninglessly acrobatic'.[79] This could be the lament of some, more conservative, versions of contemporary Christianity, both Catholic and Reformed, and it is significant that the author of the novel on which the film *Children of Men* is based was an Anglican Christian with traditional and rather conservative beliefs.[80] At the end of the film, inevitably given the investment in the good of procreation, a child redeemer is born. Edelman comments:

> Sexual practice will continue to allegorize the vicissitudes of meaning so long as the specifically heterosexual alibi of reproductive necessity obscures the drive *beyond* meaning driving the machinery of sexual meaningfulness: so long, that is, as the biological fact of heterosexual procreation bestows the imprimatur of meaning-production on hetero-genital relations. For the Child, whose mere possibility is enough to spirit away the naked truth of heterosexual sex – impregnating heterosexuality, as it were, with the future of signification by conferring upon it the cultural burden of signifying futurity – figures our identification with an always about-to-be-realized identity.[81]

By rejecting the moral and social value of reproductive futurity, Edelman has attracted criticism from other queer theorists who offer the hope of unrealized potentiality in more reparative readings.[82] Indeed, it may seem strange to engage with an author who queers the social good of redemptive futurity by investing in the death drive (if Edelman can be figured as 'investing' in anything) in a conversation with texts, both scripture and commentary, so committed to the reality of eschatological hope. But there is something compellingly theological about Edelman's non-eschatological eschatology, realized rather than inaugurated and denying a future that reinscribes the past. Edelman may be surprised to hear Song's view that 'sex BC is not the same as sex AD',[83] and that in the resurrection life, according to Christian scripture and tradition, there is no marriage and no procreative futurity. For both the early Jesus movement and for the Church Fathers, an inaugurated eschatology already relativized, if not nullified, the goods of reproductive futurity. Eunuchs, barren women, and children were to inherit the Kingdom; not children as symbols of capital and inheritors of the future, but children as pre-sexual, androgynous, unproductive beings. The New Testament suggests that the blessings of children as investment for the future have been relativized by the coming of the incarnate Child. We find echoes too in Edelman's polemic of John Chrysostom who noted that 'where there is death, there is marriage',[84] and for whom, now that the earth was populated, marriage existed only to control lust.

Curiously, Edelman's queering of the 'paramount value of futurity' and of the continuing cycle of reproduction is closer to the radically non-procreative vision of the authors of Matthew and Luke, and to most Patristic writers, than it is to the Reformed tradition that figured the family as a little church, ruled by the Pastor/Paterfamilias and modelled on the submissive hierarchy of the household codes. In a sense, Edelman has taken Song's and Shaw's eschatological intimations to a plausible terminus. Edelman and Shaw may appear to have little in common beyond their sexual orientation, but both have eschewed reproductive futurity for the attainment of jouissance.[85] For Shaw the sacrifice of heirs is not an 'end' in itself but will have been worth it for the assurance of eternal jouissance.[86] It would be deconstructing Edelman's project to claim this end – of kinships and procreation – as a Christian telos. It might even be offensive to suggest that Edelman's thesis has any telos apart from pleasure. And yet, if his work can be figured as theological, it is a theology that queers the palimpsest of Christian history, returning us to the eschatological community of the barren. It reiterates, inadvertently, those negative, ambiguous and queer traditions in which Moxnes places Jesus and that are, for Song, glimpses into an eschatology that modifies the traditionally construed creation ordinances. Song does not ask – although we might – if it is not therefore supersessionist to regard these narratives as original divine fiats, now relativized by the cross and the resurrection. We might also ask: why and how has the Church (and, indeed, the Church of England and the authors of the *Pilling Report*) chosen *this* tradition rather than *that*? It is true that *Pilling* leaves little space for reflecting on scriptural tradition and only alludes to other normative Christian readings, mostly from the Reformed tradition, in earlier Church reports and publications. The authors might not have wished to open a can of hermeneutical worms. As in the sections on the sciences and the social sciences, the authors seemed ready to privilege those voices whom they, perhaps, perceived to be orthodox, safe and 'on side'.

Robert Song was on the Working Party of *Pilling*, though it is difficult to discern the voices of the contributors, except for those sections that bear an ascription. Yet Song's vision of an alternative sexual calling, which could be faithful to Christian tradition and discipline, while also both innovative and pastoral, barely disturbs the normative protological reading of creation in which, contra early exegesis of Genesis such as that of Gregory of Nyssa, male and female are fashioned as necessary marriage partners.[87] For Gregory, protology and eschatology are linked so that, at the resurrection, the created being will return to its primal (and pristine) androgynous state.[88]

How Queer is this Art?

One of my conversation partners in this chapter, Robert Song, and the same-sex attracted adherents of Living Out, frame Christian eschatology in a new covenant that disrupts, but does not abolish, the creation goods of marriage and procreation. New charisms of non-procreative covenant relationships and abstinent celibacy are being added to the Christian calling. For Moxnes the eschatological community now includes the sterile, the ascetic and those without kin. Edelman ruptures this eschatological framework with a realized vision of non-procreative being that is in some ways more akin to that of the Church Fathers, though it abjures their valorization of ascetic discipline. None of these queries the protological claims for the Genesis texts (Edelman because he is discussing futurity rather than origin), the claims on which their neo-covenantal eschatology rests. The Christian writers assume – as do the authors of *Pilling* – that the Genesis narratives mandate marriage and procreativity. But, in reflecting on the way in which *Pilling* privileges this reading of Genesis as a creation ordinance, I wish to que(e)ry these normative, Reformed, protological claims. Could it be that the inaugurated eschatology of a new covenant is recovering the goods of the creation narratives rather than merely relativizing them? The claims that have been made for these narratives as normative readings of marriage, gender and sexuality, which are embedded in *Pilling* and in Song and in the stories in Living Out, might not be unassailable. As Ken Stone has argued, what the Bible texts are really 'about' has as much to do with our preoccupations and concerns as readers (and those of the writers of church reports) as they do with 'the texts themselves'.[89] Stone suggests that the Genesis narratives are as much 'about' food as they are 'about' sex, and, that although contemporary readers would find this parity difficult to recognize, it was one that seemed clear to the Church Fathers. For Jerome and Chrysostom, sexual congress began only after the expulsion from Eden and was made necessary by the loss of immortality. Abstinence from sexual intimacy is inseparable from abstinence from food:

> Adam received a command in Paradise to abstain from one tree though he might eat the other fruit. The blessedness of paradise could not be consecrated without absence from food. So long as he fasted he remained in paradise; he ate and he was cast out; he was no sooner cast out than he married a wife. While he fasted in paradise he continued a virgin; when he filled himself with food in the earth, he bound himself with the tie of marriage.[90]

It is not that Jerome, Tertullian and Chrysostom are 'right' in their protological reading of Genesis and that contemporary commentators, including the writers of *Pilling*, are 'wrong'; it is the case that a reading now rendered authoritative in the Church (and portrayed as 'traditional') has superseded all other possible readings. A particular protological interpretation of the Genesis accounts has not only been privileged; it has also successfully silenced the voices of other readings. Once again, despite its claims to provisionality, *Pilling* delivers inviolability. There is no recognition of the possibility that these texts do not provide a neat, binary account of cisheterosexual, and patriarchal, marriage but might rather offer something that challenges both the epistemic assumptions of the modern Church and the telos of success. In the agnostic silence of Holy Saturday and in the presence (or absence) of a dead Messiah, all possibilities are both gravid and barren, and, by dwelling in this site of queer temporality, the Church could discover that failure offers a more potent resolution than that provided by neoliberal practices of progress.

In the final chapter, I reflect upon how queerness may be expressed in this art of failure, a failure that has the tentative potential to be more redemptive than the neoliberal goal of success and progress. Indeed, the goal of progress for a church that is proclaiming the radical undoing of the gospel narrative may always prove to be chimerical. I suggest that the Church of England dwells in the queer temporality of Holy Saturday, inhabiting this site of abnegation as a redemptive space where wordiness is exchanged for Wordlessness.[91]

Notes

1 J. Halberstam, *The Queer Art of Failure* (Durham, NC: Duke University Press, 2011), 52.

2 The Archbishops' Council, *Report of the House of Bishops Working Group on Human Sexuality* (London: Church House Publishing, November 2013), 67–74: the 'distinctive hermeneutic of Dale Martin and Deryn Guest', outlined in the chapter on hermeneutic lenses, cultural meanings in scripture and translation problems, 67–74.

3 *Pilling*, 15.

4 *Pilling*, 15–16.

5 Two of the most obvious examples of readings being relativized by context or the mutability of an engagement with reason are the Church of England's position on slavery and women's orders.

6 The Archbishops' Council, *Some Issues in Human Sexuality: A Guide to the Debate* (London: Church House Publishing, 2003); Philip Groves, ed., *The Anglican Communion and Homosexuality* (London: SPCK, 2008).

7 *Some Issues* does introduce, briefly, revisionist readings by Gary Comstock, James Alison, and Bishops John Habgood, John Spong and Richard Holloway.

8 *Pilling*, 74.

9 Hugh Pyper, *The Unchained Bible: Cultural Appropriations of Biblical Texts* (London: Bloomsbury, 2010), 35–44; Ken Stone, *Practicing Safer Texts: Food, Sex and Bible in Queer Perspective* (London: T&T Clark, 2004).

10 *Pilling*, 30–36.

11 Tina Beattie argues that ha'adam in Genesis 2 is a non-gendered earthling, which only becomes male with the creation of woman, but that contra Balthasar's interpretation of the narrative as a gendered, primal man alone before God, until he is 'kenotically robbed of a part of himself', Eve (being a part of Adam) is 'not really other at all', Tina Beattie, *New Catholic Feminism: Theology and Theory* (Abingdon: Taylor & Francis, 2006), 105.

12 Although Ken Stone argues that humans, in creation mythologies, were probably created mortal but had a chance to grasp immortality by eating a food known to the Gods. In both Gilgamesh and Genesis the human is thwarted by a snake and, thus, the story of Genesis is not of a Fall into sin and death but about a failure to obtain immortality; Ken Stone, *Practicing Safer Texts*, 40.

13 Cf. C. S. Lewis's concept of chronological snobbery: 'the uncritical acceptance of the intellectual climate common to our own age and the assumption that whatever has gone out of date is on that account discredited'; C. S. Lewis, *A Mind Awake: An Anthology of C. S. Lewis* (Boston, MA: Houghton Mifflin Harcourt, 2003), 221. This is somewhat akin to the idea that Whig history is invested in the progressive improvement of human nature and culture.

14 Again, Ken Stone observes that the understanding of marriage in these narratives would not be that of most Jews and Christians today. Marriage is more akin, Stone argues, to Gayle Rubin's notion of 'the traffic in women' as (one of) the means by which men establish and manipulate relations with each other. Stone also notes that the Hebrew Bible has no words which correspond specifically with the terms 'marriage', 'husband' and 'wife', as we understand them; Ken Stone, *Practicing Safer Texts*, 82–83.

15 Robert Song, *Covenant and Calling: Towards a Theology of Same-sex Relationships* (London: SCM Press, 2014).

16 Lee Edelman, *No Future: Queer Theory and the Death Drive* (Durham, NC: Duke University Press, 2004).

17 Cf. Robert Song, *Covenant and Calling*, 13.

18 *Living Out*, http://www.livingout.org/. The organization's alternative to celibacy for gay people is reparative heterosexual marriage, if this is attainable (accessed 15.2.24).

19 Robert Song, *Covenant and Calling*, x–xi.

20 Robert Song, *Covenant and Calling*, xi.

21 Robert Song, *Covenant and Calling*, 27.

22 Robert Song, *Covenant and Calling*, 27.

23 Robert Song, *Covenant and Calling*, 84–85; he also cites difficulties such as couples who entered a 'covenant partnership' and then decided that they wanted children, or couples who married and then decided that they did not want children.

24 Some mixed-sex couples argued for a change in the law to allow them to be civilly partnered rather than (civilly) married; cf. Rebecca Steinield and Charles Keidan, in Ben Quinn, 'Couple who won battle to open up civil unions register partnership', *The Guardian*, 31 December 2019, https://www.theguardian.com/uk-news/2019/dec/31/couple-who-won-battle-to-open-up-civil-unions-register-partnership (accessed 15.2.24). See also, Equal Civil Partnerships: from the Equal Civil Partnerships Campaign Group, http://equalcivilpartnerships.org.uk/ (accessed 15.2.24). In 2020 there were 7,566 mixed-sex civil partnerships registered in England and Wales; this

was the first year that such partnerships had been recorded, 'Marriage, Cohabitation and Civil Partnerships', *Office for National Statistics*, https://www.ons.gov.uk/peoplepopulationandcommunity/birthsdeathsandmarriages/marriagecohabitationandcivilpartnerships (accessed 15.2.24).

25 It is more likely that opening civil partnerships to mixed-sex couples will have an impact on civil secular marriage rates rather than on religious ceremonies. Couples who see marriage as a sacrament or as a significant religious rite are unlikely to opt for a civil partnership; although, since some Christian same-sex couples have not converted their civil partnerships to marriages, there is a possibility that Christian mixed-sex couples may choose to enter a civil partnership rather than a civil or religious marriage. The figures from 2020 (the first year in which mixed-sex civil partnerships were available) shows that 7,566 mixed-sex civil partnerships were contracted compared with 785 between same-sex couples (in England and Wales). *Census 2021: Marriage, cohabitations and civil partnerships*, https://www.ons.gov.uk/peoplepopulationandcommunity/birthsdeathsandmarriages/marriagecohabitationandcivilpartnerships (accessed 15.2.24).

26 Robert Song, *Covenant and Calling*, 89.

27 David Nixon, 'Ecclesial Speed Dating? A Theological Reflection on One Shared Conversation', *The Expository Times*, 127, no. 8, 2016, 391, https://journals.sagepub.com/doi/abs/10.1177/0014524615592804 (accessed 15.2.24).

28 For discussions on the shifting understandings of marriage from antiquity to the present see: Allison Glazebrook and Kelly Olson, 'Greek and Roman Marriage', in Thomas K. Hubbard, ed., *A Companion to Greek and Roman Sexualities* (Hoboken, NJ: Wiley Blackwell, 2014); David L. Balch and Carolyn Osiek, eds, *Earliest Christian Families in Context: An Interdisciplinary Dialogue* (Grand Rapids, MI: Eerdmans, 2003); Philip Lyndon Reynolds, *Marriage in the Western Church: The Christianization of Marriage During the Patristic and Early Medieval Periods* (Leiden: Brill, 2001); Lawrence Stone, *The Family, Sex and Marriage in England 1500–1800* (London: Penguin, 1990); John Witte, Jr, *From Sacrament to Covenant: Marriage, Religion and Law in the Western Christian Tradition* (Louisville, KY: Westminster John Knox Press, 2012); Charlotte Methuen, 'Thinking About Marriage: What Can We Learn from Christian History?', and Augur Pearce, 'Marriage and English Law', in John Bradbury and Susannah Cornwall, eds, *Thinking Again About Marriage: Key Theological Questions* (London: SCM Press, 2016).

29 'Whether or not there was any Christian nuptial liturgy before the fourth century is a matter that remains controvertible, but there is no evidence that the Medieval Western Church ever required priestly benediction or any other liturgical form as a condition for validity. It is not until the ninth century that we find anyone declaring that a marriage is invalid unless a priest has joined and blessed the man and woman, and even then the position was undermined by the denial of nuptial benediction to remarrying widowers and widows and even to those who had not preserved their chastity before marriage', Philip Lyndon Reynolds, *Marriage in the Western Church*, xix.

30 Robert Song, *Covenant and Calling*, 40.

31 Although there is much debate on whether head means ruler or fount in this and parallel contexts.

32 Robert Song, *Covenant and Calling*, 43. For discussions on the theology of complementarity, see Adrian Thatcher, *God, Sex and Gender: An Introduction* (Hoboken, NJ: Wiley Blackwell, 2011); Tina Beattie, *New Catholic Feminism: Theology and Theory* (Abingdon: Taylor & Francis, 2006); Karen Kilby, *Balthasar: A (Very) Critical*

Introduction (Grand Rapids, MI: Eerdmans, 2012) (both on Balthasar's reading of complementarity).

33 Robert Song, *Covenant and Calling*, 43.

34 Robert Song, *Covenant and Calling*, 47.

35 'I don't see what sort of help woman was created to provide man with, if one excludes the purposes of procreation. If woman is not given to man for help in bearing children, for what help could she be? To till the earth together? If help were needed for that, man would have been a better help for man. The same goes for comfort in solitude. How much more pleasure is it for life and conversation when two friends live together than when a man and a woman cohabitate?' (De genesi ad litteram); cited in Uta Ranke-Heinemann, *Eunuchs for the Kingdom of Heaven: The Catholic Church and Sexuality* (London: Penguin, 1990), 88.

36 Robert Song, *Covenant and Calling*, 48–49, emphasis original.

37 Robert Song, *Covenant and Calling*, 49.

38 Although, for some of the early Church Fathers, who believed that the image of God was a primal androgyne and that the division into male and female was as a result of the Fall, Paul's statement in Galatians returns us to Genesis 1.26, God's primary purpose, as well as undoing Genesis 1.27, the result of human's sin. Cf. Uta Ranke-Heinemann, *Eunuchs for the Kingdom of Heaven*, 52–57.

39 In this interim time, however, a tendency towards antinomianism suggests that some societal structures remain in place.

40 1 Corinthians 15.42–45: 'So, in the same way it is with the resurrection of the dead; it is sown in corruption, it is raised incorruptible. It is sown in dishonour, it is raised in glory; it is sown in weakness, it is raised in power. It is sown an earthly body, it is raised a heavenly body. If there is an earthly body there is also a heavenly one' (my translation).

41 For example, see the references to Andrew Symes on pp. 62–3, and to John McGinley on pp. 65 and 87 n.45.

42 'Theology is a queer thing', writes Gerard Loughlin in the Introduction to Gerard Loughlin, ed., *Queer Theology: Rethinking the Western Body* (Oxford: Blackwell, 2007), 7.

43 Linn Marie Tonstad, *God and Difference: The Trinity, Sexuality, and the Transformation of Finitude* (Abingdon: Taylor & Francis, 2017), 14.

44 Halvor Moxnes suggests that it was Matthew's redaction that combined the two phrases and that the original Matthew 19.12 was an independent saying, *Putting Jesus in His Place: A Radical Vision of Household and Kingdom* (Louisville, KY: Westminster John Knox Press, 2003), 74–75.

45 More recently, those Jesus describes as eunuchs from birth have been claimed by some who do not conform to normative presentations of sex and gender as an acknowledgement, in the biblical texts, of their existence and agency; cf. Susannah Cornwall, *Sex and Uncertainty in the Body of Christ: Intersex Conditions and Christian Theology* (Abingdon: Routledge, 2010), 133–139.

46 Much as the term 'queer', originally an insult, has been repurposed by (some) LGBTIQ+ people as a badge of identity, Halvor Moxnes, *Putting Jesus in His Place*, 88–90.

47 Halvor Moxnes, *Putting Jesus in His Place*, 75–76.

48 Anna Rebecca Solevag, 'No Nuts? No Problem! Disability, Stigma and the Baptized Eunuch in Acts 8.26-40', *Biblical Interpretation* 24 (2016) 81–99.

49 Review of Arnold van de Laar, *Under the Knife: The History of Surgery in 28 Remarkable Operations*, by Gerald DeGroot, *The Times*, 12 January 2018.

50 Interestingly, this is the case in both early and contemporary readings. Jerome and Origen use the warrior trope, while Allison likens them to Spartans or Greek athletes; images replete with masculine power and self-mastery. Moxnes, *Putting Jesus in His Place*, 72–90.

51 Paul F. Paveo, 'Canons of the Council of Nicaea', *Christian History for Everyman*, https://www.christian-history.org/council-of-nicea-canons.html (accessed 15.2.24).

52 See 'Chapter 4: Leaving Male Space' and 'Chapter 5: Entering Queer Space', in Halvor Moxnes, *Putting Jesus in His Place*.

53 I am aware, as is Moxnes, that not all of Jesus' followers were male (or men). Moxnes argues that 'when ... I focus on how male identity was challenged by Jesus, it is actually a perspective that is inspired by feminist criticism', *Putting Jesus in His Place*, 73.

54 Halvor Moxnes, *Putting Jesus in His Place*, 89–90.

55 Cf. Ephesians 6.1–4.

56 'Jesus saw infants being suckled. He said to his disciples: "These infants being suckled are like those who enter the kingdom." They said to him: "Shall we, then, as children, enter the kingdom?"', in *Gospel of Thomas* 22.1–3, cited in Halvor Moxnes, *Putting Jesus in His Place*, 92.

57 There is also an exegetical tradition (found as late as the 1960s in the Exclusive Brethren) that Paul's warning to women to veil themselves (literally, have authority on her head) because of the angels, refers to randy angels who might otherwise be tempted by the women's beauty. Tertullian is the first commentator to link the warning to the Corinthian women with the lustful 'watchers' of 1 Enoch 6–7 (an extended version of the story of the Nephilim in Genesis 6). *I Enoch (Ethiopic) Parallel Translations*, http://qbible.com/enoch/7.html (accessed 15.2.24). Dale Martin in *The Corinthian Body* argues that the Genesis 6 (1 Enoch 6–7) reading of lustful angels was common in Paul's day and because, in Paul's angelology, angels are never entirely benign or morally unambiguous (2 Cor. 12.17 speaks of the 'angel of Satan' whose purpose is to torment the apostle), the angels represent some kind of threat to the sexual purity of the women prophets, 242–249.

58 *De virginitate*, 14.6 (1985), https://openlibrary.org/books/OL16542118M/St._John_Chrysostom%27s_De_virginitate_and_De_non_iterando_coniugio (accessed 15.2.24).

59 See, for example, Ruth Perrin, 'The Gift No-One Wants: Millennial Christians and Singleness', *Discipleship Research*, October 2017, https://discipleshipresearch.com/2017/10/the-gift-no-one-wants/ (accessed 15.2.24).

60 See David Bennett, 'Church Clarity on Sexuality – or Church Control?', *Christian Today*, 19 October 2017, https://www.christiantoday.com/article/church-clarity-on-sexuality-or-church-control/116440.htm (accessed 15.2.24), in which Bennett also argues that inclusive churches are 'unsafe' places for non-affirming gay Christians.

61 The Archbishops' Council, which goes on to recommend heterosexual marriage for bisexual people who are 'capable of heterophile relationships'; *Issues in Human Sexuality: A Statement by the House of Bishops* (London: Church House Publishing, 1991), 42.

62 Conversation with Sean Doherty by direct message on Twitter, 1 February 2018. Sean gave me permission to share this conversation.

63 Such as the ex-gay ministries (in a US context) in Tanya Erzen, *Straight to Jesus: Sexual and Christian Conversions in the Ex-Gay Movement* (Oakland, CA: University of California Press, 2006).

64 There is, however, an article on the *Living Out* website by Peter Ould, 'Can Your Sexuality Change?', 12 January 2021, which suggests, based on a Jones and Yarhouse study, that ex-gay therapies may effect changes in sexual identity rather than in sexual orientation, https://www.livingout.org/resources/articles/44/can-your-sexuality-change (accessed 15.2.24). The study showed that, although sexual orientation is unlikely to change to any great degree, the way in which people identify changes through alterations in self-perception and in the way in which people label their sexual preferences.

65 Sean and Gaby Doherty, 'Sean and Gaby', *Living Out*, 29 October 2020, http://www.livingout.org/stories/sean-and-gaby (accessed 15.2.24).

66 Ed Shaw, *The Plausibility Problem: The Church and Same-Sex Attraction* (Nottingham: Inter-Varsity Press, 2015), 23.

67 Ed Shaw, *The Plausibility Problem*, 23.

68 Vaughan Roberts, 'Foreword', *The Plausibility Problem*, 5.

69 Polls have suggested that an increasing number of Anglicans and Roman Catholics are in favour of same-sex marriage. Linda Woodhead commissioned a poll for the *Westminster Faith Debates*, 'Press Release "Do Christians Really Oppose Gay Marriage?"', *Religion and Society*, 18 April 2013, http://www.religionandsociety.org.uk/events/programme_events/show/press_release_do_christians_really_oppose_gay_marriage (accessed 15.2.24). In three years that number had increased. According to a YouGov poll commissioned by Jayne Ozanne, 'Same-sex Marriage – 2016 You Gov Poll', Jayne Ozanne's personal website, https://jayneozanne.com/2017/09/12/attitudes-to-same-sex-marriage-yougov-poll (accessed 15.2.24). In March 2022: 'The proportion of self-identified Anglicans who agree that same-sex marriage is "right" has exceeded 50 per cent for the first time, a new YouGov poll ... suggests', Madeleine Davies, *Church Times*, 1 March 2022, https://www.churchtimes.co.uk/articles/2022/4-march/news/uk/yougov-poll-more-than-half-of-anglicans-believe-same-sex-marriage-to-be-right (accessed 15.2.24).

70 Ed Shaw, *The Plausibility Problem*, 48.

71 Ed Shaw, *The Plausibility Problem*, 153.

72 Tanya Erzen, *Straight to Jesus*, 14.

73 David M. Halperin, *Saint Foucault: Towards a Gay Hagiography* (Oxford: Oxford University Press, 1995), 62, emphases original. Halperin's definition is cited in the Introduction to this thesis, 31.

74 Ed Shaw, *The Plausibility Problem*, 141–142.

75 Judith Butler, *Undoing Gender* (Abingdon: Routledge, 2004), 8.

76 J. Halberstam, *The Queer Art of Failure*, 52.

77 Lee Edelman, *No Future: Queer Theory and the Death Drive* (Durham, NC: Duke University Press, 2004), 3.

78 Lee Edelman, *No Future*, 21.

79 *Children of Men* is based upon a dystopian novel in which, due to male infertility, the population is dwindling, cited in Lee Edelman, *No Future*, 13.

80 P. D. James, *The Children of Men* (London: Faber & Faber, 1992).

81 Lee Edelman, *No Future*, 13, emphasis original.

82 Jose Esteban Muñoz, cited in Susannah Cornwall, 'Something There Is That Doesn't Love a Wall', *Theology and Sexuality*, 21, no. 1 (2015), 20–35; J. Halberstam, *The Queer Art of Failure*, 106–109, 120.

83 Robert Song, *Covenant and Calling*, x–xi.

84 *De virginitate*, 14.6, 1985, https://openlibrary.org/books/OL16542118M/St._John_Chrysostom%27s_De_virginitate_and_De_non_iterando_coniugio (accessed 15.2.24).

85 Jouissance is pleasure, delight or ecstasy. It is used, following the work of Jaques Lacan, to denote transgressive pleasure. The term is usually left untranslated, since there is no English term that exactly corresponds.

86 Ed Shaw, *The Plausibility Problem*, 'Marriage to Jesus will be better than sex (Revelation 21.3–4). I hear that sex can be great. But if I die a virgin, I will not be missing out: the eternal consummation of my relationship with Jesus will be far better than the temporary consummation of any human relationships. The latter always leads to death and mourning and crying and pain: the former will bring nothing but everlasting joy', 152, emphasis original.

87 Gregory understood the accounts in Genesis 1 and 2 as a double creation: the first human is an androgynous, asexual being; the making of sexual difference introduces an animality that will be stripped away at the resurrection and is contingent upon God's foreknowledge of original sin. Cf. Tina Beattie, *New Catholic Feminism: Theology and Theory* (Abingdon: Taylor & Francis, 2006), 117–118.

88 Raphael Cadenhead, 'An Ascetical Critique of "Gender Complementarity"', in John Bradbury and Susannah Cornwall, eds, *Thinking Again About Marriage*, 128–130.

89 Ken Stone *Practicing Safer Texts*, 24.

90 Jerome, *Against Jovinianus*, cited in Ken Stone, *Practicing Safer Texts*, 30–31.

91 Shelly Rambo, *Spirit and Trauma: A Theology of Remaining* (Louisville, KY: Westminster John Knox Press, 2010), 65.

5

Church Discourses and 'The Queer Art of Failure'[1]

Introduction

In this final chapter I gather together the tropes of failure as a queer art and the queer temporality of Holy Saturday as a site of, potentially, redemptive abnegation that are threaded throughout as suggested alternatives to the triumph of the neoliberal strategies that church discourses represent. Queering *Pilling*'s hermeneutic lenses entails not only que(e)rying why *these* lenses were chosen rather than *those*, but also breaching the enterprise of church reports, official discussions and synodical debates that assume that institutional constructions of privilege and authority are innate. I begin with a different kind of conversation.

> She's [Berlant] committed ... to the political project of imagining and making possible a relation to the world not shadowed by threat or the defensive dramatization of difference as existential dangers. She proposes instead that we attend to the possibility of 'making peace with' or 'being in the room with' what she calls the 'mess' of affective intensities by engaging that mess in its ordinariness instead of as inherently traumatic. What she calls her 'utopian' aspect inheres in this belief that the conditions supporting abjection, aggression, and domination by norms are susceptible to transformation in ways that won't dramatize their negativity by defensively *disavowing* that negativity, but might enable us, instead, to accept it as part of our openness to the world. Difference, conceived as 'benign variation', might thus give rise to a vitalizing experience of engagement and curiosity rather than encouraging a fearful retreat to normativity's fortified bunkers.[2]

In the extract above taken from a book that is in the form of a dialogue between Lauren Berlant and Lee Edelman on negativity, nonsovereignty and social relation, the authors use this form to explore conversation as an intimate encounter that allows engagement with what 'remains opaque or unpersuasive about the other's ideas'.³ Since I have been working throughout with the trope of failure as a way of unravelling the neoliberal, normative strands of Church of England discourse on (homo)sexuality, I find a resonance in Berlant and Edelman's understanding that the 'failures' of 'resistance, misconstruction, frustration anxiety, becoming defensive'⁴ are central to thinking relationally. Here, Edelman, writing about Berlant's commitments, notes their⁵ belief that negativity and the conception of difference as 'benign variation' lead to engagement and openness rather than retreat. This prefigures what I want to say in this chapter about the possibilities of failure and of the Church of England dwelling in the queer temporality of Holy Saturday as a site in which the 'defensive dramatizations of differences' are undone.⁶

I began thinking about queer temporality in the third lockdown in the UK following the outbreak of the Covid-19 pandemic. Lockdown is a state of queer temporality:⁷ of loss and trauma, boredom and unproductivity, depression and fear. People lost their jobs or were furloughed, companies dissolved, theatres and cinemas were closed, high streets were thinly populated, churches, schools, colleges and universities were online. As our collective sense of what is 'normal' and normative shifts, it seems apt to describe this state theologically, following Shelly Rambo and Karen Bray, as *Holy Saturday*, 'what remains in the wake of traumatized pasts and uncertain futures'.⁸ In the Holy Saturday time of lockdown we yearn for redemption from inertia, but are apprehensive that we might never return to what we once regarded as normal and natural – that productivity, activity and progression may look very different in an uncertain future. Perhaps, in this Holy Saturday period of lockdown, we learn, as Bray suggests, that what needs redeeming is not our unproductive selves, but the system that devalued and exploited us.⁹ The Church, too, seemed suspended between the hope of normality and the resigned recognition that it might be a much feebler and more provisional institution in the wake of the pandemic. At the beginning of the first lockdown, there was an optimism in the statistic that more people appeared to be joining online services than attended weekly in the flesh, but there seems to have been a decline in attendance as restrictions eased and disappeared.¹⁰

In what follows I engage with the work of Karen Bray's theology for the unredeemed, and with J. Halberstam on the queer art of failure,¹¹ to suggest ways in which institutionalized reports and the processes that they initiate of conversations, discussions and papers may inhabit the liminal time of Holy Saturday: a time when redemption is uncertain and when failure 'recognizes that alternatives are embedded already in the dominant and that power is never total or consistent; indeed failure can

CHURCH DISCOURSES AND 'THE QUEER ART OF FAILURE'

exploit the unpredictability of ideology and its indeterminate qualities'.[12] In *Grave Attending*, Bray's political theology borrows from the Holy Saturday theologies of remaining explored in Shelly Rambo's *Spirit and Trauma: A Theology of Remaining*.[13] Rambo herself engages with the mystical theology of Hans Urs von Balthasar and Adrienne von Speyr as they wrestle with the meaning – neglected in the theological and liturgical tradition – of the wordless and abandoned 'middle' between the cross and the resurrection. Balthasar and Speyr, through the latter's mystical revelations that began in the Holy Week of 1941 and continued until her death in 1967, developed an unorthodox theology of Holy Saturday. This figured Christ's descent into Hell[14] not as a triumphant rescue of lost souls, but as an experience of becoming sin and experiencing utter abandonment by the Father. Balthasar argues that a victorious Christ, active and with the agency to redeem souls on the middle day, evacuates the meaning of Holy Saturday and pre-empts the miracle of the resurrection: 'We must, in the first place, guard against that theological busyness and religious impatience which insist on anticipating the moment of fruiting of the eternal redemption through the temporal passion – on dragging forward that moment from Easter to Holy Saturday.'[15]

For Balthasar and Speyr, Holy Saturday is timeless, a space where redemption is begun in a tiny drop of love, originating in Christ's wound that will blossom and fruit, so that the site of the crucifixion itself is tenuously generative: 'This residue of love is not powerful but weary and impotent. Its movement suggests that death does not fully govern it.'[16] The descent, traditionally known as the Harrowing of Hell, is a tenet of belief with only tenuous biblical support: in 1 Peter, 'Christ ... was put to death in the flesh, but made alive in the spirit, in which he also went and made a proclamation to the spirits in prison, who in former times did not obey';[17] and two even scantier corroborations in the Apostles' and Athanasian Creeds, which mention only the descent without elaborating on Christ's purposes in being there. Nevertheless, the Harrowing of Hell, in which Adam and Eve and the righteous patriarchs are rescued from damnation by the descended and active Christ, is a doctrine of the Catholic and Orthodox Churches, and Balthasar and Speyr's reading of the descent as rejection and abandonment by the Father is potentially heterodox.[18] But, in spite of this refiguring of Holy Saturday as a wordless and liminal space, an experience of abandonment and forsakenness, Rambo argues that Balthasar and Speyr's later work elides the significance of Holy Saturday as a 'theologically underchartered site':[19]

> [T]heir increasing drive to develop a logic of redemption from the site of Holy Saturday leads them away from a vital testimony to the middle,

as expressed in the embodied and aesthetic aspects of Holy Saturday. In the course of developing a theology of Holy Saturday, their testimony to the tensions of the day are [*sic*] increasingly occluded by a particular polemic and a desire to establish theological legitimacy (both of Speyr and Holy Saturday).[20]

For Rambo, the result is that scholarship itself elides the bodily experience of Speyr and the literary theology of Balthasar in favour of their later systematic writings.[21]

Holy Saturday is (also) a Wordless space since the Word made Flesh is, according to Balthasar and Speyr's mystical theology and to its iteration in Rambo's trauma theology, now dead. The Son is forsaken by his Father and enters into a condition of suffering and separation, of passivity and failure: 'the Father and the Son are from the furthest reaches of each other in Hell'.[22] Balthasar reinterprets Hell, not as a place of busyness, but 'as a place of absence, emptiness and profound loneliness'.[23] In this vision of Holy Saturday, not only does the Son take on our suffering on the cross, but also he descends into Hell where he endures alongside the dead and damned; there is nowhere now that God has not entered and no condition, however perilous, that God has not inhabited. Balthasar and Speyr wrestle with the implications of this vision for Christian disciples, writing, '[o]n Holy Saturday the Church is invited rather to follow at a distance', and 'it is difficult to see how church or disciple can participate in this experience unless they have access to Speyr's "privileged mystical space"'.[24]

Their concept of Holy Saturday as a Wordless space – a site of absence and failure – could, I suggest, be a model for the Church's (specifically, here, I am referring to the Church of England) engagement with the troubled waters of sexuality and gender. I use the adjective 'troubled' not because gender and sexuality are troubles to be solved by teaching documents and synods but because non-normative sexualities and genders trouble the Church, which is why the Church of England has generated numerous reports and debates on the 'problem' of homosexuality. Further, I would argue, the Church of England's response to what it views as aberrant ways of being human can be troubled (or queered) in the queer temporality of Holy Saturday rupturing the cisheteronormative utopias that the Church creates and that deny – or attempt to elide – their queer beginnings.

Following Rambo's and Bray's theologies of Holy Saturday, I want to frame this 'middle' day as a Wordless site in which the Church of England can remain without anticipating the certainties and realizations of Easter Day. The Church, even in its paschal liturgies, appears to rush from the agony and failure of the crucifixion to the joy of the resurrection without pausing to experience both the abandonment and the exiguous hope of Holy Saturday.[25] In this unredeemed time, the Church can, to return to the quotation that introduces this chapter, pause and learn to abjure a 'retreat to normativity's fortified bunkers'.[26] Following the death of a naked and tortured Messiah and bereft, therefore, of hope, the Church must encounter and admit failure, so that even if rescue comes, the experience of failure will always form a part of salvation. But the Church of England baulks at the prospect, or even at the possibility of failure. The writers of *Pilling* admit that a consensus on the place of differing sexualities in the Church of England might not be possible and yet they reiterate throughout their report the belief that those not following the Church's traditional teachings on sexuality (not an uncontested claim), although they are currently 'living outside God's purposes ... will come in due course to see the need to be transformed and live lives of loving obedience in accordance with biblical revelation and orthodox church teaching'.[27]

In entering the queer temporality of this 'middle' day, the begetters of church reports could live the rupture of all certainties, encountering a provisionality that does not expect the traditional answers. They might see negativity, not as a negation of the orthodox, but as an empty space that follows the rupture of the normative. Abiding in the desolation of Holy Saturday requires, in Bray's terms, a 'grave attending' to different 'becomings', to how 'transformation' and 'living obedience' might work out for the unredeemed. In *Grave Attending* Bray writes:

> Current discourses on queer temporality seek to examine the ways in which heteronormativity and white supremacy fortify the neoliberal political economy. Many queer theorists uncover the resonance between the demand to be a productive member of society and the manipulated desire to be a reproductive member of the heteronormative family. Such demands nurture in us an optimistic belief that the straighter and whiter we become, the happier we will be. This cruelly optimistic promise (to borrow from Berlant) impedes alternate desires of community, family and self.[28]

I want to use the uncertainty, provisionality and, indeed, failure of Holy Saturday as a site for queering the hermeneutic and teleological assumptions of church discourses produced by a stable, influential, neoliberal institution – the Church of England – that reflects the values of resilience, productivity and growth promoted by the market. Bray writes of 'grave attending' that it is an attention to the lamenting cries (those released in word and affect) of those who have been crucified by neoliberalism and its concomitant heteropatriarchal, ableist, and white supremacist ethics. As such, theologically speaking, grave attending is what happens on Holy Saturday, on the day between crucifixion and resurrection. It is a style of life that does not wait for resurrection as much as it tries to remain with a difference on the day after damage and death. It does not and cannot rush toward redemption out of the gravity of such damage, because it is attendant to the damage of those who, in the wake of our resurrective impulses, we have let drown.[29]

It is not those crucified by neoliberalist ethics whom I am suggesting should inhabit the queer temporality of Holy Saturday, even though it is a site in which queer folk are often required to suffer simply because their bodies are figured by some churches and by some Christians as unredeemed. If Balthasar and Speyr and their theological followers cannot quite see how Holy Saturday can be experienced by the Church, I would suggest that the Church, as an institution, needs to be gravely attentive and to experience its queer temporality, rather than those who may already have suffered ecclesial trauma. Being able freely to inhabit a site of suffering and failure requires a level of privilege not always afforded to those whose lives are marked as unproductive or liminal. Even in an increasingly secularizing Britain, the Church of England still holds power and privilege; the Church of England is an established church with twenty-six bishops sitting in the House of Lords as the Lords Spiritual, being a permanent part of the legislature. Besides these legal rights and privileges, the Church of England has, in the twenty-first century, increasingly adopted neoliberal management, leadership and organizational models in a bid to increase both productivity and efficiency (while losing both congregations and numbers of stipendiary clergy).[30] One such initiative was launched in 2014 and chaired by Lord Green, the former HSBC chairman and UK trade minister, who was also a non-stipendiary priest in the Church of England.[31] The *Green Report* introduced a 'new modular leadership development programme for Bishops' and a 'mini-MBA' for cathedral deans and, while, in the words of the *Church Times* Leader, this wisely borrowed best practice from secular institutions, it needed also to be applicable 'to an institution that, uniquely, follows a founder whose evidence-based record of leadership involved abandonment and death'.[32] Martyn Percy, a theological educator and former Dean of Christ Church Oxford,[33] went further:

> In terms of process, there is a problem about the composition of the group who produced the report. Not one ordained woman was on the

review group – and at a time when the Church is about to welcome women bishops. This is breathtaking. Nor was there a recognized theologian, or an academic specializing in continuing professional or vocational education. And, despite the fact that the report raises secular 'MBA-style' programmes to a level of apotheosis, no recognized scholar with expertise in management or leadership from the academic world formed part of the core Working Party ... In the actual text of the Green report, there are a couple of serious issues to wrestle with. First, it has no point of origination in theological or spiritual wisdom. Instead, on offer is a dish of basic contemporary approaches to executive management, with a little theological garnish. A total absence of ecclesiology flows from this.[34]

What Percy suggests, but doesn't really develop here, is that the Church of England has, in reports such as these – both *Pilling* and *Green* – capitulated to the norms of neoliberal institutions that valorize productivity, growth and resilience.[35] These are the values of the Protestant work ethic, which, according to Weber, enabled the development of capitalism as an economic system, and so they are, perhaps, already embedded in the ecclesiologies of Reformed churches.[36] In July 2021, the *Church Times* reported on an initiative to plant 10,000 lay-led churches by 2030, an enterprise from the Gregory Centre for Church Multiplication which is led by the Rt Revd Ric Thorpe, Bishop of Islington. The vision itself is called 'Myriad'[37] and is led by Canon John McGinley, the head of church planting at New Wine[38] and a priest in the Diocese of Leicester.[39] In this article from 2 July 2021, Myriad is reported as being part of the Church of England's Vision and Strategy initiative; a week later the *Church Times* clarified that these were two separate initiatives:

> The 10,000 new lay-led churches envisaged by the Myriad project are separate from the 10,000 new worshipping communities set out in the Archbishop of York's Vision and Strategy update ... the Church's director of evangelism and discipleship Canon Dave Male said on Friday. 'We were talking about 10,000 new Christian communities coming out of revitalized parish ministry at the same time they [Myriad] were launching,' Canon Male said. 'I totally see why people were confused.' They were 'totally different things,' he said, but 'there may well be a bit of overlap'.[40]

In the week between the two articles, the church-planting initiative drew sharp criticism from some commentators, the most excoriating being in two blogs on the Modern Church website once again from Martyn Percy.

In the first of these Percy argues that the Church has yielded to instrumental neoliberalism:

> Yet all the while we continue, at least in the Church of England, to shouts of 'growth, growth, growth!'. The emerging cognitive dissonance is serious, but we should not be surprised at its appearance in a body now being run as a hegemonic organization, in which rationality and management have come to dominate. The organization, and its workers, have become tools of mechanistic management to maintain and increase production. This new system, to function, requires a constant diet of good news that raises morale and might conceivably increase production.[41]

In his second article, Percy likens the initiative's capitalist ideology of growth and an anxiety about 'size and performance' to pornography's commodification of excitement and release:

> [I]t is Maoism and Capitalism spliced together, as one might expect in the early years of the 21st century. Indeed, 'let a thousand flowers bloom' might be the new strap-line for the Church of England. But growth has become a fetish.[42]

As Bray argues, white supremacist, capitalist, heteronormative, patriarchal hegemony survives by excluding people who are poor, queer, disabled, black and single and, citing Robin James, performatively *includes* 'certain "good" (meaning healthy and resilient) women, people of colour, and gay people in its structures of power: "*this inclusion is always conditional and always instrumental*"'.[43] This, I have contended in previous chapters, is the way in which *Pilling* – and the Church of England generally – seeks to include (or, at least in some respects, accommodate) those whom it perceives as 'deserving queers': gay, lesbian and trans people who can inhabit cultural and ecclesiological norms like singleness or monogamous and/or sexually abstinent civil partnerships. Queer people are required, indeed, to model more ascetic disciplines than their cisheteronormative peers in order to be *included* in the life of the Church.

Wordlessness

Holy Saturday is Wordless. Christ has descended to the dead; he is abandoned by the Father and his mission is a failure. Only the faint hope of resurrection remains and that hope is a privilege accorded to those who know the outcome, who have experienced the redemption of Easter Day. Because as Christians we know – or think we know – the ending to this story, the resolution of the violence and desertion of the crucifixion, it is all too easy to gloss over the experience of Holy Saturday, remembering it only in the brief liturgical pause between Good Friday and Easter Sunday. The Easter lilies are already being arranged on the altar while Christ's descent to the dead is but a brief sojourn on the way to greater glory. But a Holy Saturday theology that takes seriously this queer temporality between crucifixion and an uncertain redemption keeps silent. Here there is no triumph, no assurance, no productivity; there is even little hope that this state may be interim or temporary. What would it mean for the Church to inhabit the queer temporality of Holy Saturday and to become absent and Wordless, to experience itself not as a site of striving and privilege but in a state of abandonment and negativity?

Church of England reports and debates contain and produce thousands of words written and spoken, in authorized and unauthorized discussions, blogs, videos and online interactions.[44] *Pilling* itself, besides the original published report, generated the Shared Conversations in the dioceses and at General Synod, a host of 'unauthorized' streams of words and the thousands of words that constitute the *Living in Love and Faith* resources and the further discussions on these resources. Despite this mighty torrent of writing and speech, the Church seems as far from consensus, agreement or decision on the licitness of homosexual relationships as it was fifty years ago. Perhaps it is time to abandon the persistent 'narrative of hope' for the queer art of failure: abandoning the aspiration to reach a consensus, to determine the outcome, to prevent a schism. Perhaps it is time for the Great Silence,[45] a mode of Wordlessness, a site of deliberate queer temporality for the Church in which to reflect that it is not the lives of the unproductive queers that need redemption and restoration but rather the ecclesial institution which has capitulated to the goods and gods of neoliberalism, with its commodification of Christian rites and practices, its promises of growth and success, and its privileging of hegemonic white, capitalist, male cisheteronomativity.[46]

Hermeneutic Lenses: For the Master's Tools Will Never Dismantle the Master's House[47]

I have commented in earlier chapters on the ways in which the lenses that *Pilling* employs and their order within the report reveal the assumptions of the Working Party that these are the canonical categories for examining (homo)sexuality. But why are science, social sciences and biblical scholarship deployed as the epistemological keys to unlocking the licitness of homosexual relationships in the life of the Church of England? Here, again, I would suggest that the authors of church discourses have embraced, perhaps unconsciously, the hegemonic ways of 'knowing' of the Global – and neoliberal – North. 'Disciplines, such as physics, linguistics or sociology do not exist as eternal ideas in the mind of God,'[48] writes Raewyn Connell in *The Good University*, yet Church, Academy and corporations (and in a neoliberal economy churches and academies are corporations) produce and consume knowledge as if these hegemonic epistemologies were eternal verities. The Church of England, in some of its more recent reports, adopts epistemic categories as if they were, indeed, 'eternal ideas in the mind of God'.[49] There is no que(e)rying within these documents of the epistemologies that have been deployed to examine, for instance, sexuality, and there is no awareness that using these particular tools is not a given; it is a deliberate choice. The will to include queer people within the normative boundaries of church culture is reflected in the toolkit with which *Pilling* inspects their queerness.

In the following section I will add the lenses of queer temporality to further que(e)ry the hermeneutic lenses employed by ecclesial discourses and to examine the ways in which the 'queer art of failure' might subvert their hermeneutical strategies and assumptions, beginning with how authority is constructed and how white, male, cisheteronormative perspectives are privileged in one of 'normativity's fortified bunkers'.[50]

Authority/Privilege

The Working Group set up by the House of Bishops 'to draw together and reflect upon biblical, historical and ecumenical explorations on human sexuality and material from the listening process undertaken in the light of the 1998 Lambeth Conference resolution',[51] under the chairmanship of Sir Joseph Pilling, comprised four white, male bishops. To be fair, there weren't any women bishops in 2011 and Rachel Treweek, later Bishop of Gloucester, and the Revd Dr Jessica Martin, author of the Prologue, were later appointed to assist the Working Group, as was Professor Robert Song. However, two more white men were added to support the group: the Revd Dr Malcolm Brown and Dr Martin Davie. Administrative support was provided by two women: Mrs Lauren Fenn and Mrs Caroline Kim. Further theological perspectives were provided by Professor Oliver O'Donovan and Fr Timothy Radcliffe OP, and one of the appendices (the other written by Keith Sinclair, then Bishop of Birkenhead) was provided by the Revd David Runcorn. Appendix 2 lists evidence given in oral presentations: the groups giving evidence were Anglican Mainstream, Changing Attitude, Inclusive Church, and Reform, representing a balance of two 'liberal' and two 'conservative' organizations. Of the fourteen individuals invited to give evidence only one was a woman and only one (so far as I can tell) was from the Black, Asian or Minority Ethnic communities.[52] All are academics (three professors) or senior churchmen, and one churchwoman. I do not know the sexuality of most of these people, but it is a predominantly white, male, elite, cisgender list. Even those who are Black, Asian or Minority Ethnic, or female are hardly being 'invited' to participate from the margins. There are no liminal voices here.

Running an eye over other individuals invited to contribute as part of 'an extensive process of listening to their experience', it appears that there are more women and queer people (at least those who are gay and trans), but there is a preponderance of clergy, including several bishops, and academics.[53] It could be argued that these are the voices of 'experts', people who have academic experience of the biblical, theological or ethical scholarship on sexuality, or priests who have pastoral experience of caring *for* the queer community, but, apart from the few trans and gay names I recognize on this list, most do not share the experience of *being* queer.[54] *Pilling* constructs authority, not only via those writing the words of the report, but also via those voices that are listened to, on a white, male, cisheteronormative model, and this model is taken so much for granted by the Working Party and, perhaps, by those participating that they are unconscious of inhabiting 'normativity's fortified bunker'. In the Introduction to the report, the Working Group is gracious towards those participants' voices who were 'gay, lesbian, transgendered [*sic*] and someone who had same-sex attraction'.[55]

> Everyone from the Working Group felt that the listening exercise that it had engaged in was extremely worthwhile. They felt moved and privileged to listen to the stories that were shared with them on the listening days. We are all extremely grateful and extend our thanks to all who participated, often speaking bravely and at considerable personal cost ... A number of members of the Working Group noted that they had been impressed by the quality of the relationships of the people they had met during the exercise and felt that this needed to be taken into account in any theological reflection on such relationships.[56]

These are not the words of a Working Party that is experiencing the abnegation of Holy Saturday. They are words of unacknowledged privilege, written from the normative perspective that deliberately others those outside the 'bunker': 'they' are diverse; 'they' have children; the Working

Party had 'been impressed by the quality of [their] relationships', and had 'genuine respect for the perspective of the "other"'.[57] Indeed, if there is a bunker that protects heteronormativity's prerogatives, the Working Group seems hardly aware of its fortifications, so inconspicuous are they in perpetuating the theological and cultural hegemony of the normative. There is no consciousness here of the potentialities of experiencing the state of Holy Saturday and of being abandoned by God; instead, the task is to give 'clear corporate teaching about the disciplines of Christian life, rooted in Scripture and the Christian tradition and addressing the real issues that people are facing, and setting out and upholding a clear and consistent pattern of practice for clergy and laity based on this teaching'.[58] On pages 8 and 9 of the report, after thanking the interviewees for their 'robust conversation', the authors foreclose on the outcome of conversations, interviews and theological reflection. Many words, both written and spoken, could have been spared if this privileging of one biblical and traditional view, acknowledged as normative at the outset, had not been masked by the invitation to listen to other(ed) voices. Being included on the institution's own terms is always contractual and never liberative. I suggest that only by inhabiting the site of Holy Saturday and experiencing the consequent loss of power, the consciousness of abnegation, abandonment and alterity – the sufferings of an ecclesiological precariat – could the writers of this report and the institution of the Church of England understand and restore – theologically – life outside the bunker.

The bunker exists to protect these particular hermeneutics, but it is camouflaged as 'the Church's traditional teaching on human sexuality'.[59] Despite the claims about open-ended discussion and provisionality, here is the nub of normativity. This 'traditional' teaching, iterated by a group of predominantly white, (apparently) cisheterosexual men, is the canon that reduces all other views to 'distinctive hermeneutics' and all queer people to ecclesiological precarity. Adding yet more queer hermeneutics to this normative project and inviting yet more voices from the margins will do little to redress this imbalance or to que(e)ry the privilege of the institution. Dethroning privilege requires not merely inclusion, but also resistance to the hegemonic norms that assume the cultural and religious superiority of some modes of being and knowing. In an article on queer pedagogy, Chris Greenough argues that resistance both to heteronormativity and to the elevation of queer studies/theology to an elite and arcane academic practice, requires 'practical strategies' that embody a commitment to 'risk, experimentation and failure ... inclusion, intersectionality and student-educator parity'.[60] The authors of *Pilling* and the designers of the *Pilling* process are, as I have shown, the gatekeepers of this project, for it is they who decided which voices were included and on what, and whose terms. A resistance to this hegemony and boundary marking would have meant a commitment to co-creating a narrative that interrogated normative accounts and epistemologies and embodied the mutual risks of intersectionality, experimentation and failure. Failure is anathema to the neoliberal project, but its potential for 'queer art' is particularly apt to the finitude of human attempts to categorize God. Co-writing or speaking, so that research and comment become a mutual endeavour of shared voices, rather than an asymmetrical undertaking where the voices at the margins are recruited by the magisterial researcher(s)/author(s), is exemplified in the essay, cited later in this chapter: a collaboration on theological trauma experienced by trans people and people with intersex characteristics.

Few who hold power within the institution that is the Church of England seem aware that their 'ways of being' require a 'conscious interruption' through the queer temporality of Holy Saturday, and that 'a conscious retrieval of [queer] perspectives' might enable an authentic inclusion of hitherto marginalized voices. This is not to suggest that queer perspectives should be moved to the theological centre, but rather that normative interpretations could be de-centred in acts of resistance that que(e)ry their naturalized ascendancy.[61]

Is there a Conclusion?

In the site of Holy Saturday all debate is stilled, and constructed epistemologies lose their power. Discourse; contention; privileged ways of knowing; constructions of power and authority; the neoliberal telos of productivity and growth and its production of compliant and resilient subjects; and the hegemony of canonical sexualities (or canonical anything) – all become abject, for in silence there are no voices to regulate or dominate. Here, in a place of failure, where redemption is only glimpsed provisionally – and hoped for only because, as Christians, we think we know the sequel – oppressive epistemologies are undone. The master's tools lie abandoned because the reification of the theological/epistemological 'toolkit' that is able to build or to dismantle structures that oppress and other queer people ceases in a site that queers the unacknowledged theological and epistemological presuppositions of 'before'.

And here I move to consider once again the queer art of failure as another site of rupturing the hegemonic epistemologies of church reports. In *The Queer Art of Failure*, Halberstam writes:

Queer studies offer us one method for imagining, not some fantasy of an elsewhere, but existing alternatives to hegemonic systems. What Gramsci terms 'common sense' depends heavily on the production of norms, and so the critique of dominant forms of common sense is also, in some sense, a critique of norms. Heteronormative common sense leads to the equation of success with advancement, capital accumulation, family, ethical conduct and hope. Other subordinate, queer, or counter-hegemonic modes of common sense lead to the association of failure with nonconformity, anticapitalist practices, nonreproductive lifestyles, negativity, and critique.[62]

Non-productivity and resistance to capitalist dogmas of growth and success are Holy Saturday practices, queerly embodied both by those who resist hegemonic normativity and, ideally, by the 'common sense' that others the non-conforming subjects. Halberstam disrupts the performance of 'heteronormative common sense', particularly in academic writing, with his reflections on the '"silly" archives of animated film', which 'have led to unexpected encounters between the childish, the transformative, and the queer'.[63] This is a queer echo of the gospel imperative: 'Truly I tell you, unless you change and become like children, you will never enter the kingdom of heaven ... let the little children come to me and do not stop them; for it is to such as these that the kingdom belongs' (Matt. 18.3; 19.14). This queer Kingdom ruptures normative notions of fulfilment, productivity and success, for it is the children, the eunuchs and the barren women who are its inheritors.[64]

I propose Holy Saturday as a site for silence, for sitting alongside hitherto epistemological certainties, and even for the admission that what is being attempted may never succeed on the terms on which it was established. The dream of consensus or of putting the problem back in the box and shelving it will most probably never be realized. In the queer temporality of Holy Saturday, the boundaries between deserving and underserving queers may begin to dissolve, enabling meditation on how these concepts are constructed and how they operate in church culture. Inclusion or welcome is always predicated on the willingness of LGBTIQ+ people to conform to cisheteronormative codes of marriage, family, monogamy or celibacy. Church reports, such as *Pilling*, never interrogate those codes; they are simply taken for granted as a specifically Christian cultural form of 'common sense'. The desire and hope for assimilation has long been a particular queer sensibility, principally for those alienated from the goods of heterosexual normativity by rejection and exclusion.[65] But queer people (even queer Christians) do not always hope to be conformed to heteronormativity – what Lee Edelman calls 'heterofuturity'.[66] Jose Muñoz also writes about queer failure in *Cruising Utopia*, though, unlike Edelman, he intimates the potentiality of concrete utopias, which see queerness as horizon in which the 'temporal stranglehold' of 'straight time is interrupted or stepped out of':

> Seeing queerness as horizon rescues and emboldens concepts such as freedom that have been withered by the touch of neoliberal thought and gay assimilationist politics. Pragmatic gay politics present themselves as rational and ultimately more doable. Such politics and their proponents often attempt to describe themselves as not being ideological, yet they are extremely ideological and, more precisely, are representative of a decayed ideological institution known as marriage ...The freedom that is offered by an LGBT position that does not bend to straight time's gravitational pull is akin to one of Heidegger's descriptions of freedom as unboundness.[67]

The way to queerness is, for many queer Christians who are afraid to speak of their loves and desires because inclusion is so often predicated on the adoption of straight culture, a type of homonormativity, a road less travelled. In *True Resurrection* by Harry Williams, published in 1972,[68] Williams' reflections on the pressure to perform normativity suggests that, over forty years later, the authors of *Pilling* have retreated even further into 'normativity's fortified bunkers':

> For what societies tend to require of us is that we should be satisfactory members of them. If we are not satisfactory members, or our growth as persons has made us less so than we once were, the society will exercise various pressure to make us conform to type. When this happens the societies become the gaolers of what we shall call the dead (or undead) past ... The worst off are those unaware of their bondage because with them living has been completely identified with playing a part. Instead of living to create, they exist to conform. They have been conditioned by emotional pressures to feel guilty at the very suggestion that they should break out of their role and be themselves instead ... We have to distinguish between the past as life-giving and the past as death-dealing. Salvation cannot be by way of conformity. We cannot find ourselves by playing a part. The tragedy of religion as organized in the Christian Church is that in practice this is precisely what it often asks us to do. In theory it is held that if there is a conflict between the dictates of private conscience and those of ecclesiastical authority, then we must follow our own conscience. The trouble is that the churches seldom build up personal identity enough for this conflict to occur.[69]

I have quoted Williams at length because this, in its disdain for neoliberal canons, is strikingly similar to Muñoz's argument, although here the 'cheapened and degraded version[s] of freedom' are those offered by a religion that he came to hate. Ten years later, in his autobiography, Williams wrote, 'I slept with several men, in each case fairly regularly. They were all of them friends ... Cynics, of course, will smile, but I have seldom felt more like thanking God than when having sex. I used in bed to praise Him there and then for the joy I was receiving and giving.'[70] If there were any voices willing to speak of 'the love that dare not speak its name',[71] that is, of transgressive, non-conforming queer loves, to the *Pilling* Working Party, they are strangely silent in the published report. Yet, in Holy Saturday as a queer site, a place of 'unboundedness', there can be resistance to 'straight time's gravitational pull'.[72] The powers and dominions that shape reports such as *Pilling* become both Wordless and impotent to silence the liminal voices that are hushed through being either disregarded or fearful.

Holy Saturday can be a conclusion, its queer temporality the site of failure, alterity, abjection, despair and non-resolution. It may be the cessation even of defeat: a place of unbeing and undoing where social and cultural constructs and neoliberal ways of knowing and producing vanish altogether to become (if the act of becoming isn't too generative for the extinction of Holy Saturday) a queer *tabula rasa*. Holy Saturday may also be a liminal space, an interim in which the 'weary and impotent' residue of love reaching into the depths of Wordlessness gives hope of redemption. But this redemption must not be simply a reconstruction of what has gone before, now reconstituted as an upgraded version: more tolerant, more accommodating, more generous, and less contentious, less authoritative; for that would be resuscitation rather than resurrection, a return to the systemic powers and privileges of those who frame the argument and construct the boundaries. This would, indeed, be a return to 'normativity's fortified bunkers'. Instead, it should resist the urge to seek solutions and strive for consensus and the belief that the 'problem' of homosexuality can be resolved by more effort and further work. Redemption from the 'defensive dramatization of difference'[73] can only come through the undoing of hegemonic epistemologies and privileged constructions of virtue, canonicity and normativity.

Undoing theological privilege and neoliberal, hierarchical constructions of authority effect the queer art of failure – the recognition that failure, after all, is part of the human condition and that, for Christians, it is an inherent part of our fallen nature. The theologies and ecclesiologies that the Church of England produce all too often seem predicated on growth – the production of new and acquiescent members/disciples;

success; harmony; and striving for solutions to 'problems' that are themselves constructs of the Church's own ecclesiologies and its own readings of scripture and tradition. Failure in these ventures is coded as defeat. But failure may be faithfulness to an apophatic tradition in which believers too inhabit the unknowingness of Holy Saturday, the queer temporality of as-yet unredeemed lives, living in the 'not yet'. The provisionalities habitually embedded in church reports like *Pilling* do not really disturb their over-realized eschatology, which still points towards a telic solution produced by neoliberal constructions of debate and 'listening'.

Rather than a conclusion – a telos – that resolves all of the culturally constructed 'problems', and all of the epistemological uncertainties of church reports and realizing that remaining Wordless is a pipe dream, are there ways of knowing and sharing that might embody a trinitarian way of being with sameness and difference – what Berlant called 'benign variation'?[74] One such model, which incorporates embodied ways of knowing, is represented by co-authored pieces in which the writers' embodied experiences are an integral part of the reflection. This is distinct from an authoritative Working Party inviting or welcoming the 'subjects' of discussion – usually liminal voices – to report, under terms set by that Working Party who might then select the words (and experiences) of these voices and reflect them through the report's own hermeneutical lenses. Such invitations remain a problem even in the most welcoming and inclusive of situations because the ones including and welcoming are always those with power and privilege. It is not simply that the welcome is always therefore on *their* terms, but that the invitees are inevitably powerless and othered by this process. A recent chapter, co-authored by Susannah Cornwall, Alex Clare-Young and Sara Gillingham, is a model of collaborative work.[75] Writing on trauma in Christian theological treatments of trans people and those with intersex characteristics, the authors 'focus on the trauma caused to trans people, and people with intersex characteristics, by theological and church responses which do not accord them autonomy and legitimacy as "first person knowers"'.[76] Accordingly, that chapter reflects not just the academic expertise of Cornwall, but also the epistemic authority of Clare-Young and Gillingham, who are othered 'in many theological treatments of both trans people and people with intersex characteristics, [when] others' assessments of what these persons' bodies and identities mean and signify are privileged over their own'.[77] So, in *Pilling*, the voices of gay and bi people are not heard directly, but are transmuted through the hermeneutic lenses chosen by the Working Group and in *their* interpretative words, not in the words of the outliers. Some voices, as suggested above, may be silenced altogether because they were not represented, through elision or exclusion by the Working Party or anxiety in potential participants.

But, are all such models, including this book, exemplars of the white, often male, ways of knowing of the Global North? Am I attempting here to show how the master's house might be dismantled yet still working with 'his' tools? We are all, even queer people, working in 'straight time'. My suggestion that endeavours such as *Pilling* and its offspring take a queer sabbatical is one that will most probably appeal to neither 'side'. Gay, bi and trans people desire affirmation from the Church of England of their identities and relationships, while those in the Church who are non-affirming demand closure with a definitive teaching that homosexual genital acts fall short of God's plan for creation and require repentance. Yet the wordiness of reports, discussions, synod motions, articles, books, blogs and exchanges on social media and the dalliance with 'process' provoke ennui. In the Great Silence of Christian tradition, while straight time is suspended, wordiness and constructive process might also fall into desuetude. If anything is to come from this suspension of straight time, if a telos is to be sought or desired, Church of England hierarchs must learn to deconstruct the hegemonic epistemologies in which *Pilling* and its precursors and successors have situated themselves. For an ecclesial precariat the alternatives lie in the adoption of different epistemologies and other ways of construing text, tradition and culture. Perhaps those charged with power and authority could look to the epistemologies of the Global South that aim to dismantle the white, patriarchal and colonial dominance of the Global North. In *The End of the Cognitive Empire*, Boaventura de Sousa Santos[78] writes:

> The epistemologies of the South concern the knowledges that emerge from social and political struggles and cannot be separated from such struggles. They are not, therefore, epistemologies in the conventional sense of the word. Their aim is not to study knowledge or justified belief as such, let alone the social and historical context in which they both emerge ...Their aim, rather, is to identify and valorize that which often does not even appear as knowledge in the light of the dominant epistemologies, that which emerges instead as part of the struggles of resistance against oppression and against the knowledge that legitimates such oppression. Many such ways of knowing are not thought knowledges but rather lived knowledges. The epistemologies of the South occupy the concept of epistemology in order to resignify it as an instrument for interrupting the dominant politics of knowledge. They are experiential epistemologies. They are epistemologies of the South only because, and to the extent that, there are epistemologies of the North. The epistemologies of the South exist today so that they will not be necessary someday.[79]

CHURCH DISCOURSES AND 'THE QUEER ART OF FAILURE'

I have argued throughout that queering church discourses requires that the structures of authority and power and of privileging culturally dominant ways of knowing and being are disrupted. The white, cisheteropatriarchal assumptions – largely unquestioned – need, I have claimed, to be interrogated, troubled and ruptured. The positioning of the other as a problem or subject of investigation and debate should be resisted. The selection of particular voices as representative or normative should cease. For those whose embodied experience has meant exclusion from hegemonic identities and from full participation in the rites of the Church, an *end* could be both teleological and ontological.

In this book I have suggested that by moving outside 'normativity's fortified bunkers' the Church might inhabit the queer temporality of Holy Saturday and encounter liminality, abjection, alterity and failure not as defeat, but as that 'middle time' that resists the prolepsis of redemption. Since conversations about the place of LGBTIQ+ people in church and society have been in 'process' since the time of the Wolfenden Committee, almost seventy years ago, I have also suggested that it is the ecclesial authorities rather than queer folk themselves who experience Holy Saturday as a site of desolation. As 'first-person knowers' the LGBTIQ+ community have already experienced alterity; they are in need of a liveable life[80] that might incorporate the resistances of queer theologies. But the activist potential of such theologies and queer biblical scholarship should not be subsumed by the solutionism that neoliberal ecclesial authorities espouse. This is not the place to suggest theological approaches to healing from the traumas of a context in which LGBTIQ+ people have been 'othered' and denied full access to the life of the Church. There is certainly work to be done in that site of suffering and sacrifice. I want to end with the hope that, by troubling the waters of ecclesial discourse on (homo)sexuality, I have indicated a site – a place of desertion – where the Church of England might reflect on the art of unknowing, undoing, unbecoming; on the 'queer art of failure'.

Notes

1 J. Halberstam, *The Queer Art of Failure* (Durham, NC: Duke University Press, 2011).

2 Lauren Berlant and Lee Edelman, *Sex, or the Unbearable* (Durham, NC: Duke University Press, 2014), 64, emphasis original.

3 Lauren Berlant and Lee Edelman, *Sex, or the Unbearable*, ix.

4 Lauren Berlant and Lee Edelman, *Sex, or the Unbearable*, ix.

5 Towards the end of their life Berlant began using they/them pronouns, so I use them to describe their work rather than the pronouns that Edelman uses.

6 Lauren Berlant and Lee Edelman, *Sex, or the Unbearable*, 64.

7 Karen Bray, *Grave Attending: A Political Theology for the Unredeemed* (New York: Fordham University Press, 2020).

8 Karen Bray, *Grave Attending*, 45.

9 Karen Bray, *Grave Attending*, 47.

10 Gabriella Swerling and Ben Butcher, 'Sunday church attendance almost halves in 30 years, figures show', *The Telegraph*, 9 January 2022, https://www.telegraph.co.uk/news/2022/01/09/sunday-church-service-attendance-almost-halves-30-years-figures/ (accessed 15.2.24).

11 Karen Bray, *Grave Attending*; J. Halberstam, *The Queer Art of Failure*.

12 J. Halberstam, *The Queer Art of Failure*, 88.

13 Karen Bray, *Grave Attending*, 28; citing Shelly Rambo, *Spirit and Trauma: A Theology of Remaining* (Louisville, KY: Westminster John Knox Press, 2010).

14 From the Apostles' Creed, *katotata*, literally 'the lowest', hence underworld, the dead, Hell.

15 Shelly Rambo, *Spirit and Trauma*, 63, citing Hans Urs von Balthasar, *Science, Religion and Christianity* (London: Burns & Oates, 1958).

16 Shelly Rambo, *Spirit and Trauma*, 57, writing on one of Speyr's Holy Saturday visions.

17 1 Peter 3.18–20.

18 It was deemed heretical by the scholastic theologian Alyssa Lyra Pitstick, *Light in Darkness: Hans Urs von Balthasar and the Catholic Doctrine of Christ's Descent into Hell* (Grand Rapids, MI: Eerdmans, 2007). See also the exchange between Pitstick and Edward T. Oakes, in 'Balthasar, Hell, and Heresy: An Exchange', *First Things*, December 2006, https://www.firstthings.com/article/2006/12/balthasar-hell-and-heresy-an-exchange (accessed 15.2.24).

19 Shelly Rambo, *Spirit and Trauma*, 48.

20 Shelly Rambo, *Spirit and Trauma*, 47.

21 Shelly Rambo, *Spirit and Trauma*, 48.

22 Shelly Rambo, *Spirit and Trauma*, 65.

23 Shelly Rambo, *Spirit and Trauma*, 64.

24 Rambo, *Spirit and Trauma*, 69, citing Hans Urs von Balthasar, *Mysterium Paschale*, trans by Aidan Nichols OP (San Francisco: Ignatius Press, 2000).

25 The Easter Vigil fires, which are lit after sunset on Holy Saturday and culminate in the first Mass – or Eucharist – of Easter, could arguably forestall the realizing of redemption on Easter morning.

26 Lauren Berlant and Lee Edelman, *Sex, or the Unbearable*, 64.

27 The Archbishops' Council, *Report of the House of Bishops Working Group on Human Sexuality* (London: Church House Publishing, 2013), 144.

28 Karen Bray, *Grave Attending*, 31.

29 Karen Bray, *Grave Attending*, 27.

30 'The average attendance at Sunday services fell from 740,000 in 2016 to 690,000 in 2019': Kaya Burgess, 'Church of England spends millions but fails to convert cash into congregations', *The Times*, 20 September 2021, https://www.thetimes.co.uk/article/church-of-england-spends-millions-but-fails-to-convert-cash-into-congregations-xx7hbxj8d (accessed 15.2.24); Madeleine Davies, '"Focal". "Oversight". The C of E of the future', *Church Times*, 10 September 2021, https://www.churchtimes.co.uk/articles/2021/10-september/features/features/focal-oversight-the-c-of-e-of-the-future (accessed 15.2.24).

31 The Church of England, 'Nurturing and Discerning Senior Leaders: A Report to General Synod from the Development and Appointments Group (GS2026)', https://

www.churchofengland.org/sites/default/files/2017-12/gs_2026_-_nurturing_and_discerning_senior_leaders.pdf (accessed 15.2.24).

32 'Leader: A Pooling of Talents', *Church Times*, 12 December 2014, https://www.churchtimes.co.uk/articles/2014/12-december/comment/leader-comment/a-pooling-of-talents (accessed 15.2.24).

33 Martyn Percy announced his resignation from this post in February 2022 and left in April.

34 Martin Percy, 'Are These the Leaders That We Really Want?', *Church Times*, 12 December 2014, https://www.churchtimes.co.uk/articles/2014/12-december/comment/opinion/are-these-the-leaders-that-we-really-want (accessed 15.2.24).

35 I am grateful to Sara Ahmed, *On Being Included: Racism and Diversity in Institutional Life* (Durham, NC: Duke University Press, 2012), and Louise J. Lawrence, *Refiguring the University in an Age of Neoliberalism: Creating Compassionate Campuses* (London: Palgrave Macmillan, 2021), for reflections on universities as neoliberal institutions (in need of redemption) which have informed my own reflections on the Church of England as an institution captured by the spirit of neoliberalism and in need of redemption.

36 Max Weber, *The Protestant Ethic and the Spirit of Capitalism, 1904–5*, ed. Peter Baehr and Gordon C. Wells (London: Penguin Books, 2002). Refusing the despotism of the Protestant work ethic, the queer author Quentin Crisp styled himself as *The Naked Civil Servant* (the title of his autobiography) in his refusal to frame work as life's telos, writing: 'if at first you don't succeed, failure might be your style', cited in J. Halberstam, *The Queer Art of Failure*, 96.

37 The Gregory Centre for Church Multiplication, *Myriad*, https://ccx.org.uk/myriad/ (accessed 15.2.24).

38 New Wine, which originated at St Andrew's Church Chorleywood, Hertfordshire, in 1989, is a missional movement, dedicated to releasing Spirit-filled disciples through the local church and to seeing Spirit-renewed churches change the nation, https://www.new-wine.org/ (accessed 15.2.24).

39 Madeleine Davies, 'Synod to Discuss Target of 10,000 Lay-led Churches in the Next Ten Years', *Church Times*, 2 July 2021, https://www.churchtimes.co.uk/articles/2021/2-july/news/uk/synod-to-discuss-target-of-10-000-new-lay-led-churches-in-the-next-ten-years (accessed 15.2.24); Madeleine Davies, 'Archbishop of Canterbury Endorses Urgent Plan for Church-Planting', *Church Times*, 2 July 2021, https://www.churchtimes.co.uk/articles/2021/2-july/news/uk/archbishop-of-canterbury-endorses-urgent-plan-for-church-planting (accessed 15.2.24).

40 Madeleine Davies, 'Clarification: Not 10,000 but 20,000 Lay-led Churches; Not a Strategy but a Vision', *Church Times*, 9 July 2021, https://www.churchtimes.co.uk/articles/2021/16-july/news/uk/clarification-not-10-000-but-20-000-not-a-strategy-but-a-vision (accessed 15.2.24).

41 Martyn Percy, 'The Great Leap Forward (Part One) The New Politics of Ecclesionomics for the Church of England', Modern Church, 5 July 2021, https://modernchurch.org.uk/martyn-percy-the-great-leap-forward-part-one-the-new-politics-of-ecclesionomics-for-the-church-of-england (accessed 15.2.24).

42 Martyn Percy, 'The Great Leap Forward (Part Two) The Church of England's Growth Fetish', Modern Church, 7 July 2021, https://modernchurch.org.uk/martyn-percy-the-great-leap-forward-part-two-the-church-of-englands-growth-fetish (accessed 15.2.24).

43 Karen Bray, *Grave Attending*, 50–56, citing Robin James, *Resilience and Melancholy: Pop Music, Feminism, Neoliberalism* (Ropley: John Hunt Publishing, 2015), emphasis original.

44 I am uneasily aware that, while advocating the self-denial and negativity of Wordlessness, this book is adding yet more words to the sum written about (homo)sexuality in the Church of England. There is an unfortunate irony in advocating abnegation through production.

45 The Great Silence is the period of silence kept between compline (night prayer) and morning prayer in some monastic communities.

46 See William Connolly's concept (in the US context) of the 'Evangelical-Capitalist Resonance Machine (ECRM)', which 'promising solace in the church and the family ... then cements (male) capitalist creativity to the creativity of God himself, fomenting an *aspirational politics* of identification by workers with men of prowess and privilege; these self-identifications and compensatory entitlements then encourage those sweltering in the pressure cooker to demonize selected minorities as nomadic enemies of capitalism, God, morality, and civilizational discipline', *Capitalism and Christianity, American Style* (Durham, NC: Duke University Press, 2008) 34, emphasis original, cited in Karen Bray, *Grave Attending*, 41.

47 Audre Lorde, *Sister Outsider: Essays and Speeches* (Berkeley, CA: Crossing Press, 1984, 2007), 110–113, https://edisciplinas.usp.br/pluginfile.php/4123062/mod_resource/content/1/Audre%20Lorde%20-%20S3ister%20Outsider.%20Essays%20and%20Speeches%201984.pdf (accessed 15.2.24).

48 Raewyn Connell, *The Good University: What Universities Actually Do and Why It's Time for Radical Change* (Clayton, VIC: Monash University Publishing, 2019), ch. 4.

49 Raewyn Connell, *The Good University*, ch. 4.

50 Lauren Berlant and Lee Edelman, *Sex, or the Unbearable*, 64.

51 *Pilling*, 1.

52 *Pilling*, 154.

53 *Pilling*, 155–157.

54 Of the 180 names on this list, a number of whom I recognize, I know of only 12 who are gay or trans.

55 *Pilling*, 5.

56 *Pilling*, 7–8.

57 *Pilling*, 8.

58 *Pilling*, 8–9.

59 *Pilling*, 150.

60 Chris Greenough, 'Activism in the Queer Biblical Studies Classroom', *Journal for Interdisciplinary Biblical Studies*, 2, no. 1, Autumn 2020, 108. Greenough cites the resistance of queer studies to normative methodologies and epistemologies discussed in Jane Ward, 'The Methods Gatekeepers and the Exiled Queers', in D'Lane Compton, Tey Meadow and Kristen Schilt, eds, *Other, Please Specify: Queer Methods in Sociology* (Berkeley, CA: University of California Press, 2018), 51–66.

61 On the risks of centring queer marginality, see Marcella Althaus-Reid and Lisa Isherwood, 'Thinking Theology and Queer Theory', *Feminist Theology*, 15, no. 3, 2007, 304, https://journals.sagepub.com/doi/pdf/10.1177/0966735006076168 (accessed 15.2.24).

62 J. Halberstam, *The Queer Art of Failure*, 89.

63 J. Halberstam, *The Queer Art of Failure*, 186.

64 Halvor Moxnes, *Putting Jesus in His Place: A Radical Vision of Household and Kingdom* (Louisville, KY: Westminster John Knox Press, 2003), 89–92.

65 J. Halberstam, *The Queer Art of Failure*, 72–73.

66 Cf. Chris Greenough, *Undoing Theology*, on the non-normative sexual practices and identities of Christians read as transformational.

67 Jose Esteban Muñoz, *Cruising Utopia: The Then and There of Queer Futurity* (New York: New York University Press, 2009), 32.

68 Harry Williams, *True Resurrection* (Contemporary Christian Insights) (London: Continuum Press, 2001). Williams (1919–2006) was a priest in the Church of England; gay but repressed, he suffered a serious mental breakdown and, from there, created a vision of radical love: 'We have to distinguish between the past as life-giving and the past as death-dealing. Salvation cannot be by way of conformity. We cannot find ourselves by playing a part. The tragedy of religion as organized in the Christian Church is that in practice this is precisely what it often asks us to do', quoted in Colin Coward's blog, 'What the campaign for radical new LGBTI+ Christian inclusion requires of us and the Church', Unadulterated Love, 16 July 2021, http://www.unadulteratedlove.net/blog/2021/7/16/what-the-campaign-for-radical-new-lgbtiq-christian-inclusion-requires-of-us-and-the-church (accessed 15.2.24).

69 Quoted in Colin Coward's blog, 'What the campaign for radical new LGBTI+ Christian inclusion requires of us and the Church'.

70 Harry Williams, *Some Day I'll Find You: An Autobiography* (Worthing: Littlehampton Book Services, 1982); quoted in Colin Coward, 'Some Day I'll Find You', Unadulterated Love, 13 July 2021, http://www.unadulteratedlove.net/blog/2021/7/13/some-day-ill-find-you (accessed 15.2.24).

71 'Then sighing, said the other, "Have thy will/I am the Love that dare not speak its name"' are the last lines from a poem by Lord Alfred Douglas published in 1894. It was later used in the trial of Oscar Wilde as a euphemism for homosexuality.

72 Jose Esteban Muñoz, *Cruising Utopia*, 32.

73 Lauren Berlant and Lee Edelman, *Sex, or the Unbearable*, 64.

74 Lauren Berlant and Lee Edelman, *Sex, or the Unbearable*, 64.

75 Susannah Cornwall, Alex Clare-Young and Sara Gillingham, 'Epistemic Injustice Exacerbating Trauma in Christian Theological Treatments of Trans People and People with Intersex Characteristics', in Karen O'Donnell and Katie Cross, eds, *Bearing Witness: Intersectional and Interdisciplinary Perspectives on Trauma Theology* (London: SCM Press, 2022).

76 Susannah Cornwall, Alex Clare-Young and Sara Gillingham, 'Epistemic Injustice Exacerbating Trauma in Christian Theological Treatments of Trans People and People with Intersex Characteristics'.

77 Susannah Cornwall, Alex Clare-Young and Sara Gillingham, 'Epistemic Injustice Exacerbating Trauma in Christian Theological Treatments of Trans People and People with Intersex Characteristics'.

78 Since writing this chapter, a report by the Independent Commission of the Centre for Social Studies (CES) at the University of Coimbra confirmed the evidence of abuse of power and sexual harassment by Boaventura de Sousa Santos and other senior researchers at CES. See Carlos Diogo Santos and Carolina Jesus, 'Boaventura Sousa Santos Case', 13 March 2024, Observador, https://observador.pt/2024/03/13/caso-boaventura-sousa-santos-relatorio-de-comissao-independente-confirma-indicios-de-conduta-de-abuso-de-poder-e-assedio/ (accessed 27.3.24).

79 Boaventura de Sousa Santos, *The End of the Cognitive Empire: The Coming of Age of Epistemologies of the South*, Durham, NC: Duke University Press, 2018, https://www.jstor.org/stable/pdf/j.ctv125jqvn.4 (accessed 15.2.24).

80 Judith Butler, *Undoing Gender* (Abingdon: Routledge, 2004), 8.

Bibliography

Primary Sources

The Archbishops' Council, *Issues in Human Sexuality: A Statement by the House of Bishops*, London: Church House Publishing, 1991.
The Archbishops' Council, *Some Issues in Human Sexuality: A Guide to the Debate*, London: Church House Publishing, 2003.
The Archbishops' Council, *Report of the House of Bishops Working Group on Human Sexuality*, London: Church House Publishing, November 2013.

Secondary Sources

Adams, Marilyn McCord, 'Trinitarian Friendship: Same-gender Models of Godly Love in Richard of St. Victor and Aelred of Rievaulx', in *Theology and Sexuality: Classic and Contemporary Readings*, 322–340, edited by Eugene F. Rogers, Jr, Oxford: Blackwell, 2002.
Ahmed, Sara, 'Queer Feelings', in *The Cultural Politics of Emotion*, Edinburgh: Edinburgh University Press, 2004, https://law.unimelb.edu.au/__data/assets/pdf_file/0003/3453618/ahmed_2014_queer-feelings-in-the-cultural-politics-of-emotion.pdf (accessed 15.2.24).
Ahmed, Sara, *The Promise of Happiness*, Durham, NC: Duke University Press, 2010.
Ahmed, Sara, *On Being Included: Racism and Diversity in Institutional Life*, Durham, NC: Duke University Press, 2012.
Alexander, Loveday, 'Homosexuality and the Bible: Reflections of a Biblical Scholar', in *Grace and Disagreement 2: A Reader – Writings to Resource Conversation*, Church of England, 2015, 24–51, https://www.churchofengland.org/sites/default/files/2018-05/Grace%20and%20Disagreement%202-%20A%20Reader%20E2%80%93%20writings%20to%20resource%20conversation_1.pdf (accessed 15.2.24).
Alison, James, *Faith Beyond Resentment: Fragments Catholic and Gay*, London: Darton, Longman & Todd, 2001.
Althaus-Reid, Marcella, *Indecent Theology: Theological Perversions in Sex, Gender and Politics*, Abingdon: Routledge, 2000.
Althaus-Reid, Marcella, *The Queer God*, London: Routledge, 2003.
Althaus-Reid, Marcella, 'Queer I Stand: Lifting the Skirts of God', in *The Sexual Theologian: Essays on Sex, God and Politics*, edited by Marcella Althaus-Reid and Lisa Isherwood. London: T&T Clark, 2004.
Althaus-Reid, Marcella and Lisa Isherwood, eds. *The Sexual Theologian: Essays on Sex, God and Politics*, London: T&T Clark, 2004.

BIBLIOGRAPHY

Althaus-Reid, Marcella and Lisa Isherwood, 'Thinking Theology and Queer Theory', *Feminist Theology*, 15, no. 3, 2007, 304, https://journals.sagepub.com/doi/pdf/10.1177/0966735006076168 (accessed 15.2.24).

Althaus-Reid, Marcella and Lisa Isherwood, eds, *Controversies in Body Theology*, London: SCM Press, 2008.

The Anglican Communion, 'Anglican Consultative Council (ACC)', https://www.anglicancommunion.org/structures/instruments-of-communion/acc.aspx (accessed 15.2.24).

The Anglican Consultative Council, *The Windsor Report 2004*, London: The Anglican Consultative Council, 2004.

Anglican Mainstream, https://anglicanmainstream.org/anglican-mainstream-who-we-are/ (accessed 15.2.24).

The Archbishops' Council, *Marriage: A Teaching Document from the House of Bishops of the Church of England*, London: Church House Publishing, 1999.

The Archbishops' Council, *Everyone Counts 2014*, London: The Church of England, 2014, https://www.churchofengland.org/sites/default/files/2017-10/everyonecounts_gensynodfringe15.pdf (accessed 15.2.24).

The Archbishops' Council, *Grace and Disagreement 1 – thinking through the process*, Church of England, 2014, https://www.churchofengland.org/sites/default/files/2018-05/Grace%20and%20Disagreement%201%20-%20thinking%20through%20the%20process.pdf (accessed 15.2.24).

The Archbishops' Council, *Grace and Disagreement 2: A Reader – Writings to Resource Conversation*, Church of England, 2015, https://www.churchofengland.org/sites/default/files/2018-05/Grace%20and%20Disagreement%202-%20A%20Reader%20%E2%80%93%20writings%20to%20resource%20conversation_1.pdf (accessed 15.2.24).

The Archbishops' Council, 'The Faith and Order Commission, "Communion and Disagreement"', *General Synod* (GS Misc 1139, June 2016), https://www.churchofengland.org/sites/default/files/2017-10/communion_and_disagreement_faoc_report_gs_misc_1139.pdf (accessed 15.2.24).

The Archbishops' Council, *An Update on 'Welcoming Transgender People'*, General Synod (GS Misc. 1178, 2018), https://www.churchofengland.org/sites/default/files/2018-01/gs-misc-1178-an-update-on-welcoming-transgender-people-003.pdf (accessed 15.2.24).

The Archbishops of Canterbury and York, 'Letter from the Archbishops of Canterbury and York following General Synod, February 16, 2017', https://www.churchofengland.org/more/media-centre/news/letter-archbishops-canterbury-and-york-following-general-synod (accessed 15.2.24).

The Archbishops of Canterbury and York, *General Synod, Next Steps on Human Sexuality* (GS Misc 1158, June 2017), https://www.churchofengland.org/sites/default/files/2017-11/gs-misc-1158-next-steps-on-human-sexuality.pdf (accessed 15.2.24).

Association of Internet Researchers, 'Internet Research: Ethical Guidelines 3', Unanimously Approved by the AoIR Membership 6 October 2019, https://aoir.org/reports/ethics3.pdf (accessed 15.2.24).

Atwood, Andrew, 'Shared Conversations', previously online at https://www.eggscofe.org.uk/.

Bailey, Derrick Sherwin, *Homosexuality and the Western Christian Tradition*, London: Longmans Green & Co., 1955.

Baker, Erika, 'The Shared Conversations: A Personal Reflection', *LGBTI Anglican Coalition*, 3 May 2015, https://www.lgbtianglican.org.uk/2015/05/02/accounts-of-conversations-in-sw/ (accessed 15.2.24).
Balch, David L. and Carolyn Osiek, eds, *Early Christian Families in Context: An Interdisciplinary Dialogue*, Grand Rapids and Cambridge: Eerdmans, 2003.
Balthasar, Hans Urs von, *Science, Religion and Christianity*, London: Burns & Oates, 1958.
Balthasar, Hans Urs von, *Mysterium Paschale*, trans by Aidan Nichols OP, San Francisco: Ignatius Press, 2000.
Barton, Stephen C., 'Homosexuality and the Church: Perspectives from the Social Sciences', *Theology*, xcii, no. 747, May 1989, 175–181.
Bashir, Martin, 'Church of England Votes Against Same Sex Marriage Report', *BBC News*, https://www.bbc.co.uk/news/uk-38982013 (accessed 15.2.24).
Bates, Stephen, *A Church at War: Anglicans and Homosexuality*, London: I.B. Tauris, 2004.
BBC News, 'Jeremy Timm leaves Church of England over his same-sex marriage', https://www.bbc.co.uk/news/uk-england-humber-34307063 (accessed 15.2.24).
Beattie, Tina, *New Catholic Feminism: Theology and Theory*, Abingdon: Taylor & Francis, 2006.
Beattie, Tina, 'Queen of Heaven', in *Queer Theology: Rethinking the Western Body*, edited by Gerard Loughlin, 293–304. Oxford: Blackwell, 2007.
Bennett, David, 'Church Clarity on Sexuality – or Church Control?' *Christian Today*, 19 October 2017, https://www.christiantoday.com/article/church-clarity-on-sexuality-or-church-control/116440.htm (accessed 15.2.24).
Bennett, David, 'The Bishops' Decision: My Reflection on General Synod and Participating in Shared Conversations', *Daily Roll – Reflections*, https://illuminaet.wordpress.com/2017/01/27/the-bishops-decision-my-reflection-on-general-synod-and-participating-in-shared-conversations/ (accessed 15.2.24).
Bennett, David, 'David', *Living Out*, https://www.livingout.org/stories/david (accessed 15.2.24).
Bentham, Jeremy, *Offences Against One's Self* (ca. 1785, unpublished). First published in the summer and autumn 1978 issues of *Journal of Homosexuality*, 3, no. 4, 1978, 389–405; continued in 4, no. 1, 1978.
Benzon, Nadia von, 'Social Research Using Social Media 1: Social Media as Archive', Social Research Association (n.d.), https://the-sra.org.uk/sra/blog/socialresearchusingsocialmediasocialmediaasarchive.aspx (accessed 15.2.24).
Berlant, Lauren and Lee Edelman, *Sex, or the Unbearable*, Durham, NC: Duke University Press, 2014.
Bishop Rachel, 'Shared Conversations on Scripture, Mission and Human Sexuality: Information and Ideas if you would like to join in' (Diocese of Gloucester), https://www.gloucester.anglican.org/your-ministry/shared-conversations-on-scripture-mission-and-human-sexuality/ (link no longer available).
Boswell, John, *Christianity, Social Tolerance and Homosexuality: Gay People in Western Europe from the Beginning of the Christian Era to the Fourteenth Century*, Chicago, IL: University of Chicago Press, 1980.
Bradshaw, Timothy, ed., *The Way Forward? Christian Voices on Homosexuality and the Church*, London: SCM Press, 2003.
Bray, Karen, *Grave Attending: A Political Theology for the Unredeemed*, New York: Fordham University Press, 2020.
Brooten, Bernadette J., *Love Between Women: Early Christian Responses to Female Homoeroticism*, Chicago, IL: University of Chicago Press, 1996.

Brown, Andrew, 'The Church of England: A Church that's Sick of Itself', *The Guardian*, 19 November 2013, https://www.theguardian.com/commentisfree/2013/nov/19/church-of-england-sick-of-itself (accessed 15.2.24).

Brown, Andrew and Linda Woodhead, *That Was the Church That Was: How the Church of England Lost the English People*, London: Bloomsbury, 2016.

Brown, Peter, *The Body and Society: Men, Women, & Sexual Renunciation in Early Christianity*, New York: Columbia University Press, 1988.

Brunner, Emil, *The Divine Imperative: A Study in Christian Ethics*, Cambridge: Lutterworth Press, 2003.

Burgess, Kaya, 'Church of England spends millions but fails to convert cash into congregations', *The Times*, 20 September 2021, https://www.thetimes.co.uk/article/church-of-england-spends-millions-but-fails-to-convert-cash-into-congregations-xx7hbxj8d (accessed 15.2.24).

Burke, Tarana, 'metoo', https://metoomvmt.org/get-to-know-us/tarana-burke-founder/ (accessed 15.2.24).

Burrus, Virginia, 'Queer Father: Gregory of Nyssa and the Subversion of Identity', in *Queer Theology: Rethinking the Western Body*, edited by Gerard Loughlin, 147–162. Oxford: Blackwell, 2007.

Butler, Judith, *Gender Trouble: Feminism and the Subversion of Identity*, Abingdon: Routledge, 1990.

Butler, Judith, *Undoing Gender*, Abingdon: Routledge, 2004.

Byrne, William and Bruce Parsons, 'Human Sexual Orientation', 228, in *Homosexuality: The Use of Scientific Research in the Church's Moral Debate*, edited by S. L. Jones and M. A. Yarhouse, Westmont, IL: Inter-Varsity Press, 2001.

Cadden, Joan, *Meanings of Sex Difference in the Middle Ages*, Cambridge: Cambridge University Press, 1993.

Cadenhead, Raphael, 'An ascetical critique of "gender complementarity"', in John Bradbury and Susannah Cornwall, eds, *Thinking Again About Marriage: Key Theological Questions*, London: SCM Press, 2016, 128–130.

Campbell, Douglas A., ed., *Gospel and Gender: A Trinitarian Engagement with being Male and Female in Christ*, London & New York: Continuum, 2003.

Campbell, Phillip, 'Demonic Impregnation: Incubi and Succubi', *Unam Sanctam Catholicam*, 25 May 2022, www.unamsanctamcatholicam.com/demonic-impregnation-incubi-and-succubi (accessed 15.2.24).

Carter, John, 'Positive Feedback as Diocese Holds "Shared Conversations" on Sexuality', Diocese of Leeds, 22 March 2016.

CEEC video *The Beautiful Story* launched in response to the *Living in Love and Faith* resources in 2021, https://ceec.info/resources/the-beautiful-story/ (accessed 19.4.24), https://www.leeds.anglican.org/content/positive-feedback-diocese-holds-'shared-conversations'-sexuality (link no longer available).

Census 2021, 'Marriage, cohabitations and civil partnership', https://www.ons.gov.uk/peoplepopulationandcommunity/birthsdeathsandmarriages/marriagecohabitationandcivilpartnerships (accessed 15.2.24).

Cheng, Patrick S., *Radical Love: An Introduction to Queer Theology*, New York: Seabury Press, 2011.

Cheng, Patrick S., 'Contributions from Queer Theory', in Adrian Thatcher, ed., *Redeeming Gender*, Oxford: Oxford University Press, 2016, 153–172.

Chrysostom, John, *De virginitate*, 14.6, 1985, https://openlibrary.org/books/OL16542118M/St._John_Chrysostom%27s_De_virginitate_and_De_non_iterando_coniugio (accessed 15.2.24).

The Church of England, 'Book of Common Prayer: The Form of Solemnization of Matrimony', https://www.churchofengland.org/prayer-and-worship/worship-texts-and-resources/book-common-prayer/form-solemnization-matrimony (accessed 15.2.24).

The Church of England, 'Common Worship: the Marriage Service', 2022, https://www.churchofengland.org/prayer-and-worship/worship-texts-and-resources/common-worship/marriage#mm094 (accessed 15.2.24).

The Church of England, 'Canon B 30 Of Holy Matrimony', https://www.churchofengland.org/about/leadership-and-governance/legal-services/canons-church-england/section-b (accessed 15.2.24).

Church of England, 'Canon C 26 Of the manner of life of clerks in Holy Orders', 2022, https://www.churchofengland.org/about/leadership-and-governance/legal-services/canons-church-england/section-c (accessed 15.2.24).

The Church of England, 'Civil Partnerships – A pastoral statement from the House of Bishops of the Church of England', 25 July 2005, https://www.churchofengland.org/sites/default/files/2017-11/house-of-bishops-statement-on-civil-partnerships-2005.pdf (accessed 14.4.24).

The Church of England, 'Men and Women in Marriage, GS Misc 1046' (a document from the Faith and Order Commission published with the agreement of the House of Bishops of the Church of England and approved for study), 2013, https://www.churchofengland.org/sites/default/files/2017-10/marriagetextbrochureprint.pdf (accessed 15.2.24).

The Church of England, '*Pilling Report* Published', press release, 28 November 2013, https://www.churchofengland.org/news-and-media/news-and-statements/pilling-report-published (accessed 15.2.24).

The Church of England, 'House of Bishops Pastoral Guidance on Same Sex Marriage', 15 February 2014, https://www.churchofengland.org/news-and-media/news-and-statements/house-bishops-pastoral-guidance-same-sex-marriage (accessed 15.2.24).

The Church of England, 'The Bishops of Manchester and Winchester on Shared Conversations' (SoundCloud), https://soundcloud.com/the-church-of-england/bishop-david-and-bishop-tim (accessed 15.2.24).

The Church of England, 'A Survival Guide to General Synod', 3rd edition, 2015, 18, https://www.churchofengland.org/sites/default/files/2017-11/synod_survival_guide__revised_jan_16_.pdf (accessed 15.2.24).

The Church of England, Ministry Division, 'Sending Candidates to BAP: A Guide to the Selection Process', 2017, https://www.churchofengland.org/sites/default/files/2017-10/Sending%20Candidates%20to%20BAP.pdf (accessed 15.2.24).

The Church of England, 'General Synod Shared Conversations – FAQS', 2017, https://www.churchofengland.org/sites/default/files/2017-12/160603_gs_members_faq-july2016.pdf (accessed 15.2.24).

The Church of England, 'Shared Conversations Archive', https://www.churchofengland.org/about/leadership-and-governance/general-synod/bishops/shared-conversations-archive#na (accessed 15.2.24).

The Church of England, 'Renewal and Reform: Helping Us Become a Growing Church for All People and All Places', https://www.churchofengland.org/about/renewal-reform (accessed 15.2.24).

The Church of England, 'Renewal and Reform, a Year in Numbers: 2020 Digital Report', https://www.churchofengland.org/sites/default/files/2020-10/CofE_02955_SocialMediaInfographics2020_16.9_AW.pdf (accessed 15.2.24).

BIBLIOGRAPHY

The Church of England, 'Nurturing and Discerning Senior Leaders: A Report to General Synod From the Development and Appointments Group (GS2026)', https://www.churchofengland.org/sites/default/files/2017-12/gs_2026_-_nurturing_and_discerning_senior_leaders.pdf (accessed 15.2.24).

The Church of England, 'Living in Love and Faith: Christian Teaching and Learning About Identity, Sexuality, Relationships and Marriage', https://www.churchofengland.org/resources/living-love-and-faith (accessed 15.2.24).

The Church of England, 'Prayers of Love and Faith', https://www.churchofengland.org/sites/default/files/2023-01///final-draft-prayers-of-love-and-faith.pdf (accessed 15.2.24).

The Church of England, 'Living in Love and Faith: A Response from the Bishops of the Church of England about Identity, Sexuality, Relationships and Marriage', 3, https://www.churchofengland.org/sites/default/files/2023-01/final-bishops-response-to-llf-20-jan-23.pdf (accessed 15.2.24).

The Church of England, 'Bishops Agree Key Areas for Further Work Implementing Living in Love and Faith', 19 May 2023, https://www.churchofengland.org/media-and-news/press-releases/bishops-agree-key-areas-further-work-implementing-living-love-and (accessed 15.2.24).

Clare-Young, Alex, 'Living in Love and Faith? The Construction of Contemporary Texts of Terror', *Theology and Sexuality*, 27, nos. 2–3, 5 August 2021, 118–120, https://www.tandfonline.com/doi/full/10.1080/13558358.2021.1954864?scroll=top&needAccess=true (accessed 15.2.24).

Clark, D., 'Average Weekly Attendance for the Church of England 2009–2019', *Statista*, 31 March 2021, https://www.statista.com/statistics/369080/church-of-england-attendance-by-service-uk/ (accessed 15.2.24).

Clark, Elizabeth A., 'I Corinthians 7 in Early Christian Exegesis', in *Reading Renunciation: Asceticism and Scripture in Early Christianity*, 259–329, Princeton: Princeton University Press, 1999, https://doi.org/10.1515/9781400823185.259 (accessed 15.2.24).

Clements, Ben, 'Anglicans and Attitudes towards Gay Marriage', *British Religion in Numbers*, 14 September 2012, http://www.brin.ac.uk/anglicans-and-attitudes-towards-gay-marriage/ (accessed 15.2.24).

College of Bishops, 'Statement on Shared Conversations on Scripture, Sexuality and Mission 09 October 2014', Thinking Anglicans, https://www.thinkinganglicans.org.uk/6750-2/ (accessed 15.2.24).

Collier, H. H. Peter KC, 'Marriage and/or Holy Matrimony', *Law and Religion UK*, 28 June 2023, https://lawandreligionuk.com/2023/07/06/marriage-and-or-holy-matrimony/ (accessed 15.2.24).

Conger, George, 'General Synod Shared Sex Conversations Place Unity Above Truth, Critics Claim', *Anglican Ink*, 20 July 2016, http://anglican.ink/2016/07/20/general-synod-shared-sex-conversations-place-unity-above-truth-critics-charge/ (accessed 15.2.24).

Connell, Raewyn, *The Good University: What Universities Actually Do and Why It's Time for Radical Change*, Clayton: Monash University Publishing, 2019.

The Core Issues Trust, 'Objects of Association', https://core-issues.org/about-us/ (accessed 19.4.24).

The Core Issues Trust, 'Statement of Belief', https://core-issues.org/about-us/ (accessed 19.4.24).

Corey, Benjamin L., 'If God Only Made Male & Female, What About Intersex?', Patheos, 21 August 2015, https://www.patheos.com/blogs/formerlyfundie/bio/ (accessed 15.2.24).

Cornwall, Susannah, *Sex and Uncertainty in the Body of Christ: Intersex Conditions and Christian Theology*, London: Routledge, 2010.
Cornwall, Susannah, *Controversies in Queer Theology*, London: SCM Press, 2011.
Cornwall, Susannah, 'From a Remote Rural Village in Limpopo: Colonized Bodies, Hybrid Sex and Postcolonial Theology', *Gendering Christian Ethics*, edited by Jenny Daggers, Newcastle upon Tyne: Cambridge Scholars Publishing, 2012, 147–167.
Cornwall, Susannah, 'Something There is That Doesn't Love a Wall', *Theology and Sexuality*, 21, no. 1, 2015, 20–35.
Cornwall, Susannah, Alex Clare-Young and Sara Gillingham, 'Epistemic Injustice Exacerbating Trauma in Christian Theological Treatments of Trans People and People with Intersex Characteristics', in *Bearing Witness: Intersectional and Interdisciplinary Perspectives on Trauma Theology*, edited by Karen O' Donnell and Katie Cross, London: SCM Press, 2022.
Countryman, L. William, *Dirt, Greed and Sex: Sexual Ethics in the New Testament and Their Implications for Today*, London: SCM Press, 2001.
Coward, Colin, 'What the campaign for radical new LGBTI+ Christian inclusion requires of us and the Church', Unadulterated Love, 16 July 2021, http://www.unadulteratedlove.net/blog/2021/7/16/what-the-campaign-for-radical-new-lgbtiq-christian-inclusion-requires-of-us-and-the-church (accessed 15.2.24).
Coward, Colin, 'Some Day I'll Find You', Unadulterated Love, 13 July 2021, http://www.unadulteratedlove.net/blog/2021/7/13/some-day-ill-find-you (accessed 15.2.24).
Crisp, Quentin, *The Naked Civil Servant*, London: Jonathan Cape, 1968.
Crockett, Alasdair and David Voas, 'A Divergence of Views: Attitude Change and the Religious Crisis of Homosexuality', *Sociological Research Online*, 8, no. 4, 2003, http://www.socresonline.org.uk/8/4/crockett.htm (accessed 15.2.24).
Crossley, James, 'Jewish ... But Not *That* Jewish', in *Jesus in an Age of Terror: Scholarly Projects for a New American Century*, London: Equinox, 2008, 173–194.
Crossley, James, 'The Politics of the Bibliobloggers', in *Jesus in an Age of Terror: Scholarly Projects for a New American Century*, London: Equinox, 2008, 20–55, particularly 20–23.
Dabhoiwala, Faramerz, *The Origins of Sex: A History of the First Sexual Revolution*, London: Penguin Books, 2013.
Daggers, Jenny, *Postcolonial Theology of Religions: Particularity and Pluralism in World Christianity*, Abingdon: Routledge, 2013.
Davie, Martin, 'Grace and Disagreement, Shared Conversations on Scripture, Mission and Human Sexuality', London: CEEC, 2015, http://www.ceec.info/grace-and-disagreement---martin-davie.html (link no longer available).
Davie, Martin, 'A response to GS 2055: "Marriage and Same Sex Relationships after the Shared Conversations"', Reflections of an Anglican Theologian, 1 February 2017, https://mbarrattdavie.wordpress.com/2017/02/01/a-response-to-gs-2055-marriage-and-same-sex-relationships-after-the-shared-conversations/ (accessed 15.2.24).
Davie, Martin, *Glorify God in Your Body: Human Identity and Flourishing in Marriage, Singleness and Friendship*, London: CEEC, 2018.
Davies, Madeleine, 'Synod to Discuss Target of 10,000 Lay-led Churches in the Next Ten Years', *Church Times*, 2 July 2021, https://www.churchtimes.co.uk/articles/2021/2-july/news/uk/synod-to-discuss-target-of-10-000-new-lay-led-churches-in-the-next-ten-years (accessed 15.2.24).

BIBLIOGRAPHY

Davies, Madeleine, 'Archbishop of Canterbury Endorses Urgent Plan for Church-Planting', *Church Times*, 2 July 2021, https://www.churchtimes.co.uk/articles/2021/2-july/news/uk/archbishop-of-canterbury-endorses-urgent-plan-for-church-planting (accessed 15.2.24).

Davies, Madeleine, 'Clarification: Not 10,000 but 20,000 Lay-led Churches; not a Strategy but a Vision', *Church Times*, 9 July 2021, https://www.churchtimes.co.uk/articles/2021/16-july/news/uk/clarification-not-10-000-but-20-000-not-a-strategy-but-a-vision (accessed 15.2.24).

Davies, Madeleine, '"Focal". "Oversight". The C of E of the future', *Church Times*, 10 September 2021, https://www.churchtimes.co.uk/articles/2021/10-september/features/features/focal-oversight-the-c-of-e-of-the-future (accessed 15.2.24).

Davies, Madeleine, 'YouGov poll: more than half of Anglicans believe same-sex marriage to be "right"', *Church Times*, 1 March 2022, https://www.churchtimes.co.uk/articles/2022/4-march/news/uk/yougov-poll-more-than-half-of-anglicans-believe-same-sex-marriage-to-be-right (accessed 15.2.24).

Davison, Andrew, ed., *Amazing Love: Theology for Understanding Discipleship, Sexuality and Mission*, London: Darton, Longman & Todd, 2016.

Davison, Andrew, Christina Beardsley, et al., 'A Teaching Document on Sexuality and Marriage from the Bishops of the Church of England: Some Initial Suggestions as to Questions and Themes', *LGBTI Mission*, June 2017, https://lgbtimissiondotorgdotuk.files.wordpress.com/2017/06/teachingsynopsisfinal.pdf (accessed 15.2.24).

Davison, Richard, *Flame of Yahweh: Sexuality in the Old Testament*, Grand Rapids, MI: Baker Academic Press, 2007.

DeGroot, Gerald, 'Review', *Under the Knife: The History of Surgery in 28 Remarkable Operations*, by Arnold van de Laar, *The Times*, 12 January 2018.

Diamond, Lisa M., 'Female Bisexuality from Adolescence to Adulthood: Results from a 10-Year Longitudinal Study', *Developmental Psychology*, 44, no. 1, 2008, 5–14, https://doi.org/10.1037/0012-1649.44.1.5 (accessed 15.2.24).

Diocese of Lichfield, 'Shared Conversations', https://cofelichfield.contentfiles.net/media/documents/document/2016/07/Shared_Conversations.pdf, accessed 4 December 2018; this link is no longer live and it appears that this material has been deleted from the Lichfield website.

Diocese of Oxford, 'Common Ground: Listening and Engagement: The Church and Current Issues in Sexuality', Diocese of Oxford, 8 July 2015, https://www.oxford.anglican.org/common-ground-listening-and-engagement/ (accessed 15.2.24).

Diocese of Newcastle, 'Shared Conversations', http://www.newcastle.anglican.org/news-and-events/news-article.aspx?id=3963, accessed 4 December 2018; this link is no longer live and it appears that this material has been deleted from the Newcastle website.

Diocese of Norwich, 'Shared Conversations', https://www.dioceseofnorwich.org/training/lay/discipleship/good-disagreement/, accessed 4 December 2018; this link is no longer live.

Doherty, Sean and Gaby, 'Sean and Gaby', *Living Out*, 29 October 2020, http://www.livingout.org/stories/sean-and-gaby (accessed 15.2.24).

Donohue, Caitlin, 'When Queer Nation "Bashed Back" Against Homophobia with Street Patrols and Glitter', *KQED*, 3 June 2019, https://www.kqed.org/arts/13858167/queer-nation-lgbtq-activism-90s (accessed 15.2.24).

Dormor, Duncan and Jeremy Morris, eds, *An Acceptable Sacrifice? Homosexuality and the Church*, London: SPCK, 2007.

Doughty, Steve, 'Church of England one step closer to gay marriages in church: Vote against bishops' report that supported ban is hailed as victory by liberal clergy', *Mail Online*, 16 February 2017, https://www.dailymail.co.uk/news/article-4229328/Archbishop-Canterbury-s-fails-end-gay-marriage-rift.html (accessed 15.2.24).

Dover, Kenneth J., *Greek Homosexuality*, Cambridge, MA: Harvard University Press, 1989.

Duffy, Nick, 'The shocking way newspapers wrote about the now debunked "gay gene" in 1993', *Pink News*, 30 August 2019, https://www.pinknews.co.uk/2019/08/30/gay-gene-newspapers-1993-daily-mail-ian-mckellen/ (accessed 15.2.24).

Duggan, Lisa, *The Twilight of Equality?: Neoliberalism, Cultural Politics and the Attack on Democracy*, Boston, MA: Beacon Press, 2003.

Dunnett, John, 'Shared Conversations – January 2016 – A Personal Reflection', previously online, this link is no longer live, https://www.eggscofe.org.uk/.

Edelman, Lee, *No Future: Queer Theory and the Death Drive*, Durham, NC: Duke University Press, 2004.

I Enoch (Ethiopic) Parallel Translations, http://qbible.com/enoch/7.html (accessed 15.2.24).

Epstein, Julia and Kristina Straub, eds, *Bodyguards: The Cultural Politics of Gender Ambiguity*, New York & London: Routledge, 1991.

Equal: The Campaign for Equal Marriage in the Church of England, 'Living in Love and Faith Consultation results now published', 3 September 2022, https://cofe-equal-marriage.org.uk/llf-consultation-results-published/ (accessed 15.2.24).

Equal Civil Partnerships, 'From the ECP Campaign Group', http://equalcivilpartnerships.org.uk/ (accessed 15.2.24).

Erzen, Tanya, *Straight to Jesus: Sexual and Christian Conversions in the Ex-Gay Movement*, Oakland, CA: University of California Press, 2006.

The Evangelical Alliance, *Transsexuality*, Milton Keynes: Paternoster Press, 2000.

Evangelical Group of the General Synod, http://www.eggscofe.org.uk/about.html (accessed 15.2.24).

Foucault, Michel, *Discipline and Punish: The Birth of the Prison*, New York: Random House, 1977.

Foucault, Michel, *The History of Sexuality: The Will to Knowledge*, London: Penguin Classics, 1978.

Fulcrum – renewing the evangelical centre, 'What is Fulcrum?', https://www.fulcrum-anglican.org.uk/about/ (accessed 15.2.24).

Gafney, Wilda C., *Womanist Midrash: A Reintroduction to the Women of the Torah and the Throne*, Louisville, KY: Westminster John Knox Press, 2013.

Gagnon, Robert A. J., *The Bible and Homosexual Practice*, Louisville, KY: Westminster John Knox Press, 2006.

Gagnon, Robert A. J. and Dan O. Via, *Homosexuality and the Bible: Two Views*, Philadelphia, PA: Fortress Press, 2003.

General Synod – Take Note Debate on GS2055, 15 February 2017 (YouTube), Graham James speaks at 6.20, https://www.youtube.com/watch?v=Oyj5x-fSCzMY (accessed 15.2.24).

General Synod – Take Note Debate on GS2055, 15 February 2017 (YouTube), Susie Leafe speaks at 42.24, https://www.youtube.com/watch?v=Oyj5xfSCzMY (accessed 15.2.24).

General Synod – Take Note Debate on GS2055, 15 February 2017 (YouTube), Sam Allberry speaks at 1.07.27, https://www.youtube.com/watch?v=Oyj5xfSCzMY (accessed 15.2.24).

BIBLIOGRAPHY

General Synod – Take Note Debate on GS2055, 15 February 2017 (YouTube), Justin Welby speaks at 1.59.17, https://www.youtube.com/watch?v=Oyj5x-fSCzMY (accessed 15.2.24).

General Synod, *Prayers of Love and Faith: A Note from the Legal Office* (GS Misc 1339, 2.)

The General Synod of the Church of England, *Update to General Synod of the Implementation Work for Living in Love and Faith*, The Archbishops' Council, 2023, https://www.churchofengland.org/sites/default/files/2023-06/gs-2303-living-in-love-and-faith-update.pdf (accessed 15.2.24).

Gibson, Timothy John, 'Issues in Christian Ethics: A Study of Method in Christian Ethics with Reference to the Church of England's Debate About Homosexuality', PhD dissertation, University of Exeter, 2006.

Gillett, David, 'Bishop David's Afterwords: Musings and Reflections from retirement in Norfolk', 2 December 2013, http://bishopdavidgillett.blogspot.com/2013/ (accessed 15.2.24).

Glazebrook, Allison and Kelly Olson, 'Greek and Roman Marriage', in *A Companion to Greek and Roman Sexualities*, edited by Thomas K. Hubbard. Hoboken, NJ: Wiley Blackwell, 2014.

Goddard, Andrew, 'Gay marriage would undermine a sacred institution', *The Guardian*, 1 May 2009, https://www.theguardian.com/commentisfree/belief/2009/may/01/gay-marriage-christianity (accessed 15.2.24).

Goddard, Andrew, 'James V. Brownson, Bible, Gender, Sexuality: A Critical Engagement', The Kirby Laing Institute For Christian Ethics, 2014, https://kirbylaingcentre.co.uk/wp-content/uploads/2021/01/KLICEPaper-AGoddardreviewofBrownson-BibleGenderSexuality.pdf (accessed 15.2.24).

Goddard, Andrew, 'The Bishops' Report (GS2055) The Way Forward?', *Fulcrum*, 14 February 2017, https://www.fulcrum-anglican.org.uk/articles/the-bishops-report-gs-2055-the-way-forward/ (accessed 15.2.24).

Goddard, Andrew, 'Giving and Receiving Episcopal Oversight: The Bishops' Report (GS2055)', *Fulcrum*, 8 February 2017, https://www.fulcrum-anglican.org.uk/articles/giving-and-receiving-episcopal-oversight-the-bishops-report-gs-2055/ (accessed 15.2.24).

Goddard, Andrew, 'Covenant Partnerships as a Third Calling? A Dialogue with Robert Song's *Covenant and Calling: Towards a Theology of Same-Sex Relationships*', in *Marriage, Family and Relationships: Biblical, Doctrinal and Contemporary Perspectives*, edited by Thomas A. Noble, Sarah K. Whittle and Philip S. Johnston, London: Apollos, 2017, 203–222.

Goddard, Andrew, 'Evangelical and Affirming: Pastoral Accommodation?', Psephizo, 9 January 2019, https://www.Psephizo.com/sexuality-2/evangelical-and-affirming-pastoral-accommodation/ (accessed 15.2.24).

Goddard, Andrew, 'General Synod, LLF and the mind of the church: What is the evidence?', Psephizo, 4 August 2023, https://www.psephizo.com/sexuality-2/general-synod-llf-and-the-mind-of-the-church-what-is-the-evidence/ (accessed 15.2.24).

Goddard, Andrew, *Theology and Ethics*, https://www.theologyethics.com/179-2/ (accessed 15.2.24).

Green, Marcus, *The Possibility of Difference: A Biblical Affirmation of Inclusivity*, London: Kevin Mayhew Ltd, 2018.

Greenough, Chris, *Undoing Theology: Life Stories from Non-normative Christians*, London: SCM Press, 2018

Greenough, Chris, *Queer Theologies: The Basics*, Abingdon: Routledge, 2020.

Greenough, Chris, 'Activism in the Queer Biblical Studies Classroom', *Journal for Interdisciplinary Biblical Studies*, 2, no. 1, Autumn 2020, 107–126.

The Gregory Centre for Church Multiplication, 'Myriad', https://ccx.org.uk/myriad/ (accessed 15.2.24).

Groves, Philip, ed., *The Anglican Communion and Homosexuality: A Resource to Enable Listening and Dialogue*, London: SPCK, 2008.

Groves, Philip, 'A Search for Good Disagreement', in *Grace and Disagreement 2: A Reader – Writings to Resource Conversation*, Church of England, 2015, 52–71, https://www.churchofengland.org/sites/default/files/2018-05/Grace%20and%20 Disagreement%202-%20A%20Reader%20%E2%80%93%20writings%20 to%20resource%20conversation_1.pdf (accessed 15.2.24).

Groves, Philip, John Holder and Paula Gooder, 'The Witness of Scripture', in *The Anglican Communion and Homosexuality*, London: SPCK, 2008.

Guest, Deryn, *When Deborah met Jael: Lesbian Biblical Hermeneutics*, London: SCM Press, 2005.

Guest, Deryn, Robert E. Goss, Mona West and Thomas Bohache, eds, *The Queer Bible Commentary*, London: SCM Press, 2006.

Guiliano, Zachary, 'No Winners', The Living Church: Serving the One Body of Christ, 15 February 2017, https://livingchurch.org/2017/02/15/no-winners/ (accessed 15.2.24).

Gutiérrez, Gustavo, 'Liberation Praxis and Christian Faith', in *Frontiers of Theology in Latin America*, edited by Rosino Gibellini, New York: Orbis Books, 1979.

Hai, P. E. H., 'Bridal Pregnancy in Rural England in Earlier Centuries', *Population Studies: A Journal of Demography*, 20, no. 2, 1966, 233–243.

Halberstam, J., *The Queer Art of Failure*, Durham, NC: Duke University Press, 2011.

Hall, Stuart, 'The West and the Rest: Discourse and Power', *Essential Essays, Volume II: Identity and Diaspora*, Durham, NC: Duke University Press, 2018, https://books.google.co.uk/books?hl=en&lr=&id=oCJIDwAAQBAJ&oi=fnd& pg=PA85&dq=west+and+rest&ots=qK-FCSJRiK&sig=IAQA_7Hra8IdSWJXwp-Zhc_paHA#v=onepage&q=west%20and%20rest&f=true (accessed 15.2.24).

Haller, Tobias Stanislaus, *Reasonable and Holy: Engaging Same-Sexuality*, New York: Seabury Books, 2009.

Halley, Janet E., 'Misreading Sodomy: A Critique of the Classification of "Homosexuals" in Federal Equal Protection Law', in *Body Guards: The Cultural Politics of Gender Ambiguity*, edited by Julia Epstein and Kristina Straub. New York: Routledge, 1991.

Halperin, David M., *Saint Foucault: Towards a Gay Hagiography*, Oxford: Oxford University Press, 1995.

Harrison, Glynn, *A Better Story: God, Sex and Human Flourishing*, London: Inter-Varsity Press, 2017.

Harvey, David, *A Brief History of Neoliberalism*, Oxford: Oxford University Press, 2005.

Hays, Richard B., *The Moral Vision of the New Testament*, New York: HarperCollins, 1996.

Hensman, Savitri, 'A Better Future for the Anglican Communion?', in *Ekklesia: Transforming Politics and Belief*, http://old.ekklesia.co.uk/node/10247 (accessed 15.2.24).

Hensman, Savitri, ed., 'Same- Sex Partnerships and Marriage', *Modern Believing: The Journal of Theological Liberalism – Special Issue*, 55, no. 2, 2014.

BIBLIOGRAPHY

Herek, Gregory, 'Facts about Homosexuality and Child Molestation', in *Beyond Homophobia*, https://lgbpsychology.org/html/facts_molestation.html (accessed 15.2.24).

Herman, Judith, M. D., *Trauma and Recovery: The Aftermath of Violence – From Domestic Abuse to Political Terror*, New York: Basic Books, 2015.

Higton, Mike, 'Men and Women in Marriage', *kai euthus*, March 2014, https://mikehigton.org.uk/?s=Men+and+women+in+marriage&submit=Search (accessed 15.2.24).

Higton, Mike and Rachel Muers, *The Text in Play: Experiments in Reading Scripture*, Eugene, OR: Cascade Books, 2012.

Higton, Tony, 'What Does the Bible Say on Homosexual Practice?' *Christian Teaching Resources* (n.d.), https://christianteaching.org.uk/wp-content/uploads/2021/01/biblehomosexualpractice.pdf (accessed 15.2.24).

Hornsby, Teresa J. and Ken Stone, eds, *Bible Trouble: Queer Reading at the Boundaries of Biblical Scholarship*, Atlanta, GA: SBL Press, 2011.

Hornsby, Teresa J. and Deryn Guest, *Transgender, Intersex, and Biblical Interpretation*, Atlanta, GA: SBL Press, 2016.

The House of Bishops, 'Marriage and Same-Sex Relationships after the Shared Conversations' (GS 2055, November 2016), http://www.tgdr.co.uk/documents/229P-GS2055.pdf (accessed 15.2.24).

Isherwood, Lisa and Marcella Althaus-Reid, eds, *Trans/formations*, London: SCM Press, 2009.

James, P. D., *The Children of Men*, London: Faber & Faber, 1992.

James, Robin, *Resilience and Melancholy: Pop Music, Feminism, Neoliberalism*, Ropley: John Hunt Publishing, 2015.

John, Jeffrey, *Permanent, Faithful, Stable: Christian Same-Sex Marriage*, London: Darton, Longman & Todd, 2012.

Johnson, Jay Emerson, 'Sodomy and Gendered Love: Reading Genesis 19 in the Anglican Communion', in *The Oxford Handbook of the Reception History of the Bible*, edited by Michael Lieb, Emma Mason, Jonathan Roberts and Christopher Rowland, Oxford: Oxford University Press, 2011, DOI: 10.1093/oxfordhb/9780199204540.003.0029 (accessed 9.7.22).

Johnson, Luke Timothy, 'Homosexuality & the Church: Scripture & Experience', *Commonweal*, 11 June 2007, https://www.commonwealmagazine.org/homosexuality-church-o (accessed 15.2.24).

Jones, S. L., 'Identity in Christ and Sexuality', in *Grace and Truth in the Secular Age*, edited by T. Bradshaw, Grand Rapids, MI: Eerdmans, 1998.

Jordan, Mark D., *The Invention of Sodomy in Christian Theology*, Chicago, IL: University of Chicago Press, 1997.

Jordan, Mark D., *The Ethics of Sex*, Oxford: Blackwell, 2002.

Jordan, Mark D., Meghan T. Sweeney and David M. Mellot, eds, *Authorizing Marriage? Canon, Tradition, and Critique in the Blessing of Same-Sex Unions*, Princeton, NJ: Princeton University Press, 2006.

Jordan, Mark D., 'God's Body', in *Queer Theology: Rethinking the Western Body*, edited by Gerard Loughlin, Oxford: Blackwell, 2007, 281–292.

Jung, Patricia Beattie, 'Christianity and Human Sexual Polymorphism: Are They Compatible?', *Ethics and Intersex: International Library of Ethics, Law and the New Medicine*, 29, 2006, 293–309, https://doi.org/10.1007/1-4220-4314-7_18 (accessed 15.2.24).

Kershaw, Simon, 'About Thinking Anglicans', 9 August 2003, https://www.thinkinganglicans.org.uk/65-2 (accessed 15.2.24).

Kilby, Karen, *Balthasar: A (Very) Critical Introduction*, Grand Rapids, MI: Eerdmans, 2012.
King, Helen, *The One-Sex Body on Trial: The Classical and Early Modern Evidence*, Farnham: Ashgate, 2013.
King, Helen, 'Pausanias and Agathon: "A Same-Sex Relationship"?', *Shared Conversations: Reflecting on Sexuality and Gender Identity in the Church of England*, 4 July 2016, https://shared-conversations.com/2016/07/04/pausanias-and-agathon-a-same-sex-relationship/ (accessed 15.2.24).
King, Helen, 'Temple Prostitution for Christians', *Shared Conversations: Reflecting on Sexuality and Gender Identity in the Church of England*, 14 August 2016, https://sharedconversations.wordpress.com/2016/08/14/temple-prostitution-for-christians/ (accessed 15.2.24).
LGBTI Mission, 'Press Release, Archbishops; Bold Proposal for Radical Inclusion', 19 February 2017, https://lgbtimission.org.uk/2017/02/19/press-release-archbishops-bold-proposal-for-radical-inclusion/ (accessed 15.2.24).
Laqueur, Thomas, *Making Sex: Body and Gender from the Greeks to Freud*, Cambridge, MA: Harvard University Press, 1992.
Lawrence, Louise J., *Sense and Stigma in the Gospels: Depictions of Sensory Disabled Characters*, Oxford: Oxford University Press, 2013.
Lawrence, Louise J., *Refiguring the University in an Age of Neoliberalism: Creating Compassionate Campuses*, London: Palgrave Macmillan, 2021.
Lesbian and Gay Christian Movement, 'LGCM calls on members of General Synod not to "take note"', http://www.onebodyonefaith.org.uk/news/not-take-note/ (link no longer available).
Lewis, C. S., *A Mind Awake: An Anthology of C. S. Lewis*, Boston, MA: Houghton Mifflin Harcourt, 2003.
Living Out, 'About Us', https://www.livingout.org/about-us/about (accessed 15.2.24).
Loader, William, *Sexuality in the New Testament: Understanding the Key Texts*, London: SPCK, 2010.
Lorde, Audre, *Sister Outsider: Essays and Speeches*, Berkeley, CA: Crossing Press, 2007, 110–113, https://edisciplinas.usp.br/pluginfile.php/4123062/mod_resource/content/1/Audre%20Lorde%20-%20Sister%20Outsider.%20Essays%20and%20Speeches%201984.pdf (accessed 15.2.24).
Loughlin, Gerard, ed., *Queer Theology: Rethinking the Western Body*, Oxford: Blackwell, 2007.
Loughlin, Gerard, 'Introduction', in *Queer Theology: Rethinking the Western Body*, edited by Gerard Loughlin, Oxford: Blackwell, 2007.
Loughlin, Gerard, 'What is Queer? Theology After Identity', *Theology and Sexuality*, 14.2, 2008, 143–152.
Loughlin, Gerard, 'Silent Witness: On Listening but Not Hearing in the Church of England', *ABC Religion and Ethics*, 5 April 2019, https://www.abc.net.au/religion/the-church-of-england-and-the-silence-of-gay-christians/10975666 (accessed 15.2.24).
Ludlow, Morwenna, *Gregory of Nyssa: Ancient and [Post] Modern*, Oxford: Oxford University Press, 2007.
Lynas, Peter, *Transformed: Understanding Transgender in a Changing Culture*, The Evangelical Alliance, 2018, https://www.eauk.org/assets/files/downloads/Transformed.pdf (accessed 15.2.24).
MacCulloch, Diarmaid, *Reformation: Europe's House Divided, 1490–1700*, London: Penguin, 2004.

McDonald, Chine, *God is Not a White Man*, London: Hodder and Stoughton, 2021.
McGinley, John, *Shared Conversations* (EGGS, n.d.), http://www.eggscofe.org.uk/uploads/5/5/6/3/5563632/shared_conversations_jm.pdf (accessed 15.2.24).
McTague, Tom, 'Row over bishops' left-wing manifesto spills out into the open as ministers mock Church of England's "dwindling relevance" while Welby endorses attack on MPs', *Mail Online*, 17 February 2015, https://www.dailymail.co.uk/news/article-2957106/Church-England-takes-Russell-Brand-election-boycot-call-shocked-profound-effect-young-voters.html (accessed 15.2.24).
Mann, Rachel, *Dazzling Darkness: Gender, Sexuality, Illness and God*, Glasgow: Wild Goose Publications, 2012.
Marks, Jeremy, *Exchanging the Truth of God for a Lie (Romans 1:25): One Man's Spiritual Journey to Find the Truth About Homosexuality and Same-Sex Partnerships*, Chichester: Courage UK, 2008.
Martin, Dale B., 'Heterosexism and the Interpretation of Romans 1:18 –32', *Biblical Interpretation*, 3, no. 3, 1995, 332 –55.
Martin, Dale B., 'Arsenokoités and Malakos: Meanings and Consequences', in *Biblical Ethics & Homosexuality: Listening to Scripture*, edited by Robert L. Brawley, Louisville, KY: Westminster John Knox Press, 1996.
Martin, Dale B., *The Corinthian Body*, New Haven, CT: Yale University Press, 1999.
Martin, Dale B., *Sex and the Single Savior: Gender and Sexuality in Biblical Interpretation*, Louisville, KY: Westminster John Knox Press, 2006.
Martin, Dale B., 'Familiar Idolatry and the Christian Case Against Marriage', in *Authorizing Marriage? Canon, Tradition, and Critique in the Blessing of Same-Sex Unions*, edited by Mark D. Jordan, Meghan T. Sweeney and David M. Mellot, 17 –40, Princeton, NJ: Princeton University Press, 2006.
Martin, Dale B., *New Testament History and Literature*, New Haven and London: Yale University Press, 2012.
Mason, Kathryn, 'Annulment for Non-Consummation', *Vardags*, 1 March 2016, https://vardags.com/family-law/annulment-for-non-consummation (accessed 15.2.24).
May, Callum, 'Church of England "not listening" to Gay Christians say Retired Church of England Bishops', *BBC News*, 12 February 2017, https://www.bbc.co.uk/news/uk-38940915 (accessed 15.2.24).
Meeks, Wayne A., 'The Image of the Androgyne: Some Uses of a Symbol in Earliest Christianity', *History of Religions*, 13, no. 3, February 1974, 165–208.
Merz, Annette, 'Why Did the Pure Bride of Christ (2 Cor. 11.2) Become a Wedded Wife (Eph. 5.22–23)?' *Journal for the Study of the New Testament*, 79, 2000, 131–147.
Meteyard, Belinda, 'Illegitimacy and Marriage in Eighteenth-Century England', *The Journal of Interdisciplinary History*, 10, no. 3, Winter 1980, 479–89.
Methuen, Charlotte, 'Thinking About Marriage: What Can We Learn from Christian History?', in *Thinking Again About Marriage: Key Theological Questions*, edited by John Bradbury and Susannah Cornwall, London: SCM Press, 2016.
Milbank, John, 'Gay Marriage and the Future of Human Sexuality', *ABC Religion and Ethics*, 13 March 2012, https://www.abc.net.au/religion/gay-marriage-and-the-future-of-human-sexuality/10100726 (accessed 15.2.24).
Milbank, John, 'The Impossibility of Gay Marriage and the Threat of Biopolitical Control', *ABC Religion & Ethics*, 23 April 2013, https://www.abc.net.au/religion/the-impossibility-of-gay-marriage-and-the-threat-of-biopolitical/10099888 (accessed 15.2.24).

Moberly, Elizabeth, 'Homosexuality and the Truth', *First Things*, 71, March 1997, 30–33, http://www.leaderu.com/ftissues/ft9703/opinion/moberly.html (accessed 15.2.24).

Mock, Steven E. and Richard P. Eibach, 'Stability and Change in Sexual Orientation Identity Over a 10-Year Period in Adulthood', *Archives of Sexual Behavior*, 4, 2012, https://doi.org/10.1007/s10508-011-9761-1 (accessed 15.2.24).

Modhin, Aamna, 'Brexiters tell Archbishop of Canterbury not to interfere', *The Guardian*, 27 August 2019, https://www.theguardian.com/uk-news/2019/aug/27/dont-interfere-with-brexit-archbishop-of-canterbury-justin-welby-told (accessed 15.2.24).

Monbiot, George, 'Neoliberalism – The Ideology at the Root of all our Problems', *The Guardian*, 15 April 2016, https://www.theguardian.com/books/2016/apr/15/neoliberalism-ideology-problem-george-monbiot (accessed 15.2.24).

Moore, Stephen D., *God's Gym: Divine Male Bodies of the Bible*, New York and London: Routledge, 1996.

Moore, Stephen D., *God's Beauty Parlor: And Other Queer Spaces in and Around the Bible*, Stanford, CA: Stanford University Press, 2001.

Morgan, Silas, Kate Ott, Ellen Armour, Lisa Isherwood and Ashon Crawley, 'The Queer Art of Failure', *Syndicate Symposium* (06/08/2015), https://syndicate.net work/symposia/literature/the-queer-art-of-failure/ (accessed 15.2.24).

Moxnes, Halvor, *Putting Jesus in His Place: A Radical Vision of Household and Kingdom*, Louisville, KY: Westminster John Knox Press, 2003.

Muñoz, Jose Esteban, *Cruising Utopia: The Then and There of Queer Futurity*, New York: NYU Press, 2009.

New Wine, 'Who We Are', https://www.new-wine.org/about/ (accessed 15.2.24).

Nissinen, Martti, *Homoeroticism in the Biblical World: A Historical Perspective*, Minneapolis, MN: Fortress Press, 1998.

Nixon, David, 'Ecclesial Speed Dating? A Theological Reflection on One Shared Conversation', *The Expository Times*, 127, no. 8, 2016, 390–393, 391–393, https://journals.sagepub.com/doi/abs/10.1177/0014524615592804 (accessed 15.2.24).

Noble, Thomas A., Sarah K. Whittle and Philip S. Johnston, eds, *Marriage, Family and Relationships: Biblical, Doctrinal and Contemporary Perspectives*, London: Apollos, 2017.

Nye, William, *Communion and Disagreement: A Report from the Faith and Order Commission*, General Synod (GS Misc 1139), Church of England, June 2016, https://www.churchofengland.org/sites/default/files/2017-10/communion_and_disagreement_faoc_report_gs_misc_1139.pdf (accessed 15.2.24).

O' Donnell, Karen, *Broken Bodies: The Eucharist, Mary, and the Body in Trauma Theology*, London: SCM Press, 2019.

O'Donovan, Oliver, *Transsexualism and Christian Marriage*, Cambridge: Grove Books, 1982.

O'Donovan, Oliver, 'Homosexuality in the Church: Can there be a Fruitful Theological Debate?' in *Theology and Sexuality: Classic and Contemporary Readings*, edited by Eugene F. Rogers Jr., Oxford: Blackwell, 2002, 373–386.

Office for National Statistics, 'Marriage, Cohabitation and Civil Partnerships', *Office for National Statistics*, https://www.ons.gov.uk/peoplepopulationandcom munity/birthsdeathsandmarriages/marriagecohabitationandcivilpartnerships (accessed 15.2.24).

Olyan, Saul M., '"And with a Male You Shall Not Lie the Lying Down of a Woman": On the Meaning and Significance of Leviticus 18.22 and 20.13', *Journal of the History of Sexuality*, 5, no. 2, 1994, 179–206.

Olyan, Saul M., '"Surpassing the Love of Women": Another Look at 2 Smauel 1.26 and the Relationship of David and Jonathan', in *Authorizing Marriage? Canon, Tradition, and Critique in the Blessing of Same-Sex Unions*, edited by Mark D, Jordan, Meghan T. Sweeney and David M. Mellot, Princeton, NJ: Princeton University Press, 2006, 7–16.

OneBodyOneFaith, 'A Time to Build', *One Body One Faith* (n.d.), http://www.onebodyonefaith.org.uk/news/a-time-to-build/ (link no longer available).

OneBodyOneFaith and Jeremy Pemberton, 'Church of England Synod – GS2055 Case Studies', http://www.onebodyonefaith.org.uk/news/church-of-england-synod-gs2055-case-studies/ (accessed 15.2.24).

Ould, Peter, 'Can Your Sexuality Change?', *Living Out*, 12 January 2021, https://www.livingout.org/resources/articles/44/can-your-sexuality-change (accessed 15.2.22).

Owen, Peter, 'College of Bishops – Shared Conversations', Thinking Anglicans, 19 September 2014, https://www.thinkinganglicans.org.uk/6729-2/ (accessed 15.2.24).

Owen, Peter, 'Marriage and Same-Sex Relationships After the Shared Conversations – A Report from the House of Bishops: General Synod Press Conference, 27 January 2017, Statement by the Bishop of Norwich', Thinking Anglicans, 27 January 2017, https://www.thinkinganglicans.org.uk/7440-2/ (accessed 15.2.22).

Owen, Peter, 'Debate on the Bishops' report – take note motion defeated', Thinking Anglicans, 15 February 2017, https://www.thinkinganglicans.org.uk/7469-2 (accessed 15.2.22).

Ozanne, Jayne, 'Same-sex Marriage – 2016 YouGov Poll', Jayne Ozanne's Personal Website, https://jayneozanne.com/2017/09/12/attitudes-to-same-sex-marriage-yougov-poll (accessed 15.2.22).

Paul, Ian, *Same-Sex Unions: The Key Biblical Texts*, Grove Biblical, Cambridge: Grove Books, 2014.

Paul, Ian, 'Psephizo: about', https://www.Psephizo.com/about/ (accessed 15.2.22)

Paul, Ian, 'The *Pilling Report*: Divisive and Damaging?', Psephizo, 2 December 2013, https://www.Psephizo.com/sexuality-2/the-pilling-report-divisive-and-damaging/ (accessed 15.2.22).

Paul, Ian, 'The Bible, *Pilling* and Changing One's Mind', Psephizo, 7 February 2014, https://www.Psephizo.com/biblical-studies/the-bible-pilling-and-changing-ones-mind/ (accessed 15.2.22).

Paul, Ian, 'What is at Stake for the Church and Same-Sex Marriage', Psephizo, 8 July 2015, https://www.Psephizo.com/sexuality-2/what-is-at-stake-for-the-church-and-same-sex-marriage/ (accessed 15.2.22).

Paul, Ian, 'What is at Stake for the Church and Same-Sex Marriage?', *Fulcrum*, 9 July 2015, https://www.fulcrum-anglican.org.uk/articles/what-is-at-stake-for-the-church-and-same-sex-marriage (accessed 15.2.24).

Paul, Ian, 'Are food and sex "things indifferent"?', Psephizo, 15 October 2015, https://www.psephizo.com/sexuality-2/are-food-and-sex-things-indifferent/ (accessed 15.2.24).

Paul, Ian, 'Synod's Shared Conversations', Psephizo, 13 July 2016, https://www.psephizo.com/sexuality-2/synods-shared-conversations/ (accessed 15.2.24).

Paul, Ian, 'On Synod, Sexuality, and Not Taking Note', Psephizo, 16 February 2017, https://www.psephizo.com/sexuality-2/on-synod-sexuality-and-not-taking-note/ (accessed 15.2.24).

Paul, Ian, 'Debating Transgender', Psephizo, 7 June 2017, https://www.psephizo.com/sexuality-2/debating-transgender/ (accessed 15.2.24).

Paul, Ian, 'Is the Bishops' policy on Civil Partnerships Sustainable?', Psephizo, 9 October 2018, https://www.psephizo.com/sexuality-2/is-the-bishops-policy-on-civil-partnerships-sustainable/ (accessed 15.2.24).

Paul, Ian, 'What does the Oxford Ad Clerum mean?', Psephizo, 7 November 2018, https://www.psephizo.com/sexuality-2/what-does-the-oxford-ad-clerum-mean/ (accessed 15.2.24).

Paul, Ian, 'The Biblical Case for the 'Traditional' Position', in *Grace and Disagreement 2: A Reader – Writings to Resource Conversation*, Church of England, 2015, 1–23, https://www.churchofengland.org/sites/default/files/2018-05/Grace%20and%20Disagreement%202-%20A%20Reader%20%E2%80%93%20writings%20to%20resource%20conversation_1.pdf (accessed 15.2.24).

Paveo, Paul F., 'Canons of the Council of Nicaea', *Christian History for Everyman*, https://www.christian-history.org/council-of-nicea-canons.html (accessed 15.2.24).

Pearce, Augur, 'Marriage and English Law', in *Thinking Again About Marriage: Key Theological Questions*, edited by John Bradbury and Susannah Cornwall, London: SCM Press, 2016.

Pemberton, Jeremy, 'Shared Conversations – Talking in Circles', *From the Choir Stalls, Reflection and Comment from a Priest Musician*, 14 May 2015, https://jeremypemberton.wordpress.com/2015/05/14/shared-conversations-talking-in-circles/ (accessed 15.2.24).

Pemberton, Jeremy, 'Deadly Pressure', *From the Choir Stalls, Reflection and Comment from a Priest Musician*, 23 October 2020, https://jeremypemberton.wordpress.com/2020/10/23/deadly-pressure/ (accessed 15.2.24).

Percy, Martyn, 'Are These the Leaders That We Really Want?', *Church Times*, 12 December 2014, https://www.churchtimes.co.uk/articles/2014/12-december/comment/opinion/are-these-the-leaders-that-we-really-want (accessed 15.2.24).

Percy, Martyn, 'The Great Leap Forward (Part One): The New Politics of Ecclesionomics for the Church of England', Modern Church, 5 July 2021, https://modernchurch.org.uk/martyn-percy-the-great-leap-forward-part-one-the-new-politics-of-ecclesionomics-for-the-church-of-england (accessed 15.2.24).

Percy, Martyn, 'The Great Leap Forward (Part Two): The Church of England's Growth Fetish', Modern Church, 7 July 2021, https://modernchurch.org.uk/martyn-percy-the-great-leap-forward-part-two-the-church-of-englands-growth-fetish (accessed 15.2.24).

Perrin, Ruth, 'The Gift No-one wants: Millennial Christians and Singleness', *Discipleship Research*, October 2017, https://discipleshipresearch.com/2017/10/the-gift-no-one-wants/ (accessed 15.2.24).

Phelps, Hollis and Silas Morgan, 'Special Issue: Jack Halberstam's "The Queer Art of Failure"', *The Other Journal: An Intersection of Theology and Culture*, 29 May 2015, https://theotherjournal.com/2015/07/29/special-issue-jack-halberstams-the-queer-art-of-failure/ (accessed 15.2.24).

Pike, John, 'Were loving, faithful same-sex relations known in antiquity?', Psephizo, 17 August 2017, https://www.Psephizo.com/sexuality-2/were-loving-faithful-same-sex-relations-known-in-antiquity/ (accessed 15.2.24).

Pink, Sarah et al., *Digital Ethnography: Principles and Practice*, Thousand Oaks, CA: Sage, 2006.

Pitstick, Alyssa Lyra, *Light in Darkness: Hans Urs von Balthasar and the Catholic Doctrine of Christ's Descent into Hell*, Grand Rapids, MI: Eerdmans, 2007.

Pitstick, Alyssa Lyra and Edward T. Oakes SJ, 'Balthasar, Hell, and Heresy: An Exchange', *First Things*, December 2006, https://www.firstthings.com/article/2006/12/balthasar-hell-and-heresy-an-exchange (accessed 15.2.24).
Plata, Mariana, 'Is Social Media Making Us Ruder?', *Psychology Today*, 26 February 2018, https://www.psychologytoday.com/gb/blog/the-gen-y-psy/201802/is-social-media-making-us-ruder (accessed 15.2.24).
Plummer, Kenneth, *Sexual Stigma: An Interactionist Account*, London: Routledge & Kegan Paul, 1975.
Plummer, Kenneth, 'Queer, Bodies and Post-modern Sexualities: A Note on Revisiting the "Sexual"', *Symbolic Interactionism*, https://kenplummer.com/publications/selected-writings-2/queer-bodies-and-postmodern-sexualities/ (accessed 15.2.24).
Pocklington, David, 'Shared Conversations on Sexuality, Scripture and Mission', *Law and Religion UK*, 30 June 2014, https://lawandreligionuk.com/2014/06/30/ (accessed 15.2.24).
Pomerai, David de and Glynn Harrison, 'The Witness of Science', in *The Anglican Communion and Homosexuality*, edited by Philip Groves, London: SPCK, 2008, 267–332.
Pyper, Hugh, *The Unchained Bible: Cultural Appropriations of Biblical Texts*, London: Bloomsbury, 2010.
Queer Faith Stories, 'Can you be religious and queer? | them', 3 May 2018, 6.55, https://www.youtube.com/watch?v=gnG3BSDfvhk (accessed 15.2.24).
Quero, Martin Hugo Cordova, 'Friendship with Benefits: A Queer Reading of Aelred of Rievaulx and His Theology of Friendship', in *The Sexual Theologian: Essays on Sex, God and Politics*, edited by Marcella Althaus-Reid and Lisa Isherwood. London: T & T Clark, 2004, 26–46.
Quinn, Ben, 'Couple who won battle to open up civil unions register partnership', *The Guardian*, 31 December 2019, https://www.theguardian.com/uk-news/2019/dec/31/couple-who-won-battle-to-open-up-civil-unions-register-partnership (accessed 15.2.24).
Rak, Julie, 'The Digital Queer: Weblogs and Internet Identity', *Biography*, 28, no. 1, 2005, 166–182, https://muse.jhu.edu/article/183605/summary (accessed 15.2.24).
Rambo, Shelly, *Spirit and Trauma: A Theology of Remaining*, Louisville, KY: Westminster John Knox Press, 2010.
Ramsay, Laura Monica, 'The Church of England, Homosexual Law Reform, and the Shaping of the Permissive Society, 1957–1979', *Journal of British Studies*, 57, January 2018, 108–137, doi:10.1017/jbr.2017.180 (accessed 15.2.24).
Ranke-Heinemann, Uta, *Eunuchs for the Kingdom of Heaven: The Catholic Church and Sexuality*, London: Penguin, 1990.
Reynolds, Philip Lyndon, *Marriage in the Western Church: The Christianization of Marriage During the Patristic and Early Medieval Periods*, Leiden: Brill, 2001.
Rich, Adrienne, 'Compulsory Heterosexuality and Lesbian Existence', *Signs: Journal of Women in Culture and Society. University of Chicago Press Journals*, 5, no. 4, Summer 1980, 631–660, https://law.unimelb.edu.au/__data/assets/pdf_file/0003/3453618/ahmed_2014_queer-feelings-in-the-cultural-politics-of-emotion.pdf (accessed 15.2.24).
Ricoeur, Paul, *The Conflict of Interpretations: Essays in Hermeneutics*, Evanston, IL: Northwestern University Press, 1974.
Ritchie, Angus, 'Scripture and Sexuality, Once Again: A Response to Ian Paul', *ABC Religion and Ethics*, 16 February 2016, https://www.abc.net.au/religion/scripture-and-sexuality-once-again-a-response-to-ian-paul/10097308 (accessed 15.2.24).

Roberts, Alice @theAliceRoberts, 'If the god of the bible is so clever, how come he made plants before he made the sun?' Twitter, 8 June 2021, 10.03am, https://twitter.com/thealiceroberts/status/1402189491020996609 (accessed 15.2.24).

Roberts, Christopher Chenault, *Creation and Covenant: The Significance of Sexual Difference in the Modern Theology of Marriage*, London: T&T Clarke, 2007.

Roberts, Vaughan, 'Foreword', *The Plausibility Problem: The Church and Same-sex Attraction*, Nottingham: Inter-Varsity Press, 2015.

Robinson Brown, Jarel, *Black, Gay, British, Christian, Queer: The Church and the Famine of Grace*, London: SCM Press, 2021.

Rogers, Eugene F. Jr, *Sexuality and the Christian Body: Their Way into the Triune God*, Oxford: Blackwell, 1999.

Rogers, Eugene F. Jr, ed., *Theology and Sexuality: Classic and Contemporary Readings*, Oxford: Blackwell, 2002.

Rogers, Eugene F. Jr, 'Trinity, Marriage and Homosexuality', in *Authorizing Marriage? Canon, Tradition, and Critique in the Blessing of Same-Sex Unions*, edited by Mark D. Jordan, Meghan T. Sweeney and David M. Mellot, Princeton, NJ: Princeton University Press, 2006, 151–164.

Rose, Marika, *A Theology of Failure: Žižek against Christian Innocence*, New York: Fordham University Press, 2019.

Rose, Marika, *Theology for the End of the World*, London: SCM Press, 2023.

The Royal College of Psychiatrists, 'Mission Statement', https://www.rcpsych.ac.uk/about-us/what-we-do-and-how/our-mission (accessed 14.4.24).

The Royal College of Psychiatrists, 'Statement on Sexual Orientation: Position Statement PS02/2014', April 2014, https://www.rcpsych.ac.uk/docs/default-source/improving-care/better-mh-policy/position-statements/ps02_2014.pdf?sfvrsn=b39bd77c_4 (accessed 14.4.24).

Runcorn, David, 'And how do I know when I am wrong? Evangelical faith and the Bible', *Fulcrum*, 28 January 2014, https://www.fulcrum-anglican.org.uk/articles/and-how-do-i-know-when-i-am-wrong-evangelical-faith-and-the-bible/ (accessed 15.2.24).

Runcorn, David, 'I was speaking at Trinity, Bristol yesterday ...', *Good Disagreement*, Facebook, 19 March 2015, https://www.facebook.com/groups/855137377886437/search/?q=david%20runcorn (accessed 15.2.24).

Runcorn, David, 'Public Letter on LLF Process', *Inclusive Evangelicals*, https://www.inclusiveevangelicals.com/post/public-letter-on-llf-process (accessed 15.2.24).

Runcorn, David, 'General Synod, LLF and the mind of the church', *Inclusive Evangelicals*, 24 July 2023, https://www.inclusiveevangelicals.com/post/general-synod-llf-and-the-mind-of-the-church (accessed 15.2.24).

Sarmiento, Simon, 'Reform withdraws from sexuality conversations', Thinking Anglicans, 8 October 2014, https://www.thinkinganglicans.org.uk/6750-2 (accessed 15.2.24).

Santos, Boaventura de Sousa, *The End of the Cognitive Empire: The Coming of Age of Epistemologies of the South*, Durham, NC: Duke University Press, 2018, https://www.jstor.org/stable/pdf/j.ctv125jqvn.4 (accessed 15.2.24).

Sawyer, Patrick and Olivia Rudgard, 'Anglicans Braced for New Clashes Over Gay Marriage in Church', *The Telegraph*, 11 February 2017, https://www.telegraph.co.uk/news/2017/02/11/anglicans-braced-new-clashes-gay-marriage-church/ (accessed 15.2.24).

Schüssler Fiorenza, Elisabeth, *In Memory of Her: A Feminist Theological Reconstruction of Christian Origins*, 2nd edn, London: SCM Press, 1994.

Scott, James C., *Weapons of the Weak: Everyday Forms of Peasant Resistance*, New Haven, CT: Yale University Press, 1987.
Scroggs, Robin, *The New Testament and Homosexuality: Contextual Background for the Contemporary Debate*, Philadelphia, PA: Fortress Press, 1983.
Sedgwick, Eve Kosofsky, *The Epistemology of the Closet*, London: Penguin, 1994.
Seeley, Martin, 'A Tale of Two Shared Conversations', *ViaMedia.News*, 11 March 2017, https://www.viamedia.news/category/guest-contributors/martin-seeley/ (accessed 15.2.24).
Shaw, Ed, *The Plausibility Problem: The Church and Same-Sex Attraction*, Nottingham: Inter-Varsity Press, 2015.
Shaw, Ed, 'Shared Conversations' (EGGS, n.d.), http://www.eggscofe.org.uk/uploads/5/5/6/3/5563632/ed_shaw_shared_conversations_eggs_article_v2.pdf (accessed 15.2.24).
Shaw, Jane, 'When the C of E Wanted to Talk', *Church Times*, 18 January 2012, https://www.churchtimes.co.uk/articles/2012/20-january/comment/when-the-c-of-e-wanted-to-talk (accessed 15.2.24).
Shell, Christopher, '"British Values": a Pandora's Box?', in *What Are They Teaching the Children?*, edited by Lynda Rose, London: Wilberforce Publications, 2016, 253–329.
Sherwood, Harriet, 'Church and State – An Unhappy Union?', *The Observer*, 7 October 2018, https://www.theguardian.com/global/2018/oct/07/church-and-state-an-unhappy-union (accessed 15.2.24).
Sinclair, Keith, '*The Pilling Report*: Bishop of Birkenhead's Dissenting Statement', *Virtue Online: The Voice of Global Orthodox Anglicanism*, 28 November 2013, http://www.virtueonline.org/pilling-report-bishop-birkenheads-dissenting-statement, accessed 26 April 2016, this link is no longer live.
Sinclair, Keith, 'A Conversation Hardly Begun: Reflections on the Shared Conversations, September 2015', EGGS, http://www.eggscofe.org.uk/uploads/5/5/6/3/5563632/shared_conversations_-_a_conversation_hardly_begun_-_keith_sinclair.pdf (accessed 15.2.24).
Social Media Research Group, 'Using social media for social research: an introduction', Government Social Research, May 2016, https://assets.publishing.service.gov.uk/government/uploads/system/uploads/attachment_data/file/524750/GSR_Social_Media_Research_Guidance_-_Using_social_media_for_social_research.pdf (accessed 15.2.24).
Solevag, Anna Rebecca, 'No Nuts? No Problem! Disability, Stigma and the Baptized Eunuch in Acts 8.26–40', *Biblical Interpretation* 24, 2016, 81–99.
Sommerlad, Joe, 'Section 28: What was Margaret Thatcher's controversial law and how did it affect the lives of LGBT+ people?', *Independent*, 25 May 2018, https://www.independent.co.uk/news/uk/politics/section-28-explained-lgbt-education-schools-homosexuality-gay-queer-margaret-thatcher-a8366741.html (accessed 15.2.24).
Song, Robert, *Covenant and Calling: Towards a Theology of Same-Sex Relationships*, London: SCM Press, 2014.
Spivak, Gayatri Chakravorty, 'Can the Subaltern Speak?', in *Marxism and the Interpretation of Culture*, edited by Cary Nelson and Lawrence Grossberg. Urbana, IL: University of Illinois Press, 1988.
Sprinkle, Preston, William Loader, Megan DeFranza, Wesley Hill and Stephen R. Holmes, eds, *Two Views on Homosexuality, the Bible, and the Church*, edited by Stanley N. Gundry, Counterpoints, Grand Rapids, MI: Zondervan Academic, 2016.

Stone, Ken, *Practicing Safer Texts: Food, Sex and Bible in Queer Perspective*, London: T&T Clark, 2004.

Stone, Ken, 'Queer Criticism', in *New Meanings for Ancient Texts: Recent Approaches to Biblical Criticisms and Their Applications*, edited by Steven L. McKenzie and John Kaltner, Louisville, KY: Westminster John Knox Press, 155–176.

Stone, Lawrence, *The Family, Sex and Marriage in England 1500–1800*, London: Penguin, 1979.

Stryker, Susan, Francisco J. Galarte, Jules Gill-Peterson, Grace Lavery and Abraham B. Wei, eds, *Transgender Studies Quarterly*, https://read.dukeupress.edu/tsq (accessed 15.2.24).

Stuart, Elizabeth, *Just Good Friends: Towards a Lesbian and Gay Theology of Relationships*. London: Mowbray, 1995.

Stuart, Elizabeth, *Religion is a Queer Thing: A Guide to the Christian Faith for Lesbian, Gay, Bisexual and Transgendered People*, London & Washington: Cassell, 1997.

Stuart, Elizabeth, *Gay and Lesbian Theologies: Repetitions with Critical Difference*, Aldershot: Ashgate, 2003.

Stuart, Elizabeth and Adrian Thatcher, *People of Passion: What the Churches Teach About Sex*, London: Mowbray, 1997.

Stuart, Elizabeth, 'Sacramental Flesh', in *Queer Theology: Rethinking the Western Body*, edited by Gerard Loughlin, Oxford: Blackwell, 2007, 65–75.

Stuart, Elizabeth and Adrian Thatcher, eds, *Christian Perspectives on Sexuality and Gender*, Leominster: Gracewing; Grand Rapids, MI: Eerdmans, 1996.

Sullivan, Nikki, *A Critical Introduction to Queer Theory*, New York: New York University Press, 2003.

Swerling, Gabriella and Ben Butcher, 'Sunday church attendance almost halves in 30 years, figures show', *The Telegraph*, 9 January 2022, https://www.telegraph.co.uk/news/2022/01/09/sunday-church-service-attendance-almost-halves-30-years-figures/ (accessed 15.2.24).

Symes, Andrew, 'Shared Conversations: a snapshot of the C o E, and a pointer to the future?', Anglican Mainstream, 8 March 2016, https://anglicanmainstream.org/shared-conversations-a-snapshot-of-the-c-of-e-and-a-pointer-to-the-future/ (accessed 15.2.24).

Tall, Nic, 'Living in Love and Faith: What the Church of England Really Thinks', *Equal: The Campaign for Equal Marriage in the Church of England*, 3 September 2022, https://cofe-equal-marriage.org.uk/llf-what-the-c-of-e-really-thinks/ (accessed 15.2.24).

Tanner, Kathryn, *Theories of Culture*, Minneapolis, MN: Fortress Press, 1997.

Taylor, Yvette, Emily Falconer and Ria Snowden, 'Queer Youth, Facebook and Faith: Facebook methodologies and online identities', *New Media and Society*, 16, no. 7, 201, 1138–1153, http://journals.sagepub.com/doi/abs/10.1177/1461444814544000 (accessed 15.2.24).

Thatcher, Adrian, *Liberating Sex: A Christian Sexual Theology*. London: SPCK, 1993.

Thatcher, Adrian, *The Savage Text: The Use and Abuse of the Bible*, Chichester: Wiley-Blackwell, 2008.

Thatcher, Adrian, *God, Sex and Gender: An Introduction*, Chichester: Wiley-Blackwell, 2011.

Thatcher, Adrian, *Making Sense of Sex*, London: SPCK, 2012.

Thatcher, Adrian, 'The One Sex Theory and Why It Still Matters', in *Theology and Religion Seminar*, University of Exeter, 2012.

Thatcher, Adrian, ed., *The Oxford Handbook Theology, Sexuality, and Gender*, Oxford: Oxford University Press, 2014.
Thatcher, Adrian, *Redeeming Gender*, Oxford: Oxford University Press, 2016.
Thatcher Margaret, 'Speech on October 9, 1987, Conservative Party Conference at the Winter Gardens, Blackpool', https://www.youtube.com/watch?v=8VRR Wuryb4k (accessed 15.2.24).
Thompson, Emma, 'Out of Touch Bishops are Pushing the Church to the Brink of Ruin', *The Telegraph*, 4 June 2021, https://www.telegraph.co.uk/news/2021/06/04/out-of-touch-bishops-pushing-church-brink-ruin/ (accessed 15.2.24).
Threlfall-Holmes, Miranda, 'Sex and the Bishops', 29 January 2017, http://mirandathrelfallholmes.blogspot.com/2017/01/sex-and-bishops.html (accessed 15.2.24).
Tolbert, Mary Ann, 'Marriage and Friendship in the Christian New Testament: Ancient Resources for Contemporary Same-Sex Unions', in *Authorizing Marriage? Canon, Tradition, and Critique in the Blessing of Same-Sex Unions*, edited by Mark D. Jordan, Meghan T. Sweeney and David M. Mellot, Princeton, NJ: Princeton University Press, 2006, 41–51.
Tonstad, Linn Marie, 'The Limits of Inclusion: Queer Theology and its Others', *Theology and Sexuality*, 21, no. 1, 2015, https://www.tandfonline.com/doi/full/10.1080/13558358.2015.1115599?needAccess=true (accessed 15.2.24).
Tonstad, Linn Marie 'Everything Queer, Nothing Radical?' *Svensk Teologisk Kvartalskrift. Årg*, 92, 2016, 118–129, https://journals.lub.lu.se/STK/article/view/17214/15591 (accessed 15.2.24).
Tonstad, Linn Marie, 'Ambivalent Loves: Christian Theologies, Queer Theologies', *Literature and Theology*, 31.4, December 2017, 472–489, https://doi.org/10.1093/litthe/frw043 (accessed 15.2.24).
Tonstad, Linn Marie, *God and Difference: The Trinity, Sexuality, and the Transformation of Finitude*, Abingdon: Routledge, 2017.
Tonstad, Linn Marie, *Queer Theology: Beyond Apologetics*, Eugene, OR: Cascade Books, 2018.
Townsend, Leanne and Claire Wallace, *Social Media Research: A Guide to Ethics*, University of Aberdeen, n.d., 11, https://www.gla.ac.uk/media/Media_487729_smxx.pdf (accessed 15.2.24).
True Freedom Trust, 'What is TFT?', https://www.truefreedomtrust.co.uk/ (accessed 15.2.24).
The University of Sheffield, 'Research Involving Social Media Data', Research Ethics Policy Note No. 14, https://www.sheffield.ac.uk/media/29459/download?attachment (accessed 14.4.24).
Vasey, Michael, *Strangers and Friends: A New Exploration of Homosexuality and the Bible*, London: Hodder and Stoughton, 1995.
Vasey-Saunders, Mark, *Defusing the Sexuality Debate: The Anglican Evangelical Culture War*, London: SCM Press, 2023.
Vines, Matthew, *God and the Gay Christian: The Biblical Case in Support of Same-Sex Relationships*, New York: Convergent Books, 2015.
Ward, Graham, 'There is no Sexual Difference', in *Queer Theology: Rethinking the Western Body*, edited by Gerard Loughlin, Oxford: Blackwell, 2007, 76–85.
Ward, Jane, 'The Methods Gatekeepers and the Exiled Queers', in *Other. Please Specify. Queer Methods in Sociology*, edited by D'Lane Compton, Tey Meadow and Kristen Schilt, Oakland, CA: California University Press, 2018, 51–66.
WDD Staff, 'AQ Brief History of Blogging', Web designer depot, 14 March 2011, https://www.webdesignerdepot.com/2011/03/a-brief-history-of-blogging/ (accessed 15.2.24).

Webb, William J., *Slaves, Women & Homosexuals: Exploring the Hermeneutics of Cultural Analysis*, Downers Grove, IL: Inter-Varsity Press, 2001.

Weber, Max, *The Protestant Ethic and the Spirit of Capitalism*, 1904 – 5, translated by Peter Baehr and Gordon C. Wells. London: Penguin Books, 2002.

Weed, Elizabeth and Naomi Schor, eds, *Feminism Meets Queer Theory*, Bloomington, IN: Indiana University Press, 1997.

Wigg-Stevenson, Natalie, *Ethnographic Theology: An Enquiry into the Production of Theological Knowledge*, London: Palgrave Macmillan, 2014.

Wilde, Ruth, 'Shared Conversations', 11–13 May 2015, previously online, this link is no longer live, https://www.lgbtianglican.org.uk/2015/05/15/east-midlands-conversations/.

Williams, Craig, *Roman Homosexuality*, Oxford: Oxford University Press, 2010.

Williams, Harry, *Some Day I'll Find You, An Autobiography*, Worthing: Littlehampton Book Services, 1982.

Williams, Harry, *True Resurrection* (Contemporary Christian Insights), London: Continuum Press, 2001.

Williams, Matthew, Pete Burnap and Luke Sloan, 'Ethics in social media research: Where are we now?', *NCRM News*, 7 December 2017, https://www.ncrm.ac.uk/news/show.php?article=5522 (accessed 15.2.24).

Williams, Rowan, *The Body's Grace*, London: LGCM/ISCS, 2002.

Wilson, Alan, *More Perfect Union: Understanding Same-Sex Christian Marriage*, London: Darton, Longman & Todd, 2014.

Witherington, Ben III, *Women in the Earliest Churches*, Cambridge: Cambridge University Press, 1988.

Witte, John, Jr, *From Sacrament to Contract: Marriage, Religion and Law in the Western Tradition*, Louisville, KY: Westminster John Knox Press, 1997.

Witte, John, Jr and Eliza Ellison, eds, *Covenant Marriage in Comparative Perspective*, Grand Rapids, MI: Eerdmans, 2005.

Woodhead Linda, 'Press release: 'Do Christians Really Oppose Gay Marriage?', *Westminster Faith Debates, Religion and Society*, 18 April 2013, http://www.religionandsociety.org.uk/events/programme_events/show/press_release_do_christians_really_oppose_gay_marriage (accessed 15.2.24).

Index of Biblical References

Genesis	9–10, 48, 117–20, 124, 125, 130, 136–8	**Acts** 8.27	126
1	48, 49, 62, 118–19, 130	**1 Corinthians** 6.9	47 46
2	49, 62, 118–19, 124, 130	7.29 7.31–35	121 126
1.26	141n38	11	124
1.27	125, 141n38	15.42ff	125, 141n40
1.28	10		
4	119	**2 Corinthians**	
6	129, 142n57	5.17	12
		12.17	142n57
Wisdom			
3.13–14	129	**Galatians**	
		3.28	12, 125
Matthew			
18.3	158	**Ephesians**	
19	9, 126–9	5	124
10.1–4	158		
19.4–5	119	**1 Timothy**	47
19.12	126, 141n44	1.10	46
Mark		**1 Peter**	
12.25	129	3.18–20	147, 164nn14, 17
Luke			
10.38–42	54n60	**Revelation**	
14.28	95	13.18	95
20.34–36	129	21	62
23.29	128		

Index of Names and Subjects

ableism 150
Adam 98, 119, 124, 137, 139, 147
  and Eve 147
Ahmed, Sara 16, 20-1, 28n76
AIDS 33
Alexander, Loveday 60, 66, 108
Allberry, Sam 73
Althaus-Reid, Marcella 10, 19, 20, 22
Anglican Communion and Homosexuality, The
  'Homosexuality and the Bible' 44
  'The Witness of Science' 37, 40
  'The Witness of Scripture' 44, 118
Anglican Ink 67-8
Anglican Mainstream 62, 86n21, 155
archbishops 71, 73, 80, 81
Archbishops' Council, The 98
arsenokoitai/es 46-7
ascesis 123, 125, 130
Atwood, Andrew 64, 66
Augustine 120, 124

Baker, Erika 62, 66
Bayes, Paul, former Bishop of Liverpool 109
BCP, *see Book of Common Prayer*
Bennett, David 68, 87n60
Berlant, Lauren 58-9, 74-5, 145, 146, 149, 161

Bible
  authority 45, 62, 64, 65, 68, 118
  cultural artifact 42
  cultural meaning 47
  interpretation 7-8, 12, 13, 20, 30, 42-3, 44-7, 49-51, 60, 63-4, 66, 67, 97, 99, 100-1, 103-4, 195, 109, 117, 118, 121, 123, 125, 129, 133, 135, 137, 161
  meta narrative 67, 93
  queer role models 19
  study 67
  teaching 37-8, 39, 45, 50, 62-3, 64, 68, 74, 107, 131, 132, 156
The Bible and Homosexual Practice: Texts and Hermeneutics 47, 48
Book of Common Prayer 60, 107, 119, 123
Bray, Karen 9, 11, 22, 94, 112, 146-9, 152
Broken Bodies: The Eucharist, Mary, and the Body in Trauma Theology 27n67
Butler, Judith 11, 17-18, 22, 134
Butler, Simon 98-9, 100, 107

Canons of the Church of England
Canon B2 77, 80, 82
Canon B4.2 80, 82, 91n126
Canon B5 77, 80, 82

INDEX OF NAMES AND SUBJECTS

Canon B30 60, 69, 77, 88n65, 119, 123–4
'carnal theology' 93–4, 113
CEEC, *see* Church of England Evangelical Council
celibacy 9, 16, 68, 73, 120, 121, 126–7, 130–3, 137, 158
Changing Attitude 155
Children of Men (film) 134–5,
Children of Men, The (novel) 144n80
Chrysostom, John 99, 130, 135, 137–8
Church of England Evangelical Council 61, 80, 82
cisgender 7, 9, 11–13, 18, 19, 155
cisheteronormative/cisheteronormativity 1–2, 6, 11–12, 14, 22, 40, 42, 45, 99, 113, 125, 148, 152, 154, 155, 158
civil partnerships 34, 39, 53n34, 69, 97, 119, 122–3, 140n25, 152
Clandestine Marriages Act (1753) 77
Clare-Young, Alex 6, 161
College of Bishops 60, 69–70, 78, 80
Collier, HH Peter 77
'compulsory heterosexuality' 11, 17, 20–1
Controversies in Queer Theology 18
conversion therapy, *see* reparative therapy
Core Issues Trust 37–9
Cornes, Andrew 79
Cornwall, Susannah 18, 161
Covenant and Calling: Towards a Theology of Same-sex Relationships 120–1, 123, 130

'covenant partnerships' 9–10, 120, 122–3, 129–30, 132
Creation
  narratives and ordinances 9–10, 16, 29, 37, 48, 117–19, 120, 121–5, 130, 134, 136, 137, 139n11, 144n87, 162
Cruising Utopia: The Then and There of Queer Futurity 27n62, 159

Davie, Martin 60–1, 70–1, 155
de Lauretis, Teresa 17–18
de Pomerai, David 37
de Sousa Santos, Boaventura 162, 167n78
Differences in sexual development, *see* intersex
differences, 'Queer Theory: Lesbian and Gay Sexualities 17
digital ethnography 94–5
Discipline and Punish 17
Doherty, Sean 131, 143n62
Dunnett, John 63

Edelman, Lee 9–10, 20, 22, 58–9, 74–5, 120, 134–7, 145–6, 159
EGGS, *see* Evangelical Group on General Synod
End of the Cognitive Empire, The 162
1 Enoch 142n57
Epistemology of the Closet, The 17
Erzen, Tanya 133
Ethnographic Theology 95–6
eunuchs 10, 120, 125–30, 135
Evangelical Group on General Synod 38, 61, 63, 64, 86n21
Expository Times, The 66, 75

'Facilitated Conversations', *see* Shared Conversations
failure as a 'queer art' vii–iii, 1, 2, 4, 10, 16, 29, 35, 43, 58–9, 74–6, 112, 125, 134, 145–6, 152, 154, 157–9, 161, 163
Fulcrum 71, 88n79, 100–1

Gagnon, Robert 47–8, 49, 101
gender dysphoria 12,
Gender Trouble: Feminism and the Subversion of Identity 17
General Synod 1, 4–8, 30, 32, 38, 49, 57, 59–61, 67, 69–72, 75, 76–81, 96, 98, 103, 107, 109, 111, 131, 153
Gillett, David 99
Gillingham, Sara 161
Gloucester Report, The 98
Goddard, Andrew 40, 71, 84
Gospel of Thomas, the 128
Grace and Disagreement 60
Grave Attending: A Political Theology for the Unredeemed 147, 149
'grave attending' 149–50
Green Report, The 150–1
Greenough, Chris 157
Gregory of Nyssa 22, 136

Halperin, David 14–15, 18, 20, 22, 133
Harrison, Glynn 37, 40
Hell 147–8
 Harrowing of 147
Hermeneutical/hermeneutics 1, 7, 8, 11, 12, 39, 42–3, 45–6, 50, 58, 60, 61, 64, 67, 95, 99, 100–1, 106–8, 110–13, 117–18, 136, 156
 lenses 14, 29, 30, 50, 94, 99, 103, 117, 145, 161

heteronormative/heteronormativity 16, 17, 19, 20, 21, 35, 112, 125, 134, 149, 152, 156–7, 158, 159
'Higton' motion 24n13, 32, 49, 60
History of Sexuality 17
Holy Matrimony 77–8, 88n65
homophobia 14–15, 72, 73
House of Bishops 5, 35, 57, 69, 71, 78–9, 83, 97, 105, 112, 154
Hudson-Wilkin, Rose, Bishop of Dover 81–2

Inclusive Church 155
intersex 11, 12, 13, 26n38, 36, 66, 157, 161
Issues in Human Sexuality 49, 60, 69, 76, 78, 80, 83, 131

James, Graham, former Bishop of Norwich 71
Jenkins, David, former Bishop of Durham 32
Jerome 126–7

King, Helen 82, 106–7

Lambeth 1.10 49, 60
Lambeth Conference, 1998 154
Law and Religion UK 77
Lawrence, Louise 165n35
Leafe, Susie 72–3
Lesbian and Gay Christian Movement (LGCM) 72
Living in Love and Faith vii, 1, 5, 6, 76–7, 78, 81, 83, 153
Living in Love and Faith: A response from the Bishops of the Church of England about identity, sexuality, relationships and marriage 76

INDEX OF NAMES AND SUBJECTS

Living Out 68, 121, 131, 133, 137
Lorde, Audre 17, 154, 166n47
Loughlin, Gerard 21–2

malakoi/os 46–7
Marriage and Same Sex Relationships after the Shared Conversations, see Take Note Debate, February 2017
Marriage Act (1863) 77
Marriage: A Teaching Document from the House of Bishops 69
Marriage
 civil 70, 77–8, 122
 doctrine of 122–5
 equal 30–4, 39, 68, 79, 83–4, 123, 131
Marriage (Same Sex Couples) Bill/Act 30, 32, 77
Martin, Dale 12–13, 44, 47, 49
Men and Women in Marriage, 2013 119
McGinley, John 65, 151
Modern Church 38, 152
Mounstephen, Philip, former Bishop of Truro 81
Moxnes, Halvor 9–10, 22, 125–30, 136, 137
Mullally, Sarah 78, 81
Muñoz, Jose Esteban 18, 20, 22, 159–60
Myriad 151

neoliberal/neoliberalism 1–2, 9, 11, 21, 23n4, 35, 36, 41, 43, 46, 50, 58, 94, 117, 138, 145–6, 149–53, 154, 157, 159–60, 163
Nephilim 129, 142n57
Nixon, David 66–7, 75, 123
No Future: Queer Theory and the Death Drive 9, 120, 134

O' Donnell, Karen 25n32, 27n67
OneBodyOneFaith 72–3
Origen 127
Ozanne, Jayne 73 79, 81

pastoral guidance 76–8, 80
Pastoral Guidance 82
Pastoral Reassurance 80
patriarchal/ly 14, 19, 123, 130, 138, 152, 162
Paul, Ian 60, 66, 67–8, 81, 82, 95, 97–110
Paul, Saint 47–8, 105–7, 121, 125, 142n57
'Pausanias and Agathon: a same-sex relationship?' 115n38
Pemberton, Jeremy 64, 72
Percy, Martyn 150, 152
Pilling
 'Arguments about scripture' 42–5
 'Arguments about science' 41, 45
 Biblical Lens, The 42–51
 Cultural meanings in scripture 47–8
 'Findings and Recommendations' 31–2, 43
 'Male and female in the Genesis narratives' 48–9
 'Reflecting on the Evidence' 34, 49
 Scientific Lens, The 36–42
 'Science, society and demographics' 41
 'Scripture and Theology' 43, 49–51
 'Sexuality and social trends' 33
 Social and Cultural Lens, The 30–5
 'Summarizing the Evidence' 43
 Translation problems 46–7

Pink, Sarah 94
Plausibility Problem, The 132–3
Polls
  YouGov 33–4
  Ben Clements, University of Leicester 34
  Alasdair Crockett and David Voas 34
porneia 79, 104, 126
Prayers of Love and Faith 8, 57, 76–7, 78–9, 80, 105
Procreation 10, 106, 119–22, 124–5, 130, 132, 134–6, 137
Psephizo (blog) 95, 111
  'The Bible, Pilling *and Changing One's Mind*' 97, 100–2
  'On Synod, Sexuality and Not "Taking Note"' 109–12
  'The Pilling Report: divisive and damaging?' 97–100
  'Synod's Shared Conversations' 103–8
Putting Jesus in His Place 126
Pyper, Hugh 119

'queer space' 9–10, 127–8, 130, 133
queer theology 9–10, 16–21
queer theory 9, 16–19, 134
Queer Art of Failure, The 2, 9, 58, 158
que(e)ry/ing vii, 1–5, 9, 15–17, 21, 23, 36, 41–2, 95, 112–13, 119, 123, 131, 134, 137, 145, 154, 156–7

'radical inclusion' 73–4
Rambo, Shelly 11, 146–8
Reform 61, 72, 155
Regional Conversations, *see* Shared Conversations
Reparative therapy 38, 40, 131

Rich, Adrienne 17
Royal College of Psychiatrists 37–9
Rubin, Gayle 17,
Runcie, Robert, former Archbishop of Canterbury 32
Runcorn, David 44, 47–8, 83, 84, 98, 100–2, 107, 155

Saint Foucault: Towards a Gay Hagiography 14
Saint Michael's House Protocols 60, 65, 67–8, 103
same-sex attraction 40, 54n56, 68–9, 131–3, 155
same-sex marriage, *see* marriage, equal
scripture, *see* Bible
'Section 28' (Amendment to the Local Government Act 1988) 33
Sedgwick, Eve Kosofsky 17, 28n76
Sex and the Single Savior 44
Sex, or the Unbearable 58
Shared Conversations 5, 7, 8, 31, 32, 51, 57, 59–61, 67–8, 69–76, 84, 94, 96, 103–8, 112, 123, 153
Sinclair, Keith, former Bishop of Birkenhead 43, 47–8, 64, 98, 102, 155
Society of Ordained Scientists 37
Some Issues in Human Sexuality 13, 43, 97, 118
Song, Robert 9, 120, 121, 136, 137
Spirit and Trauma: A Theology of Remaining 147
SSA, *see* same-sex attraction
Stone, Ken 119, 137
Straight to Jesus 133

INDEX OF NAMES AND SUBJECTS

Symes, Andrew 62–4, 67

Take Note Debate, February 2017 6, 69–73, 75, 84, 94, 96, 109–12
Tanner, Kathryn 93
Tattersall, Geoffrey 79, 81
Tertullian 138, 142n57
Thinking Anglicans 61, 86n21
'third gender' 127
Thomas, the Gospel of see *Gospel of Thomas*
Threlfall-Holmes, Miranda 71, 82
Tonstad, Linn Marie 19–20, 93, 125
transgender 6, 12, 13, 31, 36, 155
True Freedom Trust 131
True Resurrection 159

Undoing Gender 17

Variations in Sexual Characteristics, *see* intersex
von Balthasar, Hans Urs 22, 147–8, 150
von Speyr, Adrienne 147–8, 150

Welby, Justin, Archbishop of Canterbury 6, 30, 32, 72, 73, 84, 109, 110
white supremacy 149
Wigg-Stevenson, Natalie 94, 95, 101, 111
Wilde, Ruth 65
Williams, Harry 159
Wolfenden Committee 163
Wordless/ness 11, 138, 147–8, 153, 160–1, 166n44

www.ingramcontent.com/pod-product-compliance
Lightning Source LLC
Chambersburg PA
CBHW022056290426
44109CB00014B/1123